Just Cate

Just Cate

*A dual memoir
by lifelong friends*

Noelle Alix and Angela Martin

Authors' Note

This is a true story from the unique perspectives of the coauthors who lived and wrote it. They have painstakingly worked to ensure its accuracy. For privacy, the names and identifying details of some people and places in this book have been changed.

Permission for use of quotes is found at the end of this book.

BOOK JACKET and LOGO designed by
Elizabeth Panke Designs, http://lizpanke.com/

PHOTOGRAPHY FOR BOOK COVER by
Jane Shauck Photography, http://photojane.com/

BOOK INTERIOR DESIGN by 1106 Design, http://1106design.com/

Library of Congress Cataloging-in-Publication Data available upon request.

ISBN: 978-0-9854456-0-7

Printed in the United States of America

First Edition

http://justcate.com/

For those who simply matter most:

Tim, Josie, Stick, and Fluff,

Mom, Kim, and James;

And, you, Dad.

XO—NA

Rob, Ryan, and John—my number ones;

And, Mom, Dad, and Alex—my first and forever family.

XO—AM

(r,l) Noelle makes a surprise trip from Dublin to visit Angela during their semester abroad, junior year in college.
—London, April 1988

Ours is a story of friendship,

and the precious, sometimes fragile journey we travel.

The search for hope in what's lost,

for faith when there's inescapable sadness,

for happiness in discovering who we are.

Our understanding of things important

came bit by bit, season by season,

after the birth of an innocent, unlikely child.

A messenger of truth, who graced us without notice,

to reveal simply what matters most to each of us.

—Angela Martin

What's Inside

(This book and our hearts)

Prologue 1

1 Change.. 5

2 Awakening 15

3 Solace 29

4 Healing... 43

5 Stepping Stones 57

6 Faith.. 69

7 Parenting.. 83

8 Listening 97

9 Choices.. 109

10 Chaos 123

11 Fragility.. 141

12 Lost.. 157

13 Trust 175

14 Heaven 187

15 Pneumonia 203

16 Patience 219

17 Peace 237

18 Different.. 255

19 Compassion... 277

20 Expectations.. 295

21 Acceptance 313

    With Gratitude   331

    Permissions   335

    About the Authors   339

*Just Cate is a dual memoir written by two lifelong friends,
each in her own voice.*

Noelle's voice is set in
Adobe Caslon Pro

and

Angela's voice is set in
Gill Sans

Prologue

One's life can change in an instant. In the time it takes to blink, to breathe, or to smile, your life might never be the same, forever altered in a way you could never anticipate, never imagine. I know because it happened to me, an ordinary person whose life changed in an extraordinary way. I didn't understand the moment Cate was born that my life had changed for the better. I could only see what was right there on the surface. That something was wrong with my baby...

"It's a girl, Noelle," Dr. Meyer said, raising my new baby in the air. "Congratulations!"

I stared at her in that fragile moment as if she weren't mine, my anticipation instantly shifting to panic. *Wait, wait, wait. What's the matter with me? I've had a baby. This isn't how I'm supposed to feel.*

I tried to see my baby more clearly in Dr. Meyer's outstretched arms, but her features were out of proportion—her small eyes set into a big, round face. "What's wrong with her face, Dr. Meyer?" I asked between gasps for air.

1

"Sometimes a baby's face is a little squished when it's first delivered," he said. *No, that's not it.*

I reached out to Tim and tried to pull him toward me. "God, what's wrong with her?" I whispered. "She just looks so different." And yet I don't think he thought anything was wrong.

"She's okay," he said struggling to lift his head in reply, sick all night with the stomach flu. Anxious and upset, I was unable to catch my breath still desperate for answers. *Why isn't anyone else concerned? My God, please make this okay.*

A nurse was tending to my baby when she asked Dr. Meyer to come over. They were whispering, and then I heard her call on the delivery room phone for a neonatologist. *I knew it.* "What's wrong with my baby, Dr. Meyer?" I pleaded. "Please tell me what's going on."

"She has a bruise on her head," he said. "We'd like another doctor to examine her." *I didn't see a bruise.* I reached out to grab his hand as he was walking past me but caught the edge of his scrubs instead. He stopped and turned to me when I begged, "Please tell me what's wrong."

Dr. Meyer gazed at the floor for a moment and then fixed his eyes on me. "Noelle, we suspect your baby may have trisomy 21," he said calmly.

I could picture my fingers snapping while I sorted through the files in my mind. *Trisomy 21, trisomy 21, trisomy 21. Where have I heard that before?* Then it appeared in my head as clearly as if printed on a page from the *What to Expect* book I probably read it in: "Trisomy 21 is the medical term for Down syndrome."

Oh my God, Down syndrome…My baby has Down syndrome…

⌇

I wasn't standing by Noelle in her moment of truth, but in some deeply connected way I was. The way childhood friends who evolve into forever friends are—two lives unknowingly weaving themselves together from start to finish. Noelle and I have been friends for as long as the two of us can remember. We met in first grade at St. Mary's School in Wappingers Falls, New York. It was a small, Catholic elementary school in a small, quiet town. Classes had just resumed after the long Presidents' Day weekend in February 1974, when Sister Maurice explained a new student named Noelle Clifford would join us the following morning. She was moving upstate from New York City, and we were to welcome her.

Shy as a child, I was uneasy about meeting yet another stranger, having finally become comfortable with the thirty-some other children in class. To me, New York City was a maze our family navigated on seasonal trips to visit relatives on Long Island. We crossed the bridges and raced through the tunnels amidst hundreds of other cars, each of them going somewhere in a hurry. I wasn't exactly clear what this new girl would be like coming from such a huge, busy place.

I stopped short at the door of our classroom the next morning when I saw Noelle already sitting at her desk (having arrived early for the first and last time in her life). The doorway framed her like a portrait, and perhaps that's why I recall the moment so well. Her skin was fair as is any purebred Irishman's, and her eyes—a bright shade of blue—sat neatly above her little nose and round freckled cheeks. She fit right in with the majority at St. Mary's: the Flahertys, the O'Reillys, and the Keenans.

With an early hint of spring in the air, Noelle and I wore pastel cotton dresses that day: hers a pale yellow and mine an eggshell blue. By seventh grade, we'd opt for our plaid wool uniforms even on warmer days since the see-through dresses revealed who wore a bra and who, like the two of us, still an undershirt. To match her yellow dress on the day we met, Noelle's hair was brushed into two pigtails, each with a fuzzy yellow ribbon tied in a big bow. Her feet in their brown school shoes were crossed at the ankles and dangled a few inches above the industrial tile floor.

I was somewhat envious of Noelle's pretty features and petite stature in contrast to my sharper, Romanesque face and tall-for-first-grade height. Shapeless as a number two pencil, I was long and lean with a pouf of curly brown hair, cut short to allow a comb to pass through. My olive skin and brown eyes were complemented by the standard issue tortoiseshell eyeglasses I wore, having failed the "Which direction is the 'E' facing?" test in kindergarten.

I liked Noelle right away and she felt the same, each of us smiling when I walked in the room. In an instant my worries lifted, and we've been friends ever since. Noelle and I had no idea that our friendship would endure, rooting deep within to become part of us. Nor did we anticipate how the birth of Cate—how writing this book—would permanently seal our friendship and forever change us at the same time.

One afternoon during our writing journey, Noelle realized, "I'm not the same person I used to be." I couldn't help but agree; this was a truth we shared. And so, dear reader, we both tell this story with Noelle's words followed by mine, one leaning on the other the way best friends do.

1

CHANGE

Her Birthday

*We can never know what will happen to us next. We can
try to control the uncontrollable by looking for security
and predictability, always hoping to be comfortable and
safe. But the truth is that we can never avoid uncertainty.
This not-knowing is part of the adventure.*

Pema Chödrön
From *Comfortable with Uncertainty*

I never imagined how quickly my life could change the day Cate
was born, how radically different it would be. One minute
in labor, the next wondering how this baby could be mine. It's
hard for me to revisit that time and the hours following her fate-
ful birth. They're filled with memories I'm not proud of, with
experiences, thoughts, and emotions I've locked away like files

in a box. I was alone inside myself at that time, in a place I never thought I'd be, a place very different from where I am today.

I resisted the temptation when I was pregnant to know if my baby was a boy or a girl, though in my heart I knew I was having another daughter. When I first learned I was expecting a second baby, my thoughts were of Caroline having a sister like I had. I pictured them playing dress-up and stealing clothes from each other's closets just as my sister, Kim, and I used to. But the moment I saw my baby and Dr. Meyer told me he suspected trisomy 21, those happy daydreams vanished. Blown out like candles on a birthday cake.

I began to panic and cry, my stomach falling the instant the words "Down syndrome" popped into my brain. It was as if I'd been sucker-punched the way the news took my breath away. All the excitement and happiness that should come from having a baby were completely absent. Everything was wrong, horribly wrong.

I lay there in this surreal state of awareness yet disbelief, when Dr. Meyer approached me. "Do you have a name for the baby?" he asked nonchalantly. Tim and I looked at each other since we did have a name in mind. It was a name I loved the instant we paired the first and middle names together, brainstorming what we'd call our baby as expecting parents do. Imagining all the while the face that would match the name. "Catherine Claire," I answered, though its elegance no longer seemed fitting. *This was a name we chose for another baby.*

In the midst of my wonderings, our baby was whisked off to be screened for the preliminary diagnosis, which anchored itself firmly in my chest and weighed me down to earth. I didn't expect when they took her away to get tested or evaluated or whatever, the news would be different. I never doubted for a second my baby had Down syndrome; I knew she did.

My entire body was cold, especially my hands. I tried to warm up, pulling the blanket around me, but was still freezing. I couldn't escape this icy room, this exposed gurney. I was consciously trying to control my breathing (deep breath in, long breath out) and quiet the pace of my heart, but the grief and panic I felt were consuming.

Even though Tim was beside me, I felt isolated with my awful thoughts—thoughts a mother shouldn't have for her baby. *If only I could go back one day so this didn't happen.* And I was flooded with images of the baby I saw, but didn't expect to…

…Her big round face, her little eyes, her flat, thick neck…

Somehow, for whatever reason, my baby had Down syndrome. Everything was fine when I was pregnant. My AFP results were average, no cause for alarm. And, I had just turned twenty-nine. *Didn't this happen to older mothers?* It was as if it wasn't I who was experiencing this, though I knew it was. I guess it was like any unexpected event, where you're present in the moment, but your mind isn't totally there with you. Where you believe what happened, whatever it is, but don't yet understand.

We were moved to a recovery room where I lay on a bed, and Tim sat on the floor next to me. The two of us were crying, unable to comfort one another even though we tried. We reassured each other that everything was going to be okay, but we had no idea what was happening or what was ahead of us. We had just found out our daughter was mentally retarded, at least that's all we knew about this disability. It all seemed so impossible, so unreal.

We were at Lenox Hill Hospital on the Upper East Side of Manhattan. This was the same hospital where Caroline was born, though it seemed completely different—sterile, institutional, heartless. Through the doorway I saw a passing doctor ask my nurse, "What's wrong with that couple in there?" She said, "Well, they just found out their baby has trisomy 21." I watched as he continued along. *Our lives have changed forever, and this doctor can walk away, and nothing is different for him.*

The first phone call I made was to my parents who were at our apartment taking care of Caroline. I was barely able to speak when I heard the sound of my dad's voice, the tears drowning away my words. He consoled me, almost as if he knew what I was desperately trying to tell him. "I know honey, it'll be okay," he said. "Let me get your mother." *What does he mean he knows? He didn't even ask me if I had the baby.*

When my mother got on the phone, I told her we had a baby girl and then cried as I told her, "but, Mom, she has Down syndrome." It was the first time I said these words aloud, though I will say it wasn't that I'd acknowledged the truth so much as I was simply stating the fact. Through my tears I heard her say, "It's going to be just fine, Noelle. Everything is going to be okay." My mom continued to reassure me as I cried. The repetitive words she used and the calm of her voice were the safety net I needed. "Noelle, you're going to be okay."

The hours Tim and I spent in the recovery room were some of the most emotional we've experienced as a couple. Other than the two phone calls to my parents and his parents, we didn't talk much. Tim, still too sick to stand, was sitting on the floor propped up against my bed. Despite our silence and the distance between us, I felt connected to him. We held hands even though it was in this awkward position with me reaching out for him, and him reaching up to me.

The delivery room nurse was kind enough to get us a private room, which we eventually settled in. Both of us were relieved for the privacy and quiet as Tim closed the door and lay down next to me. "I love you," he said holding on to me, shivering from the chills of his virus and probably the shock over our circumstances as well. I knew he was trying to be strong for both of us even though he couldn't tell me so.

Word soon came it was time to see our baby in the nursery. My nurse couldn't bring Catherine to us because she was under the lights for jaundice, which meant I wouldn't be able to hold her either. "This will just be a looking visit," the nurse conceded. Right now, even a glimpse of her was enough. A new memory to erase that initial image my mind was replaying.

Tim took my hand and we walked through Lenox Hill's obstetrics ward—a dreamlike journey that led me to believe I was there one minute and invisible the next. It was crushing to witness family celebrations while we passed each room filled with guests, flowers, and laughter. Visitors brushed past us carrying fistfuls of balloons, stuffed animals, and wrapped gifts. It was as if everyone was going to a party we weren't invited to. I gripped Tim's hand more tightly. *Everyone is happy.*

On the final turn for the nursery, we saw visitors waving and cooing at the newborns through the glass. I felt like a foreigner, oddly misplaced in this cheerful scene. Tim and I weren't the happy parents we were supposed to be. I tried to tell Tim what I was feeling, but the words got caught in my throat. *This is just so different.*

When we looked through the oversized nursery window, Tim and I saw two nurses crowded around Catherine, who lay in a clear, deep bassinet. I have to say, it gave me a glimmer of hope since it seemed they both wanted a turn with her. We stood at the window crying, our gaze intently focused on the activity encircling our baby. Much as we tried, we weren't able to see her and eventually decided to go back to our room.

Shortly after we returned to my room, my brother, James, who lived in Manhattan, appeared in the doorway. He caught me by surprise looking so much like our dad in a trench coat and knit cap instead of the sweatshirt and Yankee baseball hat I was accustomed to seeing him wear. James hesitated a moment before coming in, "Hey, Noelle."

James and I got along well enough, but there was a six-year age gap between us. We rarely were in the same school at the same time, always at separate stages in our lives. But here he was my first visitor, happening to arrive at the right time. Tim needed to go home, but didn't want to leave me alone. The stomach virus, sleeplessness, and sadness had won. James promised he would stay and after some prodding, Tim conceded.

"I'll be back before you wake up," he whispered, leaning in to kiss me goodbye.

"Go get some sleep," I said, honestly wanting him to rest, and then I lied, "I'll be all right." He tried to smile, but couldn't and instead reached out for his coat. He threw it over his shoulder and walked out of the room, his head hanging low.

James pulled up a chair and sat down next to me. It was odd for the two of us to be alone in this emotional instance. It was forever him calling me for help, or me doling out unwanted advice he didn't take. We never had a serious conversation about anything. Now here he was, just this young guy, not wanting to leave his big sister alone. I was reminded of our dad, who never abandoned anyone—even perfect strangers.

More than anything, people mattered most to our dad. Often on his commute home from Manhattan, he'd swing by someone's house for a visit. "Hey, I'll be late tonight," he'd call to tell us. "I gotta go see Gubby." He had the same instinct to stop whenever he got within spitting distance of a stranded motorist. Taking his foot off the accelerator, he'd say, "Oh, the poor bastard. I should stop."

If ever James, Kim, and I were with him, we'd cry out, "Oh, c'mon, Dad, please! We're never gonna get home." But it didn't matter what we said, or how hard we protested. He'd never listen. The detour would inevitably become this black hole of time, where there might be a stop at the service station, then a drop off at the person's house, and the "Oh, sure I'd love to come in for a cup of coffee" reply once we got there. Our dad always had all the time in the world.

So, tonight, James was my Good Samaritan. The change of partners provided some needed levity, with one person after the next referring to us as Mr. and Mrs. Alix. After the last such comment from my nurse, "Just press the call button if you need anything, Mr. and Mrs. Alix," James leaned in and said, "Hey, want your husband to make any phone calls for ya?"

"No, I can do it myself, thanks," I said, realizing I hadn't spoken with anyone. He handed me the phone, and I made one or two calls, then handed the phone back to him. I didn't feel like talking.

Despite it all, James decided to go only after my urging. I watched him put on his coat and hat, getting ready to leave, when it occurred to me that my brother had grown up. There was so much I wanted to say to him right then, but all I could do was lift my hand to wave goodbye. *Thank you, James.*

An obstetrician from my practice came through the door after James left, asking me to try and sleep, even though my plan was to stay awake forever. *I can't go to sleep because then I'll have to wake up and face this.* Eventually she ordered some sleeping medication, which I must have taken though I have no memory of it. And then I fell asleep.

I'm not sure what time it was when I got the call about Noelle from our high school friend, Carolyn. The sun was out, but the hours were blurred by the unpredictable newborn schedule I was keeping, my second child, John, only six weeks old. I remember Carolyn being guarded with her words, trying to temper concern with compassion. "I have some news," she began slowly. "Noelle had a baby girl and everyone is okay, but, Ange, the baby has Down syndrome."

I dropped to my knees as if in prayer on the living room floor where I was standing, stunned by what she said. I didn't cry, which was strange because I'm such a crier. Sad or happy, my rivers flow. Maybe it was because I wasn't sure how I felt, the news catching me by surprise. I hung up with Carolyn and sat down right where I was, unable to let go of the receiver and questioning how this could possibly be.

I recalled the moments after I delivered John, and asked the doctor if he was okay. Her nonchalant "Yes, he's fine" response, was like "Of course, aren't they all?" No, I reasoned without understanding exactly why. No, I guess not all babies are born healthy even when you assume they should be.

I could only imagine how devastated Noelle must be. I had just delivered the healthy baby I expected, but Noelle, with the same hopes—the same naïve assumptions—did not. It was all too close to my heart. This might have been my child and my life as easily as it was hers. I couldn't help but wonder why this happened to Noelle and not to me.

It was hours later when I heard Rob come in from work and say, "Hi, Sparky, how was your day?" I ran up and threw my arms around his shoulders, sobbing when I told him about Noelle.

"Oh, no, you're kidding," he said, hugging me back and then becoming very quiet.

"You and I just had this perfect, beautiful baby boy—but it could have been us, Rob. What if this was us?"

"I guess I never thought our baby wouldn't be okay," he said gripping me more tightly. "But even if things were different, we could handle it."

"I hope so, but how can it be that life is so random?" I said and then began to wonder if my own well-planned, thoughtful life that I did my very best to control might just up and turn around one day.

It was the first time in my experience that a close friend had to face something tragic—at least that's how it seemed then. And I couldn't believe it had happened to Noelle. She was always the popular one, with a ton of friends, and the highest of hopes. I thought of her innocence (an innocence we shared), the uncertainty of her future, and the courage she'd have to summon in the hours and days to come.

At the same time, I worried Noelle couldn't share this news with each of her friends. She was a girlfriend's girlfriend—always on the phone, always up for ladies' night, always ready to blow off work for a cup of coffee. We were her therapy. I thought about how awful she must have felt not to want to talk. It saddened me to think about all the difficult hours she endured without the comfort of her friends. And so we reached out, innately the way women do, beginning a chain of calls, one linking to the next to share news and hope, "Say a little prayer, okay? Could you call Colleen next?"

I knew it was selfish, but I hoped Noelle would call me. How I wanted to hear her voice and console her, to tell her all that our friendship meant to me. I felt far away from her, but resolved that I would always be there, that she wouldn't go through this alone, that this baby wasn't just hers; somehow she was mine, too.

2

AWAKENING

The Next Day

*Believe more deeply. Hold your face up to the light,
even though for the moment you do not see.*

Bill Wilson
From *As Bill Sees It*

I opened my eyes the following morning, and it didn't take long to realize where I was and why. The same sinking feeling I had after seeing my baby returned. *Yesterday really did happen.* I was lying in my hospital bed, isolated in that quiet room without flowers, cards, or the people I cared about. There was no baby in a bassinet next to me, and Tim hadn't come yet, so I was alone with my thoughts.

There I was in the wake of it all, reliving everything I saw, heard, and felt the day before. I was at the lowest point I've ever been, so anxious about what had happened, so anxious about what was to come. I wasn't looking for someone to blame that morning or for some explanation why this happened to me. Quite simply, I was in shock about how unreal this all still seemed.

I went to the hospital to have my second baby. I was supposed to be this content new mom. It was supposed to be me and Tim and Caroline and our new baby all together here, with family visiting us. But it was nothing like that. I grieved for what I thought was lost, for what I thought would never be. My life was going to be so different than I ever imagined. And, I didn't think it would be happy.

Growing up I used to daydream about my future. It was hardly unique and probably similar to the vision most of my friends had for themselves. I hoped to have a good job, be married, and have kids—and that's pretty much how my life turned out. I went to college and then on to law school, got a job at a large Manhattan law firm, was married, and had a healthy baby girl. I didn't consciously think about it, but I guess I expected the next chapter in my life to unfold as planned, with a second child, maybe a third someday. I was looking forward to raising the kind of family I grew up in. Kim and I were only a year apart. This was how I thought it would be for Caroline.

As I lay there, these happy images were replaced by depressing thoughts. I pictured a difficult life for this baby—and us—and a sad life for Caroline because she wouldn't have a "normal" sister. Gone from my mind were the hopeful dreams of our family life to be, all the fun stuff I grew up doing and wanted to recapture with my own kids: the Saturday morning hikes, the big family picnics, the way we'd drive to Chinatown in lower Manhattan for lunch on a whim. Erased along with my dreams were the smiling faces in the family portraits I'd hang on walls. Now the pictures would include a baby who looked so different from Caroline, so different from a typical baby.

My thoughts were all over the place, jumping in an instant from the future into the past. I recalled a day the summer before when I was newly pregnant with Catherine and vacationing with my family in Myrtle Beach, South Carolina. My mom, Kim, and I were at a carousel when I noticed a young couple helping their little girl off the ride. She had Down syndrome. My eyes lingered on this family. "Look at that couple," I said to my mom and sister who were standing next to me. "They seem young to have a child with Down syndrome." Knowing I was the queen of hypochondriacs, my mom said, "Noelle, what—what? Now you think you're gonna have a baby with Down syndrome?" She made me feel neurotic, because after all she was right: the thought did cross my mind.

Tim finally showed up and although he still wasn't feeling well, thankfully I wasn't alone anymore. Despite our heavy sorrow, we promised each other that we could do this, that together we would be okay. It made me feel better to have him there, to hug me, to pull me up. After wiping away each other's tears with a blanket, we asked if we could see our baby.

While we waited for her to be brought from the nursery, a nurse who had a teenager with Down syndrome stopped in to talk with us. She was very nice, though not the energetic sort. "Catherine, that's a pretty name, but maybe a little long," she said candidly and added, "You might want to think about shortening that so she can spell it."

My stomach dropped. *My daughter won't be able to spell?* The second she left the room, I started to cry and grabbed Tim's shirt,

"We shouldn't have named her Catherine. We picked the wrong name. What are we going to call her? Let's call her, Cate, okay? We'll just call her Cate."

"Okay, Noelle, okay. Just Cate," he said calmly, letting me work this through as he usually did. This was his job in our marriage—to be the steady force, the one who calms me down, the one who lets me emote everything and then tells me, "Just breathe. It's going to be fine."

I scooped up Cate out of her bassinet once my nurse wheeled her in. I wanted to see her up close since we hadn't had the chance to do so until now. She didn't look like our baby as I scanned her face, running my hand along her cheek. There were no distinguishing family features, no trademark that made her ours. When Caroline was born, she was unmistakably Tim's daughter, so much so we called her Timothina. But there was no trace of either of us in this baby's face.

Cate's most striking feature was her sky blue eyes. They were as stunning as they were telling. The color captivated me while their slanted almond-shape revealed her secret. I was reminded of it every time I looked at her, my subconscious echoing the truth inside my head: *My baby has Down syndrome.*

Beyond her eyes, Cate was different in other ways. She had wispy black hair that stood on end like a mohawk. Her body was part linebacker, part Buddha with a round abdomen and a thick neck that ran right up into the base of her head (most of us have a gentle curve here). I found myself searching her face for the baby I expected, but all that stared back was Down syndrome. *Will I ever see her just as my baby?*

She was able to stay in my room from then on, which I was glad about. Every once in a while I'd let Tim hold her, but then I'd ask for her back. "Okay, my turn now." As the afternoon wore on, Tim could barely hold his head up. I urged him to go home and sleep, but he shook his head insisting, "I don't want to leave you and Cate." Even though I wanted him to stay, to have some sense of family, of togetherness, I insisted otherwise. "Don't worry about us. Come back in a few hours when you feel better. We'll be here."

I watched the door slowly close behind him and then turned to Cate. It was just the two of us now, my baby with Down syndrome and me. She was tightly swaddled in a white receiving blanket with alternating pink and blue stripes, sleeping contentedly, her mouth open. I leaned in to kiss her cheeks, which were pink and round, the rest of her skin a creamy white. I stopped short of smoothing down Cate's hair, instead just looking at her eyes that were noticeably close-set and watery even though they were closed.

I pulled the covers of my bed up around us and snuggled Cate in with both arms. We lay this way for hours. I wanted her with me so much so I couldn't put her back in the bassinet. I thought that if I held her I would feel better. That my awful feelings of sadness and the guilt about being sad would fade away. I thought that maybe if I held her close, I would begin to feel differently.

Later that day, my nurse asked if I wanted to speak with someone. I imagine it was impossible not to sense my despair. "Yes, I would," I replied almost immediately. *I'll talk with anyone who can help me feel better.* A nun soon appeared at my door, introducing herself in a soft voice, though I missed her name (I was sort of expecting a psychiatrist). She was cherubic and quite short, with porcelain-white skin. Her very presence radiated a peace that wrapped around me like a hug.

Seeing her made me realize I'd never had a deeply personal conversation with a religious person. Even though I spent eight years in Catholic school and four more at a Catholic college, faith hadn't played a conscious role in my life. It seemed there was always some concrete answer for my little problems that cropped up. Needless to say, I was nervous at the prospect of speaking with this woman. I just wanted to talk and not worry about what I was going to say.

I welcomed the nun into my room, and she reached out to me, held my hands, and asked me how I was. With that I started crying and opened up to her like an old friend, sharing every thought, every emotion, and every fear. "I don't want this to be happening. I feel so guilty. Will I ever not be upset? Will I love Cate as much as I love Caroline?"

She soothed me with words, deep in faith. "God will give you the strength to do this, Noelle. It's not going to happen overnight, but He handpicked you." When she left, even amidst all the emotion, I had a tiny sense of calm. That maybe someday it would be okay. I remember her as an angel, the first person who shed light on my darkness.

Shortly after, Father Larry, a Catholic priest and distant relative, came to visit from his parish on the West Side. It was good to see him, though part of me hoped when I heard the knock at my door that it was my family. I wasn't this hugely religious person, yet two out of my first three visitors were. For as much as it was different to have what amounted to strangers with me then, I felt free to be honest with them. That they would keep secret whatever it was I might say—a penance without consequence.

When he came through the door, I instantly recognized Father Larry, a humble little man, who was always smiling. He removed his cap and overcoat, revealing his balding head and ring of white hair; his black clerics with white roman collar were wrinkled at the knee. Father Larry sat down next to me and said, "Noelle, your Aunt Anne called and asked me to come and visit with you." He reached out his hand and touched my arm. "She loves you very much."

"I know," I said and smiled when I thought of her, "I love her so much, too."

"How are you?" he asked and through my tears I told him how desperately I wanted to change my emotions, yet how powerless I was to do so. "You need to mourn the baby you thought you were having before you can accept the baby God gave you. Let yourself go through this process. You will love your baby, of that I am sure. Just give yourself time."

Father Larry assured me that all my thoughts and emotions were perfectly natural, that this was how anyone in my situation would feel. He absolved me of the overwhelming guilt I carried with his words and calm manner, explaining why I felt the way I did. My baby Catherine died the day Cate was born, he said, at least my image of her did. Father Larry told me the mourning process was happening inside me and I had to let myself go through it.

"Know she is a special baby by God's design," he continued. "Have faith that this is His plan." I was trying to believe what he said, to look at this from a bigger perspective. Still it was hard to interject myself into this equation, to believe that I was meant to have this child. The nun's words echoed a similar theme as I thought back on them. "God handpicked you," she had said knowingly. I wanted to believe what they told me, but it was difficult to gauge if this was truth or simply what a religious person says to someone in crisis. *Are these only words to help me make sense out of the unexpected?*

Although I was alone again after Father Larry left, I did have the company of my sister who called about ten times that day. My parents were the ones to tell her about Cate and after pulling herself together, Kim inundated me with phone calls.

She was trying to be upbeat, but couldn't keep from crying. We recalled the day at Myrtle Beach, "Kim, remember the family on the carousel?"

"Oh my God," she said with relief to get it off her chest, "that was the first thing I thought of."

When Kim wasn't on the phone with me, she was calling her friends and friends of friends, gathering information on Down syndrome and searching for another mom I could talk to. This was before the Internet existed, so spending hours on the phone was her only means of outreach. She eventually got the name of a woman who had a child with the disability and after speaking to her, Kim asked that she call me.

I have to say, as much as my conversations with the nun and Father Larry imparted love and hope for the future, my talk with this woman did just the opposite. She wasn't overly positive about her own experience and, in fact, she made me feel worse. Even so, Kim's outreach meant so much. She started what seemed impossible to me at the time. When I couldn't imagine taking a step forward, she did. For both of us.

I spent much of the rest of my stay at Lenox Hill with Cate in my arms. I needed this physical connection with her: to breathe in her new-baby smell, to kiss her tiny upturned nose, to feed her when she was hungry. How I wished my mind would feel differently. Even though Father Larry said I wasn't a bad person, I felt like one. I buried the guilt I had over these feelings in the deepest recesses of my being, not sharing it with anyone. Not Tim, my parents, or Kim.

Maybe I needed to grieve then, to experience guilt, pain, and loss before I could welcome this child, before I could take the preliminary steps toward healing, acceptance, and love.

But I didn't understand this at the time. I was very much alone, withdrawn inside myself as if this was a burden I would carry and these emotions were my own to sort out.

In between calls from my sister and my time alone was a lighthearted visit. My secretary and good friend Linda burst into my room like a hurricane with an enormous balloon bouquet and shopping bag full of gifts from the Disney store. She was determined to celebrate the birth of this baby in the same jubilant fashion she had Caroline's. Linda's grand entrance in her boisterous New-Yorker-style made me laugh, and I couldn't recall the last time I did that.

In one motion Linda put down her things and reached out her arms. "Give me that baby," she demanded in her throaty Brooklynese. I indulged Linda at once, stretching my arms to meet hers, as we passed Cate, this little bundled nugget, between us. Cradling the baby about two inches from her nose, Linda immediately introduced herself, "Hello, little mosquito. I'm your Aunt Linda." She visited for a long while and never expressed a sentiment other than joy at the birth of this baby. Not that day or ever. I knew Linda was upbeat for me and I'll always remember that, always be grateful for her bright, spirited visit when there was so much sadness.

When she left, I was alone again. I didn't seem to have Tim or my parents around much during those times. My father joked that he crossed the George Washington Bridge ten times in three days, but never got out of the car. It was a chaotic time when I thought about it with nothing going as it should have: Tim in bed too sick to function, my mom not being able to get to me because my daughter needed her more (Caroline got the virus Tim had), and my dad, too haphazard to know what the hell to do, like a cabbie between fares. Perhaps this was a foreshadowing of my new life, where everything would be placed just beyond my control.

A neonatologist came after a time with some test results. (It was the same doctor from the recovery room.) He said my baby had good tone and I remember thinking, *Okay, tone, whatever, she's got good tone,* but having no idea what tone was. He explained her heart was okay, that she didn't have the congenital heart defect common among children with Down syndrome. *What, she could have had a heart defect?* "Oh, thank God," I said out loud, both surprised and relieved by the news.

"Aren't you singing a different tune today?" the doctor said abruptly. I stared at him, desperately wishing to say what I was thinking: *You're an asshole.* I dismissed him from that point on even though he kept rattling off data. Whatever he had to say, I didn't listen. Then he walked away just as he had before. I will say, though, for as much as this doctor had no bedside manner, he was perceptive. I was ashamed of how I felt after delivering Cate and although my wounds were still fresh, it was a new day.

I spent many hours thinking about Noelle while I cared for my children over the next few days. I would look at my new baby John and my toddler Ryan and thank God for their health, feeling both blessed and guilty they were okay. I felt strangely disconnected from Noelle, since my life went along while hers had changed so dramatically. I wondered where she was, how she was, and what she was doing.

Every time I tried to picture Noelle in the hospital with Catherine, my mind reflected back to St. Mary's and our early days, the memories vividly sharp. I recalled a day in third grade when we were in Sister Kieran's class. It was noontime, and we just had retrieved our brown paper bag lunches from the closet at the back of the classroom to eat at our seats. But Noelle couldn't find hers. She went up to Sister Kieran and said her lunch wasn't there. "I'm sure I brought it."

"Go back and look again," Sister Kieran said, shaking her head.

Noelle turned and scanned the room, her eyes stopping to stare at Billy Gallagher who was already eating. She went up to him, and with steely conviction said, "Give me back my lunch."

"Go away," I heard him say obnoxiously. "It's *my* lunch." With that Noelle returned to Sister Kieran and said, "Billy took my lunch!"

"How could that be?"

"But, Sister Kieran, it is my lunch. I know it is. It's what I bring everyday."

Billy smirked while taking bites of her chicken roll sandwich with mayo on white bread and store brand chocolate sugar cookies.

"You will come to the convent with me, and you can get a peanut butter and jelly sandwich."

The convent? No one had ever been sent to the convent— and Noelle hated peanut butter and jelly. "She's telling the truth!" I wanted to shout. "Billy's so mean to us. He even stepped on my carton of milk when it fell on the floor last week!" But I sat there, frozen to my seat, while Noelle was escorted out. I watched through the classroom's metal venetian blinds while she and Sister Kieran crossed the parking lot and disappeared into the convent. *I'm scared for you. I don't know where you are. I want to help you, but I don't know how.* Every single feeling I was having right now.

My thoughts were persistent when I tried to drift off to sleep at night. I'd shimmy up close to Rob so that we were nose to nose and share all of my wonderings. "Noelle is probably finishing up with the baby's nighttime bottle like I just did with John…Unless the baby can't drink from a bottle for some reason…What if there's something wrong…Oh my gosh, Rob, do you think they're okay? I wish she'd call."

"Why don't you just call her?" he asked one night eager to hear how they were as well.

"I don't think I should quite yet."

"But why not? She's your good friend."

And I knew that, but I hesitated calling Noelle and her family, wanting to give them the distance I thought they needed. I was raised to respect people's privacy and not to pry. But the not-knowing was becoming too much for me. By the next morning, I still hadn't heard from Noelle so I broke down and called her parents at their house. "Hello, Mr. Clifford," I said quietly when Noelle's dad answered the phone. "It's Angela Guadagno Martin." With his thick New York accent he boomed, "Angela Gwa-dan-yo Martin, the friend with three names. How the hell are ya?"

"Okay," I said wanting to say more, but he seemed out of breath. "Did I get you at a bad time?"

"No, I'm glad ya caught me. I'm just walking in the door here to pick up a few things. We've been at Noelle's. Did you hear about the baby?"

"I did. How's Noelle? How is she, really?" I asked and in his most genuine, softhearted way, he said, "Oh, you know Noelle. She's a mother bear." At first I wasn't sure how to read his analogy. Was she angry and growling at her circumstance or embracing and defending this fragile child? When he continued, I was happy to learn it was the latter. "I'll be damned if I can get in to see her. Carol tells me Noelle can't put the baby down."

I sensed from the way he spoke that even though so much had changed, some things hadn't. Her parents were the same loving, supportive people I remembered, embracing their daughter and granddaughter no matter what. I had the comforting feeling that

Noelle would be all right, that she was trying to accept this, even though it was all so new, so uncertain.

Reassuring as our talk was, I still needed to reach out to Noelle. Late one night a few days later, I pulled a pad of paper into my lap from the basket next to my bed, and started to write. To compose a letter or poem or whatever would pour from my pen and my heart. I was always a binge writer this way, jotting down my thoughts when the urge would strike in order to see them more clearly. A diffident child, writing was often my only means to express the words I couldn't possibly say.

I had kept my early writings private in a Holly Hobby diary that had a pink gingham cover and built-in brass lock. It came with two of the smallest keys I've ever seen, in case you lost one, or your brother stole one, I guess. When I had something particularly secretive to write, I'd sit Indian-style with the diary in my lap under the long white Formica desk my father built for me, which stretched across the far wall in my bedroom like a countertop.

This was my hideaway of sorts, the place where I could escape from the world. I would jot down what was bothering me, silly things about my friends, what boys I liked, what I hoped for someday. Looking at the blank page before me now, I thought about my friend and prayed the right words would come to me when I needed them to.

I found as I wrote, the questions circling my mind about the randomness of fate were replaced by the assurance of my faith that this baby came to Noelle for a reason. Deep within my conscience, I knew that one day we would understand why. That our uncertainty would someday give way to understanding. I decided not to send her my thoughts that went on page after page. Instead the final version of my musings was simple and from the heart.

I copied the note into a baby card and bundled up my little ones to mail it at the post office. This card was too important to leave in my mailbox at home, where I would impatiently wait for it to be collected. I opened the door of the post office box and dropped the card through the slot, checking twice to be sure it slid out of sight. I felt better that Noelle soon would know how much I cared.

3

SOLACE

Coming Home

I believe that when all is said and done, all you can do is show up for someone in crisis, which seems so inadequate. But then when you do, it can radically change everything.

Anne Lamott
From *Traveling Mercies*

Cate and I were released from the hospital after a few days as any typical mother and baby would be. And I imagine we left in the same manner that all new families do, completing the formalities of signing discharge papers, collecting our things, and packing up our new little baby into her car seat. That said, it was unmistakably atypical in the mood we went about it all. While it was good to be on our way, to get out of the hospital, and to leave the memories of the past few days behind us, there was this inescapable somber feeling hanging over Tim and me. To add to our sorrow, we were going to a new apartment in suburbia. A place that just didn't feel like home.

The week before, I'd resigned my job as an attorney in a large New York City law firm and retreated with my family from Manhattan to a two-bedroom apartment in northern New Jersey. Part of me was still upset about having to leave the city that had become my home and the job I'd worked so hard for, but I wanted to be with my kids. The long hours, the nanny, and the cramped apartment were hard enough with just one child and seemed impossible with two.

We planned that Tim would commute and I would stay home with the kids, at least for a while anyway. Having just moved, I didn't even know where the grocery store was to buy diapers, wipes, and ready-to-serve formula. We hadn't unpacked either, with boxes stacked in corners and the disassembled crib propped up against a wall in our bedroom.

We arrived at our apartment to find my parents, Caroline, and to my surprise, my brother-in-law, Dave, from Virginia. Dave was away on business when Kim called him with the news. He decided to reroute his return trip so he could be there for Cate's homecoming. As Tim and I made our way inside and hugged everyone hello, Dave began unbuckling the baby from her car seat and asked, "Can I hold Catherine?" before anyone else could beat him to it. "Sure, of course, but we're calling her Cate," I said eager to get off on the right foot.

I swooped up Caroline and hugged her as if it were more than only a few days since I'd seen her last. "I missed you so much, Josie," I said.

"Me, too, Mommy."

It was hard to let go as I was hit with a wave of loss for her, for the sister that she wasn't going to have. Needless to say, I was a basket case, all over the map of emotion: crying, worrying, trying to be upbeat and strong, and at the same time physically feeling like I'd gone a few too many rounds in the ring.

My dad was weepy as he reached his arms wide, wrapping me in a big, warm hug and holding on extra long. This was the way he hugged, with all of himself. He was dressed in his Saturday garb: these ugly green sweatpants, splattered with dried paintbrush strokes, a flannel shirt, and work boots that curled up at the toes. It was good to see him, since he never did make it to my hospital room, just dropping off my mom to visit so he could be at the apartment with Caroline.

I felt myself starting to cry, but not wanting to. It was his hug that made me kind of crumble, his sense of sadness—or something like it—which made me feel sad, too. My dad wasn't the rock-solid type my mom was. She knew everything was going to be okay, because in her head you make it okay. "You can do this, Noelle. The doctors said she has great tone. She's alert already. She drinks from a bottle so well. She started off so big, no heart defect. This is going to be just fine." I needed both of my parents each in their own way giving me the support they could. My mom sharing her strength, and my dad his emotion.

I always knew I had a wonderful dad, even growing up when you're not supposed to have such positive thoughts about your parents. It was one of those things no one had to tell me or remind me about. My dad was an insurance adjuster by trade who, like the superhero Mr. Incredible, often found coverage for those who might not have it otherwise, as long as they were decent and maybe offered him a cup of coffee. His work attire consisted of a short-sleeved dress shirt, usually stained with soup or coffee, and dress pants, which sat below his huge belly and dragged three inches under his heels.

I commuted with him to work one summer, having landed the most boring job in history at his insurance company: literally, putting the insurance policy in the typewriter, typing the start and end dates, taking it out, and then going on to the next one in the never-ending pile. Unfortunately it paid more than fast food restaurants, so I was there.

Driving into work, we'd pick up a cast of characters along the way. Our first stop was for his boss, Big Al, who was heavyset and doused himself in cologne. Then we picked up his good friend, Keith, who had a prosthetic leg and would die much too young from cancer. Last, we collected the usual suspects who worked in his building from a bus stop at the entrance to his office park. "I'll be back to get ya," he'd say through an open window while we'd drop off the first crew, and go back to the bus stop for the second. Some afternoons after finishing his lunch and settling a few claims, he'd head back to his car for a nap, whispering to me on the way out, "Honey, I gotta go grab five."

He wasn't your average dad as dads went in our day either. After tag-teaming with my mom when school let out (she worked second shift), he'd drive us wherever we needed to go and was always up for an impromptu outing. Some afternoons we went out for ice cream, for a McDonalds run, or to buy scratch tickets. If we ever won, we spent the money right away. If it were a $1 or a $5 winner, we'd buy more scratchers. With a big one, like a $20 winner, we'd order Chinese for dinner.

My mom was the sane, structured one in our family—someone had to be. If not for my mom, I wouldn't have the work ethic I do, I might not have gone away to college, and probably wouldn't have continued on to law school. She was my biggest supporter, even in high school when I cared more about boys than grades. "Noelle if you only put in as much time on your homework as you do on your hair, you could get straight As," she'd tell me every Friday night when I headed out the door to another party. I finally hit my academic stride in college when my mom encouraged me to stretch further and apply to law school right away. "Go while you're in the mode of going to school. We'll work through the finances somehow."

The afternoon we arrived at our apartment was my dad's first time meeting Cate, and I have to say it was love at first sight. (Corny, yes, but true.) He passionately loved each of his grandchildren, couldn't get enough of them really. It makes my throat close up to think of it and the way he was with all of them, so I don't do it often. He held Cate most of the day in a chair we had in the corner of what we called the living room.

When the grandkids were newborns, he held them horizontally above his belly, the way you'd carry a ham home from the butcher. It was such a production. He couldn't just take the baby, sit down, and hold it all on his own. First, he'd sit down, next you had to place the baby in his arms, and then he'd never move from the position. I'm sure he holds the record for the longest ham-baby-hold in history. I watched the two of them sit there, Cate looking as if she was being sacrificed before a god, and my father as content as could be.

My mom had a roast beef cooking in the oven and a pot of cut, peeled potatoes boiling on the stove ready to be mashed. The apartment was much more pulled together than when I had left, and Caroline had been bathed and was on the mend. I suppose that was my mom's way, jumping right in to handle whatever needed to be done. She brought a sense of order and normalcy to the occasion, which otherwise would have been, well, just kind of sad.

To walk into this strange place and see a celebration for us, a celebration with my family was the welcome I needed.

The smell of food cooking, the smiling faces, the hugs and laughter were everything to me. Although I missed not having my brother or sister there (Kim was planning a long visit in a day or two), I have to say the sorrow that overcame me in the car lifted just a touch. This wasn't home, yet in some small measure, it felt that way.

I figured Noelle would receive my card in a few days and then I would call and see how she was doing. In the meantime, I distracted myself amidst the routine of my own life, which my new baby folded neatly into. It felt right, the four of us. With the addition of John, I knew my family was complete: two boys, two years apart almost to the day. As brothers, they would have in each other a playmate and a sparring partner.

It seemed so easy, how the miracle of a healthy baby just came to me. I don't think I would have appreciated that had I not been preoccupied about how Noelle was welcoming into her family, Catherine—a baby who was different, a baby she didn't expect. How could she possibly have the same contented feeling about her family I had for mine?

Ryan quickly got past his big brother anxiety, understanding that John wasn't going anywhere—he was home. And John was truly at ease, seven weeks old and starting to smile and coo—the milestones ticking away ahead of schedule, effortlessly, innately. I'd smile at him and he'd smile right back, dimples dotting his cheeks even then. Sometimes when I smiled at him, or looked at him and he responded in kind, I thought of Noelle and her new baby. *Will Catherine be able to do the same things with you?*

This all still didn't seem possible in the world I once knew, that my carefree friend from Wappingers Falls gave birth to a child with a disability. I always pictured Noelle with a litter of blonde-haired girls with pigtails. Girls who played dolls and dress-up, who wanted to be Cinderella, who were as pretty and popular as she was.

It was my emergent faith—a faith I always had, but never stood up for as my own—that shed a new light over the question of what was supposed to be. It was an inviting door to open wider, to contemplate more deeply why this happened to Noelle, to float about in the idea that Catherine's birth wasn't chance, but purposeful. And, yet, I found myself dropping back to the days when life wasn't so heavy, when our friendship was as easy as picking up the phone and talking about what now seemed to be nothing of any significance.

So it went, as if the door to my little New Jersey apartment was a turnstile ushering in and out an endless flow of visitors. People from all corners of my life came to visit or called on the phone, each of them assuring Tim and me we would be able to handle this, that everything would be okay, that we would be wonderful parents for Cate. While I didn't believe their sentiments were true (I'm no different than anyone), they were words I needed to hear. The more I heard them, the more I began to gain the courage to believe them.

At the same time, it was the elephant in the room no one wanted to mention, that the baby we brought home had Down syndrome. While visitors carried a positive energy with them, there was also this knowing that no one said how they really felt. People consoled us the way you might at a funeral, saying only the good, when honestly it was just so hard.

Almost everyone spoke to us of their encounters with people with Down syndrome and how well they were doing. My mom constantly reminded me about Alison Byrnes, a girl from Wappingers Falls who was on Ange's and my swim team growing up. Her mom was the coach. "Remember how good she was, Noelle?" I thought back to picture Alison. I never paid any attention to her, other than to look at her a little longer than maybe I should have. She was just kind of there—not part of my life, not part of my circle of friends.

I thought about myself as a child on those early morning swim meets and after-school practices. *Why didn't I ever talk with Alison, offer any friendship?* I guess I was self-absorbed, oblivious to most things other than my friends and what mattered to me. And at twenty-something, I wondered how far I'd come. In my defense, perhaps I hated swimming so much that nothing else registered except counting the minutes until it was over.

My mother had insisted I join the swim team, thinking it would make me a good swimmer. I pretty much stunk at all sports, so it came as no surprise that I was the worst one on the team. When the relay teams were handed out (this being the only race I swam because it was the only one I qualified for), I'd hear the girls from my team say, "Man, we got Clifford. We're never gonna win." The more I thought about it, Alison and I did have a connection. Both of us were enthusiastically cheered when we finished a race: Alison because people were genuinely happy for her, and me so they could finally get on with the next heat.

Noelle and I were always friends from that very first day in Sister Maurice's class. We played at recess on the blacktop at school and went to each other's birthday parties—the basic sort, without themes and mystery drop-off locations. As we got older, Noelle and I chatted for long stretches on the telephone and met at the roller derby on weekends. There were the days we spent staring dreamy-eyed at the life-sized poster of Shaun Cassidy taped to Noelle's bedroom ceiling, while painting our fingernails and talking about the latest Tom McCann woodwork wedge sandals our mothers wouldn't let us buy.

There was the first boy-girl party at the end of sixth grade where spin-the-bottle broke out and all the weekend nights in high school driving to the latest party when her old Nova broke down. There was the graduation trip to the Jersey shore ("Are you sure about this turn because I think that truck is headed straight for us!"), and the day trips and bar hopping during breaks from college.

For all of our adventures, my most endearing memories with Noelle are those of us at her house. She lived in a small ranch home built in the 1960s in a neighborhood that must have been an orchard once with street names like Applesauce and McIntosh Lane and her own of Crabapple Court. Her house was at the end of a cul-de-sac and perched atop a hill that led down to a small body of water Noelle referred to simply as The Lake, even though it was really more of a pond. In the winter, Mr. Clifford would jump up and down on the lake's icy surface to test it before he'd let us skate. "Okay, if it can take that you girls are safe," he'd say, and head off while we sat down on large overturned buckets to lace up our white skates with white laces.

What I remember most about Noelle's house is how it was always filled with people. I'd walk through the front door since it was never locked, and find neighbors, Mrs. Clifford's sisters, or our friend, Brian Murphy, who was practically a fixture there. I'd often catch him rummaging his way through Noelle's fridge or debating with Mr. Clifford about inane topics, like the merits of "going to couch." Because of Mr. Clifford's awful snoring, he was banished to sleep on the couch in the basement at night—every night.

I bet Brian had the same affinity for Noelle's house that I did. I loved being there. It reminded me of my Italian grandmother's home that was cozy and welcoming, a place where visiting mattered. People would come up, give me a hug, and say, "Angela, how are you?" as though I belonged. A shy kid, it made me feel part of something bigger. Family has a way of doing that, and that's exactly how I felt when I was at Noelle's, like I was a member of her family.

Our friendship was closer some years than others, the way most friendships are. There was that quirky ninth grade junior high school year wedged between St. Mary's and Roy C. Ketcham High School. Only a few of us from grammar school would even acknowledge each other. We were trying our best to find new friends, attempting to be cool, and fit in. Noelle and I would glance at each other when passing in the hallways and smile, but quickly turn away as if to say, "Yeah, we're still friends, but we've got to make it on our own here for a while."

Every visit, phone call, and letter was a gift to me, distracting me however temporarily from Down syndrome. One visit came hours later than planned, which was right on time for my family. At about 10:00 p.m., my Uncle John and Aunt Anne (my dad's brother and his wife) arrived along with my parents and a hodgepodge of cousins. In they came loud and exuberant, as if it were 1:00 in the afternoon, with happy greetings and congratulations, loaded down with bags and bags of groceries and gifts. They took countless trips back and forth from the car to unload.

I got Caroline out of bed, her blue eyes blinking to adjust to the light from her open bedroom door. "Me-Ma, Pop Pop, Aunt Anne, and Uncle John are here," I whispered. Carrying her on my hip into the living room, she was swooped up into a barrage of hugs and kisses. Almost immediately, my Uncle John began working in the kitchen. He was the cook in the family, at the stove at every occasion. Dressed as if he'd just come from a meeting, he maneuvered about my kitchen in his wing tips and button-down shirt, which stretched over his large belly and tucked into his dress pants. Rather than cook one entrée at a gathering, say roast beef, he'd also prepare salmon, chicken, lamb chops, and hamburgers. Now, this wasn't because he was indecisive, it's because that's what he was serving. That night we had a spiral ham, steaks, lamb chops, and liver and onions.

While he cooked, my Aunt Anne gave me one of her biggest hugs—the kind where the breath is squeezed out of you—and pulled out three shopping bags from Bloomingdale's filled with dresses and clothes for Cate and Caroline. She had three boys and nothing brought her more joy than going to Bloomies to buy dresses for little girls. This was how she spent her money, how they both did—on others.

Aunt Anne was as striking as always. Her silver hair was freshly cut at chin length, and she was elegantly dressed in a silk blouse, tailored pants and a blazer.

"Would you like to meet Cate?" I asked after squeezing her and thanking her many times over.

"Yes, Noelle, if you wouldn't mind getting her up. I'd love to."

I found Cate curled in a ball up against the crib rails in her furry pink-footed sleeper. Scooping her up, I carried her to my Aunt Anne's outstretched arms.

"You are God's blessing," I heard her whisper to Cate when she held her close.

For my Aunt Anne and Uncle John, Cate's birth was an occasion to be celebrated. They taught me the most basic lesson of generosity and goodness not just with this visit, but also consistently throughout my life. I remember that evening as if it were a dream. The wonderful thing is, it really happened.

My sister came the next day, and she and my mom stayed with me. Without being asked, they moved in and simply took over. They helped with everything and cared for me in a way Tim couldn't. I'm a big believer that women need women—they just get it. The three of us passed the time reminiscing and talking about everyone else in the family because that's what we do. We went shopping, out to eat, and to the park. There was nowhere we had to be, no meetings to attend, no appointments to keep. It was as if we were on vacation.

Kim held the baby for long stretches during the day on our red, floral, living room couch. Cate often had a paci in her mouth, and her hands and feet were lost in the three-month size stretchy that fit Caroline when she was a newborn. In the evenings, my mom insisted—as she did with all the grandchildren—that we establish a nighttime routine for Cate: "Even if she's sleeping, you wake her at 11:00 p.m. for a bath and then feed her a bottle."

My mom would sponge bathe Cate on the dressing table and afterwards gently smooth her newborn eczema patches with baby lotion. I watched my mom adeptly work, her professional nursing skills coming so naturally. All the while, Cate was calm, her alert eyes staring at the bottles of Johnson & Johnson and Baby Magic set next to her. When my mom finished her routine, I dressed Cate and settled down into the one comfortable chair we owned to give her the nighttime bottle.

My mom and Kim consoled me at random breakdowns, which happened often. When we were taking a walk one afternoon through the center of town with the girls in the double stroller, I saw two teenagers walking toward us and I burst into tears thinking Cate would never have friends.

"Yes she will," they insisted.

Late one night when we were watching TV, I woke up

from dozing off to see a disabled actress on the screen. "Does that woman have Down syndrome?" I blurted out between sobs.

"See, Mom, I told you we should have turned this show off."

"Oh, Kim, stop it."

"No, I knew she'd get upset."

And all the while I just sat there crying.

I was a mess, beyond the typical emotional new mother whose hormones are all out of whack. Anything that remotely reminded me of Down syndrome or pointed to Cate's future had me in fits. At every opportunity, I talked through my insane worries with them. Neither one showed signs they were tired of listening, though I'm sure the conversations were all about me when I left the room.

Then one day, I knew it was time for Kim and my mom to go home. A big piece of me wanted them to stay forever, to continue on with this escape-from-reality time of just being together, but I needed to take some steps forward on my own. Although I didn't want to begin down what was a new road, I had this fleeting moment of inner drive, which was something I used to have a lot of. Even though I cried when they left, and the steady stream of visitors began to dwindle, I was ready to be on my own with the kids. Or, at least, I hoped I was.

Noelle and I seemed to defy the odds with our friendship, since the years have a tendency to pull old friends apart. We hung on, our connection remaining even after we finished college and found jobs, the physical tie of our hometown helping to keep us close. We were able to catch up with each other and step back at the same time—

"Hey Noelle, are you going to Wappingers for Christmas?"

"Yeah, let's try and meet up with Brian and Carolyn if they're around. Maybe we can go to Mulligan's one night."

In great measure, our friendship thrived because we were different personalities, yet shared common values. I craved her zip, her spontaneity, her lightheartedness and she our long talks, my thoughtful answers, and, as she says, the way it only takes a bit of prodding to get me to walk on the wild side. In important ways we were the same. We didn't have a lot of material things when we were young (we still don't), we had curfews, we had jobs, we were Catholic school kids much as we tried to drop the stereotype, and we agreed on most subjects. Noelle and I occasionally wrote letters, but we mostly stayed in touch by phone. Even if months had passed, it always seemed like yesterday whenever we spoke.

Our last conversation had been a few months earlier, both of us expecting our second babies—she with Catherine and me with John. Noelle called me at home in Connecticut from her Manhattan law office to gripe over her workload, her student loans, and how she wished to be home full-time with Caroline. "Do you love being home with Ryan?"

"I do, but it's kind of bittersweet. I wouldn't change my decision, but sometimes I feel a little lost."

"But it's gotta be better than this."

We laughed and the subject changed, to what I don't recall. Little did we know that the next time we would speak, Noelle's life would have changed in a way we never could have anticipated. So I waited for time to pass, for my letter to be delivered and received, for the chance to pick up with my friend where we left off and set sail through unchartered waters.

4

HEALING

Finding My Way

…have patience with everything
that remains unsolved in your heart.
Try to love the questions themselves,
like locked rooms and like books written in a foreign language.
Do not now look for the answers.
They cannot now be given to you because you could not live them.
It is a question of experiencing everything.
At present you need to live the question.
Perhaps you will gradually, without even noticing it,
find yourself experiencing the answer, some distant day.

Rainer Maria Rilke
From *Letters to a Young Poet*

It was the happiest time of my life when Caroline was born and I was on maternity leave. I couldn't wait to start the day. I used to put her in her bouncy seat on the kitchen table and talk away, making plans for our daily escape for bagels and coffee, a bowl of soup, or a walk in Central Park. I was thinking about new baby things back then like counting to be sure she had enough wet diapers, whether or not she burped after her last bottle, remembering to swab her belly button with rubbing alcohol.

Now, I lived my days with more of a forced energy, a constant prodding from within to get myself going, to get out of bed and on with the day. *You can do this.* It's not as though I was never happy or smiling, but it was distinctly different than after Caroline was born. I wasn't this happy new mother, without a care. I was more like a malted, with a swirl of emotions stirring inside. Up one minute unloading the dishwasher and singing along to my favorite CDs, and then down the next. I guess I was a little depressed, too. I don't know. There was just this melancholy about me I couldn't seem to shake as hard as I tried.

Thankfully the newborn care for Cate was the same as it was for Caroline. There wasn't anything extra to do for her because she had Down syndrome. Some babies need heart surgery, some have digestive problems, and so on. Cate and I got into the cyclical routine that mothers and typical babies do—the feedings, the naps, the diaper changes—yet my mind wasn't simply focused on what needed to be done here and now the way it was when Caroline was born. With Cate, my thoughts sporadically jumped into the future, sometimes two weeks ahead, sometimes twenty years ahead.

There was one afternoon not long after my mom and Kim left, when I was sitting on the couch feeding Cate a bottle and watching Caroline play. Caroline was wearing her new big-girl underwear and rain boots, singing a Barney song while jumping up and down on the bubble wrap left over from our move. My mind spilled over into a cascade of random worries: *Will Cate be able to be potty-trained? Will she be able to play on her own? Will she be able to sing?*

These weren't notions I pined over; I quickly pushed them out of my mind the instant they entered. Nevertheless new thoughts and questions would soon replace them, surfacing out of the blue without my insistence. I'd find myself in the shower thinking about group homes: *Will Cate have to live in one?* I'd be pulling dinner out of the fridge and wonder: *Where will she go to school?* I'd be folding clothes with a soap opera on in the background and my stomach would fall: *Will Cate be able to get married?* I'd see Caroline bending down to kiss Cate's forehead and ask myself: *What will it be like for Caroline to have a sister like Cate?*

I continued my self-therapy of holding Cate to make myself feel better, always taking her out of the infant seat, cuddling her in both arms, and burying my face in the crook of her neck. I especially loved stealing her out of the crib at night so she could fall back to sleep in my arms. It was as much a conscious act as it was a willing one. Holding her was something I needed to do. Something I could do to draw positive energy inside me.

I guess it didn't help my mood that I also missed living in the city. It would have been better not to have so much change all at once, but here we were. I thought the best way back to life as usual was to start my old routine in this new place. To get out of the house the way I did in Manhattan, to find something to do beyond our apartment walls. I began to bundle up my girls and take them for a walk every day to the bakery or the playground or wherever, to get to know this new place and establish some sense of normalcy. Although, I will say, my life hadn't been what some might consider normal in quite some time.

Tim and I had both accepted jobs in New York City after I graduated from law school, finding a tiny one-bedroom apartment on the Upper East Side. It's the place where I have the best memories of Tim and me as a couple. The apartment was scarcely 400 square feet, and had an exposed brick wall. One weekend, when we were newly married, we spent two full days snowed in together there during a blizzard. Through our window we watched a woman in the apartment building across the street who was reading on her bed. It must have been a really good book because I don't think she moved the whole time. She probably had the opposite perspective of Tim and me, thinking something along the lines of, "Holy crap, aren't those two people sick of watching TV yet?"

On weekends, Tim and I would go for a run in Central Park. I would do the big loop, he would cut through below the reservoir, and we'd meet back up at the 86th Street entrance and then go out for coffee and bagels. We would go to Yankee games on Saturday afternoons and then head down to Pete's Tavern in Gramercy Park for beers. After the games we'd grab a cab home and order Chinese, trying, if possible, to get in a little fun before the delivery guy came. It's a running joke in New York City that they cook on the bike, so you had to be quick.

I worked the way an associate lawyer in a big New York City law firm does, logging from eight to eighteen hours a day, depending on what deal I was working on. Billable hours mattered, the transactions were complex, and I was green. There was this macho-type atmosphere with lots of boasting in the elevator: "I was here until midnight last night," as if somehow it meant you were working harder than the rest.

I went back to work when Caroline was three months old and hated every minute of it. All I wanted was to be home with her. I set my sights on doing just that by triple paying student loans as often as I could. Like most working couples, we learned to roll with the all too often glitches with babysitting coverage.

Tim left by 5 a.m. to be home to relieve the babysitter at night. I'd do everything in my power to get my work done to be home by seven. But despite the effort, I had little control over my hours.

Many nights I jumped a cab from work to our apartment to spend two hours with Caroline, only to cab it back to the office. This was before the age of cell phones, laptops, and wireless e-mail so I couldn't work from home. Then I'd hop a car service home at midnight just to do it all over again the next day. When I found out I was pregnant with my second child, I knew I couldn't do it any longer. Tim and I both realized we needed to make some changes.

We decided I wouldn't go back to work after this baby was born, and we'd move out of Manhattan and try and make it on Tim's salary for a while. So I resigned a few days before my due date, after having the whole departure party with good-byes and well wishes, and moved to New Jersey. Tim and I thought our only worries would be surviving on one salary and making new friends.

I eagerly anticipated when the phone would ring, the mailman would arrive, or someone would visit to break up the day and clear my mind. Every now and then my dad would show up with a cup of tea and my favorite black-and-white cookies, just to stop in, and say hi, hold the baby, and tell me how Caroline drove him nuts, just like everybody drove him nuts. He was the quintessential visitor the way he came without notice—a happy surprise smack in the middle of the day. In many ways, I think visiting is a lost art because few have the time to practice it. How I loved when he did.

Letters and baby cards continued to trickle in. One morning, a card from Angela arrived. It was the only card that came that day. Realizing I hadn't talked with her since a few months before

Cate was born, I recalled our conversation with me grumbling about work and wanting to change my life, and her listening. God, and here I was. She had drifted from my mind, but as always she was my friend who arrived just when I needed her to. Inside the card was a handwritten note:

Dear Noelle and Tim,

I read a poem once that spoke of children as angels who from Heaven choose the family they will join. How lucky Catherine is to have chosen yours, where there is and will be so much love. Most people never find their true mission in life, but Catherine knows hers. She was born to give love, receive love, and teach us all how precious life is. How lucky we are to have her. Please know she has us as family. You are all our family. Congratulations.

Love,

Angela, Rob, Ryan and John

Her words resonated with me in a way no one else's had. Their positive, spiritual thread was similar to what I heard from the nun and Father Larry. Yet at that moment, her words meant more to me. I listened to the nun and Father Larry, and I tried to believe them, but Ange's words—arriving as they did, in a single card, at this time—sat with me in a different way. I don't know exactly why other than to say that Angela was the smartest friend I had, she was always herself, and always honest. If she said something was true, I believed her. I trusted in these words because she wrote them, and that trust made me hope. *Ange knows I was meant to have Cate.*

I had never really thought about it, that my life—the everyday person's life—had special purpose, that maybe each and every one of us was here for a reason. Ange's card, her written words, opened my mind to this line of thinking, to this bit of faith. *What if there is more to life than I think there is?* While we'd never spoken of religion or spirituality before (our friendship being easy and fun), we were older now and life had made an unexpected turn. Up to now, we'd never had cause to think more deeply about our circumstances. About why things were the way they were.

I took her card to bed with me that night and after reading it probably for the tenth time, tucked it in my nightstand. I very purposely put it where I could get to it (it's still the one thing in my house I can find, unlike my morning mug of coffee, the car keys, or my cell phone that's hiding in an undisclosed location in vibrate mode). I needed her card at an arm's length the way some people keep the Bible. I pulled it out of the drawer when I was upset. I looked at it when I was overwhelmed with fear of the future. I cried over it when I doubted myself. "She was born to give love, receive love, and teach us all..." These were the words that stuck with me most. It wasn't the full sentence Ange had written, but the fragment where her handwriting ended on the line before finishing on the next. It pierced through all my thoughts, all my worries. "She was born to give love, receive love, and teach us all..." *God, is Angela right? She must believe it. Do I?*

The first time Noelle and I spoke after Catherine was born is a fleeting memory. Although I was eager to talk with her, part of me was scared, too. What would I say? Should I gloss over what was going on here in Connecticut with Ryan and John and just focus on her family? Or, does Noelle need the distraction of idle chatter? Maybe that's why I avoided calling her longer than I should have.

Despite my Guadagno work ethic (story goes that Pop Pops had a job before he stepped foot on Ellis Island), I'm pathetic about things I'd rather dodge. Too much time had gone by and the more I dragged my feet the harder it was to call. In the beginning it was because I thought Noelle needed the time, but now it was because I did. I was thinking about this too much and just had to pick up the phone.

This initial call was short by comparison to our usual marathons. Perhaps that's why it's such a blur, akin to pulling a band-aid from a child's knee. *Hurry up and get it over with, and you won't feel the pain.* For as much as my phone call was meant to be an outreach of compassion to my good friend, it was also an acknowledgement of the truth. Her baby had Down syndrome and mine didn't. Her family wasn't what she expected, and mine was. While I believed every word I wrote in the baby card I sent to her, I also felt sorry for Noelle.

She thanked me for my card, "God, it really means so much, Ange. You can't possibly know." All the while I was thinking about what an awful friend I was for only having sent a card instead of visiting and for taking too much time to call her. Even though my mother had taught me the importance of sending a card that conveyed my true feelings to someone (my mom takes great care in selecting cards for those she loves), Noelle was one of the few people to appreciate my doing so. Perhaps I shouldn't have been surprised.

I will say it was awkward to talk to Noelle that day in a way it never was before. Almost like we'd just met and I didn't know her well enough to comfort her. Noelle said she was okay, though both of us knew she wasn't. "Cate's really healthy," she added, and I blinked back tears. I recall needing to choose my words carefully, but I don't know exactly what I said. I'm quite certain I didn't say what I wanted to: "I'm really worried about you, Noelle, and I have to tell you how guilty I feel that my baby is okay and yours isn't. Please understand I didn't expect this to happen, and I'm sorry that it did even though I know there's a greater plan in the works."

I'm sure amidst my fumbling, I did say words like: "We'll always be friends" and "I'm here to help you," because I felt them in my heart. Yes, friendship and support, these were tangible promises I could offer. Promises I vowed deep within my soul to keep. While so much was uncertain for Noelle, being there for her was one way I could make things better.

∽

The girls and I headed out just before lunchtime for our daily stroller walks in New Jersey. It seemed this was the earliest I could escape from the apartment with a toddler and a baby. By now spring had arrived, so the dressing was easier—no snowsuits, boots, or other paraphernalia required. I smiled watching Caroline put her hands on mine as I gripped the top of a pair of navy tights and pulled them up her endless legs. *You'll be taller than me someday, Josie.* But when I pulled the dotted onesie over Cate's abdomen and snapped it around the inside of her legs it made me question her independence. *Will you always need me to help you get dressed?*

When I used to walk in Manhattan with Caroline, I found a stroller was a magnet for attracting attention. Inevitably someone would approach the carriage, look in and say, "Aw, a little baby girl. How old?" I used to love that with her, just laughing and chatting on with total strangers about my baby, naively thinking everyone was as entranced by my child as I was.

Now, every time a person poked her head in the carriage, I felt the need to explain my baby had Down syndrome. Honestly, I'm not really sure why I'd say it, but there was always this pull to share the truth. "She's four weeks old blah, blah, blah and she has Down syndrome." I don't know, perhaps I assumed people could tell right away, so I would just say it aloud to get it out there. Maybe no one even noticed, but it was the first thing I saw so I assumed it was the first thing everyone else could see, too.

"Oh, she's so cute," some would say to my news of her disability. Others made personal connections, "Oh, my cousin has Down syndrome." I would always walk away from these encounters regretting my need to say too much to complete strangers. *Why do I do that?*

Besides our daily walks, there were plenty of errands that pulled me out of the apartment as well. One afternoon, I made my way into the grocery store with the girls, holding Caroline by the hand and with Cate slung over my arm in her infant seat. All at once I noticed a nicely dressed middle-aged black woman being escorted out of the store by two police officers. *Gosh, that doesn't look right.*

I continued along, latching Cate's car seat to the front of a grocery cart and lifting Caroline into the back. We meandered around the produce section, picking up what I thought we needed, not having checked the refrigerator or made a list before we left. I was tying up a bag of apples when my eyes fell on this young man at the front of the store, near the end of one of the aisles. He was in a reclining-type wheelchair and significantly disabled. *Oh my God, how hard.*

"Can I have a piece of cheese, Mommy?" Caroline asked when I lifted a bunch of bananas into the cart. "Yep, that's our next stop." We headed for the deli counter and I asked her to pull a number from the machine. I maneuvered the cart out of the way to wait our turn when I overheard two women whispering about me. "She looks too young to have a child with Down syndrome," they said, attempting to be discreet by looking away. In an instant, I was transported back to Myrtle Beach and my own curiosity about the young family I'd seen.

I brushed off the incident, finished up our shopping, and headed for the cashier with the shortest line. After checking out, I saw the same woman who had been accompanied by the police officers out of the store. She was struggling to push the wheelchair that held the young disabled man I saw earlier, and at the same time pull her grocery cart behind her. I asked if she needed help and she said, "Yes, thank you, I do." So I asked her to wait there while I quickly put my groceries in my car and went back with the girls for her.

The woman pushed the wheelchair while I pushed her grocery cart with one hand, held Cate in her car seat with the other, and had Caroline hold onto the cart. We stopped alongside her handicapped van so I could load in her groceries while she waited for the mechanical lift to reach the ground. After the woman maneuvered her son into the van, she put her hands on my cheeks, kissed me, and said, "Thank you, dear." She told me that she had left her son in the van with the windows down while she ran into the grocery store. "I was quickly shopping when an announcement came over the loudspeaker asking that the owner of a van that sounded like mine report to the customer service desk.

"When I approached the desk I was met by two police officers responding to a report of a disabled person being left alone in a parked car. I explained that it was my car and my son, that I had to run into the store for just a moment and couldn't maneuver the wheelchair and the grocery cart at the same time. And that I couldn't leave him home alone," she said, closing the door of the van. "Since I'd already gone through the monumental effort to get here, I decided to go back in and bring my son with me. Don't you know, neither the police nor anyone from the store offered to help?"

"Oh, I'm so sorry," I said.

"My son was a perfectly fine and healthy young man until a roofing accident left him physically and mentally disabled," she explained. "My other son is autistic and I thought this was the harder path that God had given me. But now he helps care for his disabled brother. You never know what the good Lord has in store for you, but rest assured there are angels all around us," she said pulling her keys out of a pocket. She hugged me goodbye, leaned down to smile at Cate, and then went on her way.

Even though I tried to be conscious of Ange's words that Cate's birth was purposeful, it wasn't a miraculous recovery for me. I still relied on family and friends to coach me out of my funk every day. They encouraged me to take things slowly, to concentrate on the present. But living in the present with an eye towards the future was my nature. During law school I had become more focused. A person who had a plan for her life, a clear idea about what she should be doing next. So not looking ahead, not knowing what to expect from the future, much less day to day, was not only unnatural, but scary as hell. I'd never traveled down life's path without a map before.

It was this uncertainty, not just my sadness, which made these early days with my girls so tough. I knew there was so much to come, so much I didn't even understand. For me, this wasn't bringing home a baby and simply doing what comes naturally as a mom, that maternal instinct rallying from within. My first thought was to read. I began with the primer on Down syndrome and was determined to read it cover to cover. It explained everything one needed to know about the disability, but all that I focused on were the negative things—the what-could-be-wrong-with-Cate kinds of things. I sobbed every time I opened that damn book.

Still, I was drawn to it like an addict, to that glimmer of hope the next chapter might provide, only to be let down by another round of hard facts. It was devastating to learn of the medical problems Cate might encounter, everything from a higher incidence of mental illness to digestive problems and the early onset of Alzheimer's. I spent hours obsessing over the possibility of every scenario, placing myself on high alert for signs of these maladies. I was convinced Cate would have leukemia, and I pined over that for a week. Another week was spent staring into her eyes looking for cataracts. The instant one eye strayed, and every baby's eyes do, I was convinced she had wandering eyes.

When my mind didn't have enough to worry over medically, it began to consider what Cate would not be able to do socially. I had it figured she wouldn't have friends to play with, wouldn't be asked to the prom, and might never have a boyfriend. These thoughts were relentless. They followed me into the kitchen when I was making lunch, to the park on our walks, and into bed at night.

One afternoon while sitting in my favorite club chair with Cate nestled in one arm and the book in the other, I was done. "Forget this!" I said out loud, having read my last unfortunate statistic, and chucked the book over my shoulder. It landed on the floor behind me, where it collected dust for a few months. I could hardly look at that book, let alone move it to a shelf. I'd never been much of a researcher, anyway. I usually just called Ange for her opinion like: "Hey, did you get that chicken pox vaccine for Ryan?" and that was good enough for me.

When I took Cate to the pediatrician for a checkup, the doctor suggested I call the mom of one of her patients with Down syndrome. This was more my style. The pediatrician prefaced that the woman might be a little intense, but was very knowledgeable. I was thrilled to have a name and called her as soon as I got home. Only seconds into our conversation, I realized the pediatrician was right on both counts. Although we didn't have much in common, she was eager to share her knowledge and for that I was grateful.

This phone call was an important first step. With it I'd entered the world of Down syndrome in earnest. To this day, everything I know about the disability I learned from talking with anyone who would talk to me. It was clear from these early conversations that being a mom of a child with Down syndrome would mean doctor appointments with specialists, having more patience than I currently possessed, and something called early intervention.

5

STEPPING STONES

Everything Down Syndrome

Whatever comes your way,
give it meaning and transform it into something of value.
A precious stone cannot be polished without friction,
nor humanity perfected without trials.

Author Unknown

Early intervention was a term that came up often when I spoke to the pediatrician, friends, and even an acquaintance from childhood whom I happened to run into. "You need to get Cate into early intervention," or, "So, have you started Cate in early intervention, yet?" Now, I considered myself an educated human being, but for the life of me I just didn't get it. *Is early intervention some kind of special school you enroll in?*

It was as frustrating as it was truly hilarious. I can't help but laugh when I remember how insane getting started was. Maybe I was simply asking the wrong people, having just moved to New Jersey and not knowing a soul, but it was as if I were looking for Oz. No one had a contact person, a phone number, or map of the Yellow Brick Road to set us on our way. There was just this amorphous term—early intervention—and the need to get Cate involved right away.

After talking to a bunch of people, I figured out that early intervention is a set of services, including occupational, physical, and speech therapies, that would help Cate develop and progress. Although the advice to enroll Cate in early intervention was well intentioned, it created a false sense of urgency within me. I was consumed with getting her started in a program, worrying that Cate's every hope was pinned on immediate action, lest the promise of her life be swallowed up in some abyss.

What lunacy it was. I mean, here I was with a newborn. I shouldn't have worried so much, but my obsessive brain wouldn't let it go. Starting Cate in early intervention at six months old instead of six weeks old would have been okay, too. I was completely unsure of myself—unsure of what I was supposed to do for Cate. It was different with Caroline, when I didn't dwell on anything and simply took my mom's lead.

"Noelle, this baby was born at ten pounds, she needs cereal," my mom said, dishing out her advice when visiting two weeks after Caroline was born. From a kitchen shelf she pulled a box of Gerber rice cereal someone had given us as a baby gift along with all the needed sundries: Balmex, baby power, and medicine droppers. After pouring a little mound of rice cereal into a baby bowl, she headed to the refrigerator in search of the bottle of Enfamil I made earlier.

"But, Caroline's only two weeks old. The doctor said a baby should be six months old before you introduce that," I implored, though I had no idea. My mom stopped stirring the formula into the rice cereal to sprinkle a pinch of sugar on it and said, "The doctors today with all these new rules."

"Oh, I know," I said, assuming she knew what she was doing. *Are you supposed to put sugar in baby cereal?* I put Caroline in her bouncy seat on the kitchen table and watched my mom feed her. Caroline ate every bite and that was that.

Because of my self-induced pressure, Tim and I were eager to start Cate in early intervention and made an appointment to preview Stepping Stones. It was a program based in northern New Jersey offering birth-to-pre-K early intervention services designed specifically for children with Down syndrome. This was a big day for us. Tim took the day off, and we were excited to get Cate started. I even dressed her and Caroline in matching yellow jumpers for the occasion and tried unsuccessfully to clip a white bow into Cate's thin hair that still stood straight up. I didn't think this would be a hard day; I thought it would be an enlightening one.

We pulled up to the annex of an older church where Stepping Stones was located. A young woman with Down syndrome stood at the front door. I couldn't take my eyes off her, and I have to say I was heartbroken. It was the first time I'd seen a person with Down syndrome since I'd had Cate and, honestly, I think it was the first time I ever really looked at a person with the disability. I couldn't believe this would be my daughter some day. My baby was standing before me as an adult—all the years of growing up instantly accelerated before my eyes.

"Did you see her?" I asked Tim under my breath as he pulled open the door for me.

"Yeah, Noelle, I know."

Come to find out, the woman we met was an early participant in the program and now worked as a volunteer. I was unable to see how independent, social, and responsible she was. All I saw was a young woman who was talking to herself. Adding to my heartache, I heard she was their star pupil, their success story. The promise of Cate's life seemed anything but hopeful.

And then we met the staff.

A conservatively dressed woman in her early fifties approached us and extended her hand. "Hi, I'm Betty Mitchell, the director here," she said in a soft-spoken voice.

"So nice to meet you. I'm Noelle," I said, shaking her hand before she bent down to greet Caroline who sheepishly peeked out from behind me.

"You must be Caroline," Betty said. "We have a playroom for the older sisters and brothers." Betty stood up and looked at Cate who was in the infant seat that was still hanging on my arm. She tickled Cate's knees, while looking at her with a wide smile. "She's so bright-eyed," Betty said, now holding the tips of Cate's toes. "That's a great sign, Noelle."

I have to say her words went a long way to help alleviate my fear of having a child with a glazed appearance, who (it's awful to say or think) looked retarded. It was a word Ange and I tossed around so loosely in high school. "Oh my God, you're such a retard," we'd say to each other and laugh. Now it may as well have been a swear word—one of the few swears I'd never say again.

The professionals we met that day spoke in only positive terms about Cate's potential. They told us she would achieve the milestones a typical child does. The only difference was that it would take her a little longer to do so. "They all get there, Mr. and Mrs. Alix," a therapist said with one caveat: "They all get there differently, but they all get there." Stepping Stones was not only where Cate began her developmental therapy, but also where I began my own rebirth.

We entered the therapy room where Cate's classes would be held and I saw a mom holding a baby girl with Down syndrome. I immediately connected with this woman without speaking a word to her. Like me, she was young, gorgeous, impeccably dressed (sorry, I couldn't help myself). Actually, she looked about my age and seemed so sad, so unsure and in that way was just like me. I felt badly for her, thinking this was as improbable a turn in her life as it was in mine. We became friends and she later admitted feeling the same way about me that morning. Very sorry to see how sad I was, too.

Tim and I sat down and I busied myself, lifting Cate from the car seat and unzipping her snuggly, which I tucked into the diaper bag. I cuddled Cate into my lap and quietly scanned the room while we waited for the class to start. There was so much stuff there I'd never seen before: a custom swing, modified chairs, mirror-lined walls, and three-dimensional geometric mats. Eventually, three more children and their parents joined us. It was so much to take in: the children, the parents, the equipment, and the staff. Yet, I have to say, I concentrated on the children most of all. Here were other babies with Down syndrome. Babies just like Cate.

We found ourselves in a place where having a baby with Down syndrome was totally normal. It was never about what Cate couldn't do, but what she would do. It was reassuring that these people knew what they were talking about, that Cate would be okay. I guess the greatest leap was for me to acknowledge that this was part of my life now: our child had Down syndrome and—wow—this was how I'd be spending my time even though it was completely foreign to me.

～

It was as if our kids took turns being sick, preventing Noelle and me from seeing each other. For a couple of months we visited by phone, which Noelle was quite accustomed to doing. She was a prolific phone-talker, especially in high school when she would stretch the extra-long phone cord from the kitchen to her bedroom at the end of the hall, flop on her bed, and talk long into the night. As it happened, the phone calls with friends after Cate was born were just as essential to Noelle. She said they meant more to her than any of us probably knew.

In those early days it was difficult to gauge how Noelle was doing since our phone calls centered on Cate. She was a master at avoiding the subject, deftly steering us away from her and on to the baby. Although I prodded to find some glimmer of truth about her every time we spoke ("How are you? Be honest."), she never answered the question completely enough to satisfy me. Her preference was to take charge of the conversation and do all of the asking.

She posed leading questions, which were impossible to disagree with. "Okay, I'm probably nuts, but Cate will talk, right?" She'd listen for my answer in her favor, "Yes, she'll be able to talk," and immediately ask another: "She'll have friends, right?" Again, I'd consent, "Yes, she'll have friends. You're her mom. Cate will probably have more friends than she'll know what to do with."

These answers came to me as quickly as her questions were offered. For the most part, I believed what I said. Although I suppose my responses were made in part to appease her, to encourage her to believe something I had no idea about—any real authority to promise. Yes, good Catholic that I was, I was slipping half-truths under her radar. Yet how could I respond any differently? I'd never say something like, "Actually, Noelle, there may be a chance that she won't be able to speak very well." Sometimes honesty isn't the best medicine with your best friend.

Noelle was always one to get the answer she was looking for, even when we were younger. It was just her way. When thinking about how all our friends would celebrate after high school graduation, she said, "You're going to New Jersey with us, right Ange? Of course you're going." I don't imagine it was all personality after Cate was born, but part coping mechanism, too. With her leading questions, Noelle got the reassurances she needed to hear. And, yet, there were other times, every now and then kind of times, when she brushed the edge of harder topics. When I didn't have an answer other than the truth.

"Ange, remember the classroom at Ketcham, down in the basement? And the kids we saw for only a minute?"

"Coming off the short bus…Yes, I do. God, yes I do." And I did. The images of them ghostlike in my memory the way I must have seen them, but really didn't. Almost as if they weren't there at all.

As great a facility as Stepping Stones was, beginning wasn't easy. It wasn't just adapting to the therapies, but the actual getting there twice a week that had me in a twist. The only route was via the Garden State Parkway, which for lack of a better description, totally sucked. It was years before the E-Z Pass, when the Parkway had thirty-five cent tolls every ten miles, each one causing a twenty-minute backup. I spent the drive with my stomach in knots, knowing I'd be late yet again. Despite the hideous traffic, I never left as early as I wanted to. And that, ladies and gentlemen, is the story of my life.

I would fly in the door dragging Caroline by one arm and holding the fifty-pound car seat in the other looking as if I'd just come from a class at the gym. I'd quickly drop Caroline at sibling support services (a.k.a., the babysitting room) and take Cate to her therapy. If it was a Tuesday, a volunteer stayed with Cate and I ran to a parent support group. On Thursdays I stayed with Cate to learn and to see what the therapists were doing. In either instance, disheveled from the fiasco of trying to get there on time, I'd attempt to gain my composure before I'd walk into the room. Putting a hand to my chest, I'd catch my breath and pitch my standard line, "Oh, hi everyone. Sorry I'm late."

The Tuesday parent support group was guided by a social worker, and my particular session was attended exclusively by moms, each with a child Cate's age. We were a group of women who might not have otherwise connected, and yet we clicked right from the start. There was this pure human connection for us—a bond by circumstance—that melted away the pretenses women often have on first meeting. (How is she dressed? Where does she live? Does she seem nice? What kind of job does she have? How did she have time to do her hair and makeup before she got here?) We all knew without saying the words that what we shared was far more important than what we did not.

We met in a classroom, sitting on little kid chairs arranged in a circle. While the babies were next door getting their therapies, we were getting a brand of our own. There was plenty of banter about fitting back into our favorite jeans, our clueless husbands, and dysfunctional families, though most often we spoke of our fears: Would our kids go to a regular school? Would they walk? Would they be overweight? Would they talk normally? Would they ever work one day? Would they get married and have kids? Would they live with us forever?

Our sessions were open and brutally honest, without any social pressure to be politically correct. We talked about how we spent a little more money to buy cute outfits for our babies, how we would never give them a "bowl" haircut, how we hated when their tongues stuck out of their mouths. We wondered what our other kids' lives would be like having a sibling with Down syndrome. We discussed the possibility of having more children and being scared about that. It was refreshing to open up with these women. To have thoughts I imagined were exclusively my own sprout from someone else's lips.

Within the first few weeks there was a predictable comfort in going. I knew that I'd leave feeling better than when I arrived, and that I wasn't in this alone. Tim, my parents, Kim, and Angela always listened and were sympathetic to my concerns, but this group of women understood me in a way no one else could. We learned from each other that maybe life with a child we didn't expect would be okay. How I loved Tuesdays.

Noelle and I were finally able to visit early that spring at my childhood home on Monroe Drive. While Noelle's streets were named for apples, ours honored past presidents and were dotted with cookie-cutter split-level homes on modest half-acre lots. I remember Noelle coming through my parents' front door count-less times growing up, every time for something fun. To play dolls and dress up when we were little girls, for sleepovers as teens, for pictures on my wedding day as young women. It was wonderful to finally be able to see her and yet this was a happy-sad visit. I didn't recall ever having had one of those with her before.

Noelle had Cate in her arms while Caroline followed timidly behind her. "It's good to see you," I said and spread my arms wide to hug Noelle. "Here, let me hold Cate," I said eager for the chance to get to know this baby. It was as if Noelle passed me a sandbag when I quickly threw a second arm under Cate to support her weight. Yet it wasn't just her size that made me feel I had to hold her with two arms. There was a looseness about her like she didn't have any bones.

"Wow, she's solid," I said with surprise.

"I know, she weighs a ton, doesn't she?" laughed Noelle and then more seriously added, "Babies with Down syndrome have low muscle tone. We were told to hold her securely, so you may need to support her head a bit more." I found that I had to cradle her arms in, too, or else they dangled to the side like those of my baby doll Susie whom I had while growing up, whose floppy cotton arms and legs would hang to the ground if I didn't hold her tight.

Cate didn't fuss the way some babies do after leaving the comfort of their mothers' arms. She was the gentlest of babies and beautiful—a beautiful baby who looked like she had Down syndrome. Her eyes, the bright blue of beach glass, were turned up at the corners and set into her circular face. I was compelled to press my cheek against hers, which was warm and soft next to mine. While Noelle ran to get her bag from the car, I squatted down still holding Cate and reached out a hand to Caroline. "You're such a good big sister," I said, my voice cracking. To see Noelle and her girls was to understand this was all very real.

We made our way to the backyard where my parents were watching Ryan and John. There were greetings all around, and we sat for a time making a fuss over the baby and catching up. My mom wanted to hold Cate and sat her up in her lap already knowing how to prop Cate's head, without instructions from Noelle. She lovingly cradled Cate's neck and chin in her right hand as if she'd done it all her life. I know my mother, who is a deeply faithful person, was filled with nothing but love for this precious, most innocent of babies.

This was one of those cordial visits where you skim the surface and don't really talk about what you should. To get into a deep conversation didn't seem the right thing to do that day. Maybe it was because my parents were there and it would have been awkward, but still I think it was for the best that we didn't talk about anything too serious that afternoon. It was the opportunity to see Noelle and meet Cate. There would be plenty of time for getting to the heart of things in the months and years to come.

Aside from receiving the emotional support, at Stepping Stones we learned how to raise a baby with Down syndrome. Typical milestones that happen naturally with most babies might happen differently for Cate, so they gave us the information we needed to help her progress. Perhaps the biggest general obstacle for people with Down syndrome comes from having low muscle tone. For babies, low muscle tone can make everything from speaking, to feeding, to crawling and walking more difficult.

When we fed Cate, we were told to support her chin with one hand to prevent open mouth posture; hold her tight to strengthen her stomach muscles; put a thickening agent in her drinks so she wouldn't choke on them; teach her how to drink from a straw (which to me seemed crazy for an infant) so she could develop stronger muscles in her lips; tap her lips and say, "lips together," so that her tongue would stay in there. They told us not to use pacifiers or sippy cups because they promoted tongue-thrusting. *I'll never remember all this stuff.*

This was great advice, but some of it ran contrary to the practicalities of life and remaining sane. Who doesn't need a pacifier to calm a baby? I for one would plug that paci in as soon as we got in the car for yet another heinous trip down the Garden State Parkway. Still, there was the nagging guilt I felt every time I put it in her mouth, the same guilt I had eight years later when she was still drinking from a sippy cup because I had already cleaned up fifty-five spills that day and couldn't take one more.

We were told to constantly stimulate Cate, at least that's how my Type A brain took it. It wasn't enough for me that Cate had an older sister jumping around in her face, acting out children's TV shows, and putting on spontaneous performances. Cate couldn't sit in her bouncy seat and not be active because it made me feel guilty. I had to hang black-and-white mobiles in front of her; I put her in colorful rattle socks, so when she kicked her legs she'd be stimulated; I bought the rattles that were recommended to me with specific handles to build her fine motor skills.

Cate would be content sitting in her infant seat, her perfectly round face smiling at me when I was washing dishes or doing whatever, and I'd call out to Caroline: "Go talk to your sister." Caroline would saunter in and say, "Hi Cate, hi Cate, hi Cate" over and over. The monotone way she'd say it made me insane, but it was better than nothing.

I was always thinking about what I should be doing for Cate, and when I wasn't, I felt guilty that I should be. I never worried whether Caroline would crawl, walk correctly, or speak in complete sentences. I didn't even think about it. With Cate, everything was a big question mark, and I didn't want to fail her. I was worried she wouldn't reach the new ivy-league benchmark I'd set for her: to be a high-functioning person with Down syndrome.

6

FAITH

Her Baptism

We cannot restrict our God to one building;
the very earth and heaven could not contain him.
God cannot be captured in books, for he is too mighty;
He cannot be pressed between pages like a flower.
He roams freely and comes to each one of us.
God hides within each of us, waiting to be found:
Our God waits to be discovered within his creation.

David Adam
From *Music of the Heart*

Tim and I had been talking about when to get Cate baptized, and we had this feeling that we wanted to do it sooner rather than later, both of us not really articulating why. I called Father Larry and asked if he would baptize Cate for us, and he assured me he would love to. As with Caroline, we decided to have the baptism at St. Mary's in Wappingers Falls, the church I grew up in. We went ahead with our plans against my mother's strong advice, "Let's hold off until summer or at least late spring so we can have the party outside. My house is too small for that many people."

I was dead set against waiting.

Cate at 3 months old: Makes good eye contact; tracks objects and people with her eyes; beginning to bat and swat at toys; inspects her own hands; responds to sounds and voices; starting to eat cereal from a spoon; beginning to roll over from her stomach to her back.

Up until the time I had Caroline, I don't think I truly thought about religion or my faith. I went to Catholic grammar school where it was part of my daily education. Every Sunday my family and I would go to church and, probably like most kids, I never liked going. I don't remember paying much attention or reflecting on anything other than whether or not we were going out for breakfast afterward or if any of my friends were there.

I went to a Catholic college more by chance than design, and I took some religion courses because they were required. In my late teens and early twenties, I wouldn't have called myself religious and I rarely talked to God or prayed on my own. There was a period in college and law school where I didn't go to church at all, except when I was home for weekend visits with my parents. When I did go to church, it was more the aerobics of it—the sitting, the standing, the kneeling, and the ritual of the mass—that engaged me more than genuine faith. I was

Catholic because of what I did and how I acted rather than how I felt in my soul.

As is the case with most Catholics, my family had its church routines. We attended the 11:15 a.m. mass every Sunday and sat in the same pew near the back of the church—the one with a structural column right in the middle of it. I have no idea why we chose to sit in that row since my dad could barely squeeze his stomach by the column. We'd all make our way around it, contorting our bodies in whatever way worked. My dad was usually last man in, inhaling all the air he could into his lungs to carry him past the obstruction. "Jesus, why the hell do we gotta sit here," he'd say, even though he stopped at the same pew week after week, motioning with his arm like a traffic cop for us to file in.

Church was a time for trouble with my dad. He'd pass us crazy notes written on the church bulletin: "Don't look now. I think there's a Colossian behind us." Or he'd randomly begin to giggle and tell me, "Don't get me started. Your mother's gonna be pissed." Before long one of us would be in a laughing fit so unshakable we'd have to leave. He'd scope out where the local mortician was sitting and whisper, "There's McCauley, looking to see who's coughing, hoping for his next customer." Then he'd spy the woman with the tight-fitting white pants sitting a few rows ahead of us and ask, "If she had a quarter in her back pocket, ya think we could read the date?"

I'm sure my dad believed in God. He certainly believed in doing good for others, always lending a hand, always helping someone out no matter what. He had no tolerance, however, for what he would call "the bullshit." He never liked being told what to do in terms of practicing his faith. My dad was the most Christian person I've ever known, but he was by far the least holy. For him religion happened at the corner deli, around the kitchen table, on the city streets—every place he traveled and well beyond the confines of church.

〜

Mr. Clifford was unlike any of the other fathers I knew, and for that matter, unlike any other man I'd ever met. He was always interested in you, specifically, in the moment, and would talk to me like I was a person, not a kid. "Angela Gwa-dan-yo," he'd bellow, as if announcing me at a Yankee game. He'd smile and ask me a pertinent question, knowing all that was going on with our friends, "So, did ya go to Sofia's last night? I hope you girls stayed out of trouble." I'd quickly reply, "Yes, Noelle dragged me along. And, yes, we were good," and then wait, seeing the twinkle in his eye, for the zinger of a wisecrack about to fly out of his mouth. "Where the hell do ya think they get their dough? Stocks, bonds, the mob?"

I'd often find Mr. Clifford in the driveway about to get into his car, his oversized glasses sitting halfway down his nose and cocked to one side. "Ah, I gotta go drop off something to my brother, John," he said one afternoon, opening the door to his company car, while I walked up the driveway to see Noelle.

"Isn't that like an hour away?"

"Yeah, and damned if I wasn't just there yesterday."

"Couldn't you just mail it?"

"You're a smart one Angela Gwa-dan-yo," he'd say with a chuckle and get in the car. I cannot begin to count the number of similar conversations he and I had in this exact setting—me coming to see Noelle, him heading off in the car. I like to remember him this way, to think of him living his life in a uniquely faithful way. Caring for others by showing up.

Although my dad was the polar opposite of Mr. Clifford, he had a similar passion for people, eagerly putting himself out there.

An IBM executive by day and all-around handyman on weekends, he installed dishwashers, toilets, and garbage disposals for many of the neighbors and loved every job. "You've got to do it right," he'd say, be it your homework, the way you fixed something, or the way you put your family first. Noelle would often show up at my house and find him in the middle of a job—under a car hood, up a ladder, on the roof—and belt her typical comment, "Geez, Mr. G. Why don't you just call somebody?"

For my dad, doing things right was not only how you worked, it was also what made you a good Catholic. To be sure, Sunday mass was never to be missed, and my dad knew his prayers and said them loud enough to be heard by anyone within earshot. He and my mom together said the special prayers at funeral masses and burials, prayers that came in a certain order, prayers I didn't know.

This piece of him used to surprise me even though, like my mom, he'd gone to Catholic school all his life. He was my dad who worked twelve hours a day at the office and then two more at home, who could do anything, who was our life raft. "Don't worry, I'll take care of it," he'd say when something wasn't right. Faith lived deep inside him and I see now it was part of what made him a strong man.

After Caroline was born, I distinctly remember having the genuine desire to go to church, which I don't recall having felt before then. I was so happy, so thankful for this little baby. I couldn't believe she was mine. I needed to say thank you to God, and maybe going to church was the way to do that.

The first time we went to church in Manhattan we left our apartment at the start of mass, walking as fast as two people could behind a stroller. "Do we wheel the baby into church?" I asked Tim, when we were about to walk in, clueless about this piece of church etiquette. Instead we grabbed Caroline and ditched the stroller at the back, attempting to sneak unnoticed into an open pew, while the priest was finishing up his sermon.

Attending church in the city was unlike anywhere else I've ever been; it was truly a cross section of city life. There was the younger, transient population to whom church was just one of many Sunday stops. Some would carry in groceries, while others wore exercise clothing, fitting church into their busy modern lives. Then there were the elderly who, I'm sure like my own relatives, had lived in the same city neighborhood their whole lives, surrounded by this younger crowd whose faces would come and go.

It was about this time that I began saying silent bedtime prayers in my head the way I used to when I was little. There was something about having Caroline that awakened a faith in me I'd never really known. The prayers I said were familiar ones I could recite from memory—the Hail Mary, the Our Father—when I closed my eyes and lay down on my bed. There was no order to how I said them or set number I had to reach to make it count.

This is not to say I made it to church every Sunday, or that I remembered to pray every night. I was a Catholic on the rebound, trying my best to connect with God. When I skipped mass or fell asleep before saying my prayers, it felt like I had missed something. I welcomed this glimmer of faith in my life and, along with it, the wider perspective I gained as a parent. As if it were a new idea, I realized life wasn't simply about making decisions that affected me—that self-centered, twenty-something take on things.

We began planning Caroline's christening shortly after she was born, thinking mostly about the party we would have to celebrate. This was the perfect opportunity to see our friends and family and have them over to meet Caroline. I didn't consider the true meaning of baptism as a sacrament for her. I thought about the christening dress, the formality of the event, of celebrating the gift of Caroline.

～

Caroline was a beautiful baby, and beyond her years even then on her christening day, looking around inquisitively at everyone there, seeming to take it all in. She was remarkably tall, too, probably taller than any baby I'd ever held, her long legs in knit booties stretching beyond the hem of her gown. After the ceremony was over, we went to Noelle's parents' house to celebrate. Her mom had rented a white party tent, which was pitched in their backyard to hold everyone who came. There were coolers lined up on the grass like soldiers, one after the next, filled with beer, wine and soda, and food was marched out of the house—a parade of women carrying long, deep aluminum trays of ziti, casseroles, and salads.

Watching Noelle's mom and aunts run about, chat, mingle, laugh, and dish out food, reminded me of the women in my family who mattered most to me, women I wanted to emulate. How they celebrated religious events in a big, jubilant way. And how faith was laced into their lives, even on quiet, uneventful days.

I can still see my Grandma Guadagno walking down the steep hills of Tarentum, Pennsylvania, returning from daily mass with a rosary dangling from her fingers and a dog-eared Bible clutched to her chest. Her home was adorned with religious paraphernalia, my favorites being a plaster mini-Pieta set on her bedroom dresser and a small plaque hung over the kitchen doorway to her cellar asking for God's blessing on her home, "Dio mi benedici questa casa."

Just as vivid are the memories of my Grandma Froning, my maternal grandmother, rocking in a chair reading her prayer books or saying the rosary. She owned her fair share of spiritual knick-knacks, including a framed print of the face of Jesus. It was incredibly lifelike the way his eyes seemed to follow you wherever you went. I used to be frightened of it until my mother set me at ease, "Jesus isn't watching you, he's watching over you." It was a trying day when we cleared out my grandmother's apartment after she died, but we were heartened to find a statue of Mary and an open bottle of holy water on the table next to her bed.

My mom's faith was equally visible, from the magazines and prayer cards that arrived in the mail, to her favorite statue of Mary, cracked and glued in every possible place. "Your mom is like Sister Maurice," Noelle murmured to me when we were little girls, sitting at the kitchen table staring at Mary, waiting for my mom to dole out a homemade snack. The statue of Mary still graces the center of the kitchen table forty years later, along with my mother's mantra—"Let go, let God"—and framed prayers for those lost on September 11 and for the soldiers in Iraq and Afghanistan. My mom had actually planned on being a nun when she finished college, until she met my dad at a party. Thankfully for my brother, Alex, and me, it was love at first sight.

My mom put everyone else first, which I assumed was a character trait and not the manifestation of her faith, which it was. Clothing, jewelry, make-up, and name brands were not important to her. "Things will never make you happy," she'd tell me in an attempt to explain how faith affected her life. As a teenager, it was hard for me to follow suit; I was easily tempted by shopping with friends and the Calvin Klein jeans Brooke Shields was modeling. My mom let me get the things I thought I needed without lecturing, quietly slipping faith in without my knowing.

~

Tim, Caroline, and I continued to go to church right up until Cate was born, because it had become part of our weekend schedule. Although I felt good about going, I honestly didn't attend mass with the hopes of being filled up by faith; it just seemed the right thing to do. But after Cate was born, there was a spiritual pull for me to go. At least that's the best way I can describe it, having never had that draw before. It wasn't a feeling of obligation to attend church because I should, but rather because I needed to.

I was inspired by the words Ange wrote to me in her baby card, beyond the encouragement I reaped from them at first. I continued to pull her card out of my nightstand many times a day even though I'd already memorized it. To see the words written in her handwriting was to know she believed them, and that she wanted me to believe them, too. *"She was born to give love, receive love and teach us all..."*

I caught myself thinking about Ange's words all the time, stepping back in my memory to listen to my conversations with the nun and Father Larry. *There's a reason Cate's here, a reason she's mine.* Without any sort of conscious decision, I let go of the comforting words I heard after Cate was born to take hold of these spiritual ones. To allow myself to move on from the "Hey, you can do it!" pep talk that goes a long way when you think you can't, to the faithful sentiments that now consumed me. I needed something more substantive for the long haul, as if the comforting words were the life raft that kept me afloat and the spiritual words were the ones that would ultimately save me.

That life and faith were intertwined was news to me, even though Ange and I sat through all the same catechism classes in elementary school. But I have to say, I wouldn't have wished to make this connection in any way other than through my best friend. That Ange's words helped open my mind or my soul or whatever it was to this faith growing inside me made it okay, made it real. That said, I couldn't simply release into the idea that there was a big master plan beyond my hopes for my own life. I was seeking a deeper reassurance—a guarantee if one could be found—that the words were true. I needed to believe as much as Ange, the nun, and Father Larry did, that this was as it was meant to be.

That's probably why there was an urgency to have Cate baptized, why I was so driven to set a date and stick with it. Whether that reassurance or support was from the church, or my family, or God, I don't know. I just needed it. I wanted her to be blessed. There was an importance to the sacrament this time. The thoughts of a party and the christening dress were secondary to me, if I even considered them at all. As it happened, this was the reawakening of my faith journey—an invisible course I didn't realize I was embarking on until I was well underway.

I always thought Cate was blessed from the start. More than the rest of us, I mean. That she was a special baby in ways we didn't yet understand. It seemed that Cate, at only a few months old, knew things about life and what mattered that Noelle and I didn't. Things she came to teach us, things we might not otherwise learn, things we were supposed to see. With Cate's birth, pieces of this world, people in this world, who had moved imperceptibly through my days, now came into view.

There was the young mechanic at the garage with the limp and extra-thick sole on his left shoe. The sign for The American School for the Deaf on North Main Street I used to drive by every day without a thought. The older man riding his bike about town like Santa Claus with a garbage bag of deposit cans slung over his shoulder. The inspiring words in Natalie Merchant's song, *Wonder,* I played over and over in my car—words that made me weep: "… laughed as she came to my cradle…know this child will be able…" The middle-aged man with Down syndrome who sat next to his elderly father at church. And dozens more images, words, and faces, multiplying by the day. *Pay attention, Angela. There's more to faith in this life than you realize.*

When I was young, I couldn't imagine having dinner or going to sleep without thanking God first, or having Sunday begin in any way other than going to mass. My family even went to church on vacation. "God doesn't get a day off," my dad still says. Most Sundays we attended the same service as Noelle, passing her family on the way up to our pew (also on the right but closer to the altar). Noelle often said it was easy to spot my family since we all stood the same height—the four Gs all in a row—the way you spied your friends instead of paying attention to the service.

It saddens me to say when I left for college, part of my faith left, too. I don't know if it was the freedom of that time or getting away from the routine, but one Sunday I didn't go to church. And that one Sunday turned into many Sundays. The first few times, it hurt that I skipped mass, but the guilt faded as the weeks went by. I slept in, hung out with my friends, or studied without giving church a thought. It became very easy without my family standing next to me to forget that faith was important.

I spontaneously asked Noelle about it when we were home from college for Christmas break on our way out to meet friends. "Do you go to church at school," I blurted out, assuming she probably did go. That it was a social thing at Catholic University in D.C where she went.

"Almost never."

"Really? Me either. Do you ever feel guilty about it?"

"Almost always. But, honestly, I think God gets it. It's not that we don't care, it's just, you know, we're in college." Yet, unknowingly to Noelle and I that evening out on the town, faith had rooted itself deeply in our souls, hidden only by the distractions of young adulthood.

My faith didn't resurface until Rob and I talked about getting married. He was Protestant and I told him I wanted to remain Catholic, for our children to be Catholic. I couldn't imagine my life without Rob, but I began to realize I couldn't imagine my life without my faith even more. I saw it was an intricate part of the person I was, and I didn't want to change that about me. I wanted my children to receive the sacraments, to be raised in the same faith traditions I was. I told Rob that I would walk away from the relationship if he felt otherwise. It was the most courageous thing I've ever done.

Rob and I did marry and when I was expecting our first child, he mentioned wanting to become Catholic. I never pressured him to do so, but he felt it would bring us closer as a family. "This is something I want to do for the three of us," he told me after church one Sunday, having made the final decision. Overcome with emotion, I thought the least I could do for him would be to trade my allegiance from the Yankees to the Red Sox—there's still much debate about who had the tougher conversion.

What we didn't expect with Rob's choice, however, was how it brought us closer as a couple. He often talked about what he was learning in his RCIA (Right of Christian Initiation for Adults) classes and I shared with him the spiritual thoughts Cate's birth inspired inside me. I didn't fear his admonishment that I'd found religion. In our own ways, we both had.

I walked into my parents' bedroom the morning of the baptism carrying Cate who was wearing only a diaper. My mom had neatly laid out the christening gown sewn with Irish lace on her floral bedspread, the same way she set out school uniforms on our beds when we were kids. The dress was showing its age, dotted with yellow stains, the netting slightly ripped in a few places. Its imperfections were beautiful to me, revealing all the memories it held. This was the dress Kim, James, and I wore—that all the grandchildren would wear—my mother carefully storing it after each christening for the next baby. Cate's eyes were fixed on mine while I dressed her in all the layers: the gown, the netting overlay, the bonnet, the socks, and the shoes.

Father Larry baptized Cate at St. Mary's Church on a sunny Sunday afternoon as he had Caroline two years earlier. I can't recall anything he said, though I hung on his every word. I cried when he spoke, feeling so much emotion that I cannot fully describe, other than to say it wasn't sadness and it wasn't joy. There was a peacefulness about his presence, about his voice, that was almost holy. Though I didn't share any of my thoughts with Father Larry, I felt this bond with him then. His faith had helped me through some important days of my children's lives, of my own. I both admired and envied the faith he had, mine being so fragile, so new.

After the christening, a crowd of family and friends gathered at my parents' house and, contrary to my mom's thinking, everyone fit. At one point that afternoon, something made me stop and look around the room at everyone who was there. It came to me that I was never appreciative of all the people in my life before this moment. *I'm so lucky.* I think we all felt grateful in some way, the hugs from each one a little stronger than usual. Even though Angela couldn't be with us, I wished she were there. I smiled when I thought of what she wrote, what she knew. The day reminded me that I was not alone in this life and whatever it was that lay ahead.

7

PARENTING

On Being a Mother

We have held others close and been held close.
We have been lifted up and lifted others up.
We have swung each other until, dizzy with laughter,
we have fallen together in a happy heap.
For the difficult maneuvers we have been given good tutors.
We have known the comfort of following
and the pleasure of improvising.
We are able simply to dance well enough.

Virginia Rickeman
From *The Well Is Deep*

Mothering wasn't quite what Noelle and I had anticipated at the start, each of us taking a different path—she as a working mom and I as a mom who was home with my kids. It took a while to make our way, to find a comfortable stride, a confidence in being the moms we wanted to be. Loving our children more with their every breath, we traveled the imperfect road of motherhood that turned as much on our perceived failings, as it did our maternal instincts.

The only thing I knew about being a mom when I had taken the job two years earlier was that I wanted to be one. I was twenty-seven years old when Ryan was born, empowered, as I'd never been in my life. To follow in my mom's footsteps, step away from my public relations career, and jump-start it when I was ready. Yet being at ease with mothering after Ryan was born came slowly. My heart was there, but it took a while for my head to follow.

There was the brainpower piece of working I missed. For months, I'd set Ryan in his swing in front of the morning news and together we'd watch while I ate breakfast. It was harder than I thought it would be to leave behind my old profession, to turn on *Sesame Street* and embrace my new one. Then there was my perfectionist self that didn't want to screw up. The stakes were higher: this was my child, not a project. I was relieved to be rid of the stress at the office, but I created my own stress at home by making mothering my new job.

I had set a daily schedule for eating, food shopping and errands, naptime, and playtime. But I didn't have the sense of community I was hoping for the way I did growing up. It was a strangely solitary time. No one was hanging out in the neighborhood, taking stroller walks, or playing in the driveway with her kids. So I enrolled us in read-aloud programs at the library with Miss Sophie, pet-the-bunny programs at the local farm, gym and movement classes at the community center—every free or inexpensive program I could find. It bothered me, but it seemed this was the way to raise your children in suburbia.

The whole approach was foreign to Noelle who in our call a few months before John and Cate were born advised, "Just make some friends, have a glass of wine, and relax a little."

"I know, I've tried, but I haven't really clicked with anyone. So many of the women I meet are babysitters or grandmothers."

Eventually though, I made a friend at a Halloween party who invited me to join a playgroup with other stay-at-home moms from our church. Her outreach was just what I needed—the exact remedy Noelle prescribed. When the boys and I attended our first playgroup, I instantly felt at ease. *These women are just like me.* Each of them had put aside college degrees and promising careers to be home with their kids. Having new friends to talk with gave me renewed energy in my own choice: that being a full-time mom was the right job for me right now.

I was beginning to get comfortable with Stepping Stones and our new routines, when I received an unexpected phone call from the partner I used to work for. After the typical "Hi how are you?" pleasantries, he said he had a couple of things he wanted to run by me. Without really going into any reason why, he offered me a host of opportunities from extending my health insurance coverage, to coming back to work, possibly working part time with a flexible schedule, even the chance to telecommute. This was unheard of for a large New York City law firm in the nineties since this was prior to the advent of flextime and mobile technology, when things weren't as adaptable as they are now.

I knew my old firm offered me these options not because I was such a brilliant legal mind, but more likely because they felt sorry for me. I'd heard that this partner was emotional when he learned about Cate, and my guess is he didn't know how to help and asked my colorful secretary, Linda, what they could do for me. I'm sure after some quick brainstorming, she threw out a bunch of options, thinking most of all about what would suit me best. You may think that law firms and lawyers don't have hearts, and don't make accommodations, but they did, especially for me, especially then.

I'd had such a tough time working and being a mom—an issue I thought I'd just put to rest for a while. But with such uncertainty about the costs we might incur with Cate, I had to consider that we probably needed the money. Stepping Stones was already an expense we hadn't budgeted for when I resigned the first time. I must have called Ange five times for help weighing out my options.

"Maybe you could work three or four days a week and have long weekends with the girls."

"I wish, but it conflicts with Stepping Stones." No matter how many schedule variations I examined, there wasn't a perfect answer. I decided to accept their offer, given our circumstances and the salary they offered. But it was with a heavy heart.

The commitment to go back to work meant beginning a childcare search, which was always hard for me, as I think it is for all women who travel down that road. You're looking for yourself in someone else, and that person can never be found. I wanted to find someone who had no pretenses about Down syndrome and would give both girls the attention I wanted each of them to have. So much emphasis was placed on Cate that I always worried about Caroline getting enough. I did find someone I liked, but as with any childcare situation it wasn't perfect because it wasn't me.

℘

At the same time, I began to have my own worries, different worries, for Ryan. He was more than two-years-old now and with every passing day, still didn't talk much. While not uncommon among children his age, I took seriously the alerts in the parenting books I read to be vigilant. There was this small piece of me that began to wonder if my working, even just part time, would have been better after all. *If he were in day care, he'd be around kids more often. Maybe he'd be further along.* And, yet, deep inside—to a place only mothers go—I had this sense that something was wrong.

Of his language deficit, the pediatrician confidently said, "That's a boy for you, Mrs. Martin." In my heart this was what I wanted to hear. I tried to push my concerns aside, but it was hard for me to let go of the worry completely. My girlfriends talked about how their toddlers inundated them with questions to which I'd often concur, "Oh, I know." The truth I shared only with Noelle when chatting after Cate's baptism. Keeping things light, she, too, spoke of Caroline's endless inquisitions. "Sometimes I tell her we're gonna play the quiet game."

"I wish I could say the same, but Ryan really doesn't talk much. Should I be worried?"

"I don't think so. James didn't talk until he was three—not a word. Then again, maybe we shouldn't use my brother as a benchmark," she said and we laughed. "But, seriously, if you're really worried, I hear good things about Birth to Three, now that I've finally figured out what it is. Why don't you look into it?"

"Here I pledged to help you with Cate and now I'm the clueless basket case."

"For the record, it goes both ways. We can take turns being clueless."

"Deal. How are you? How's Cate?"

"We're okay. She can roll over both ways now. But ya know me. I'm obsessed with what she should be doing next. John's, what, six months? He must be starting to crawl."

"Yep," I sort of lied. He was crawling everywhere. I didn't have the heart to tell her and instead blurted out my deepest hope, "Cate will get there, too."

"I know. One step at a time, right?"

One step at a time for all of us, I guess. We hung up and I made a slew of calls to find our town did have a Birth to Three program that offered speech evaluations—and Ryan was eligible.

Once again, the insanity began. It was as if I were wrapping up a maternity leave, instead of having formally left the firm. My baby was four months old, Caroline was now a two-year-old, and I was back to work as a busy associate and my kids' mom, too. I think the only way I got through it was to know my working wasn't a choice. It was something I had to do for my family.

I did telecommute, which was difficult because the technology wasn't great back then, and most lawyers weren't supportive of it. There wasn't a precedent for this kind of arrangement at my firm or any other large firm I was aware of. I had to make my own way, much the same as I was doing in the world of Down syndrome. Nothing seemed easy then, personally or professionally. Everything took a very conscious effort.

I worked from my apartment and would go to the office in Manhattan as needed. It didn't take me long to learn there was no such thing as part-time legal work. One week there might be fifteen hours of work and the next week seventy-five hours, and that's just the way it was. It didn't matter that I was part time. If clients needed their work done, my job was to do it. So I often found myself obsessing into the early morning hours over debt covenants, definitions, events of default—you know, the stuff dreams are made of.

Tim was supportive, but it wasn't an equal division of labor between us. It's probably true of most working couples, especially if one of them works from home. I was at our apartment, but I had a babysitter because I was working. Even with this seemingly tidy situation, I was still in charge of everything. I didn't just have my job during the day the way Tim did. The daily to-do list that automatically registered in my head never popped into his.

We didn't discuss what needed to be done every day, or how it would all be accomplished. I just did it the way one of those circus clowns keeps twelve dishes spinning at once. I was working, but constantly making accommodations to my day for unplanned illnesses, doctor appointments, birthday parties and all the other things that came up. My experience proved that "working mom" was an accurate term and far from what it meant to be a father—extra adjectives not required. I was always working at one thing or another and at the same time always a mom.

On our scheduled date, I took Ryan to one of the elementary schools in town where he would be evaluated by a speech therapist. I hadn't anticipated how a trek with my toddler through the hallways of a school would set my over-zealous brain into action, calculating exactly how long we had to resolve this issue before he started kindergarten. *His speech will be fine by then.* I laughed at myself for having such a concern, and pointed at the artwork on the wall to show Ryan. "Look at all the beautiful things you'll do when you go to school."

So much for this glimpse at maternal confidence, however, as my self-doubt returned the instant I introduced myself to the therapist. "Hi, I'm Angela and this is Ryan," I said smiling and extending my hand to shake hers. *What if I've blown this whole thing out of proportion?* The therapist seemed pleasant enough and asked me to leave the room so she could evaluate Ryan.

"What a sweet boy," she said after asking me to join them. "But he's a tough one to figure out." She thought he did have a speech problem and that it might be physiological, where the muscles in his mouth weren't fully formed. Her diagnosis didn't seem quite right, though for whatever reason I was unable to verbalize my thoughts. *What's my problem?*

The therapist prescribed monthly visits and a series of daily tongue and jaw strengthening exercises for Ryan and I to do at home. And so we did the exercises, because that's who I am: first-born, road-paver, rule-abider. It wasn't fun, but I needed to fix this. Our nursing hadn't gone well and I thought that maybe this was the source of the problem...that I needed to help Ryan catch up before he started school...that his challenges were not only my fault, but mine to cure.

ꝰ

Cate at 8 months old: Responds when her name is called; beginning to imitate familiar social games with gestures ("clapping hands," "so big"); beginning to look for a hidden object; has a head tilt to the right; can sit up on her own but still falls backwards; smiles often and beginning to giggle.

Life went along without me having much say in it, working nutty hours, going to Stepping Stones, worrying about the time I wasn't spending on my job or with my family. I was fragmented and stressed, but didn't realize it because I was focused on trying to keep everything going. God knows if I'd stopped I probably wouldn't have known where to start up again. One by one, the dishes would fall and break. I was always anxious because I was doing the best I could at everything, yet never felt I had enough time for any of it. My life was one massive guilt trip as I transformed myself from lawyer to mother to wife to therapeutic assistant to lawyer, over and over again.

On Tuesdays and Thursdays, I drove Cate to and from Stepping Stones and attended the group and therapy sessions when I was supposed to be working. Linda covered for me, telling people I was on the phone or in a meeting. Thankfully, she had a velvet tongue, where the white lies flowed as smoothly as the truth.

Not only was I pressured by what I wasn't doing at work, but also by what I hadn't done with Cate. Every session ended with the therapist saying, "Now, it's really important to practice blah, blah, blah, if you want your child to blah, blah, blah." *Shit, I haven't done this since last Tuesday's class.* All I could do was race back to meet the babysitter at our apartment and then be a lawyer for the rest of the day.

Here and there I tried to catch up on Cate's daily homework, which lately focused on crawling. The physical therapist at Stepping Stones gave us a pair of "hot pants," which were made of spandex and similar to bike shorts, except that the legs were sewn together and you had to put them on over Cate's clothes. It was like stuffing a sausage into its casing. Cate would squirm and fuss, making it nearly impossible to get them on. But once I did, it was easy to pick her up since she was so tightly constrained, turn her upside-down and attack her with kisses. "Ah, I got you!"

"Eh, eh, eh," she'd chuckle, unable to wriggle her legs free. Her laugh was reminiscent of the sound my Nova used to make when I'd turn the key in the ignition and the engine wouldn't turnover. Eventually we'd settle down and get to the business of crawling.

The hot pants were designed to keep Cate's legs together so she could learn to crawl on all fours. With low muscle tone, a natural position for a baby with Down syndrome is to have her legs splayed out wide like a frog. Funny thing is, now Cate's claim to fame is her obscene straddle split where her pelvis is on the floor and her legs stretch beyond a radius of 180 degrees—with her feet pointing backwards!

Cate's early attempts at crawling without the hot pants propelled her backward rather than forward. She'd push up on her hands, lifting her body off the floor from the waist up and, not yet using her legs, would slide in reverse. Our apartment was so small that she'd quickly work her way under our couch, the skirt framing her round face like a nun's habit. The busy couch fabric easily camouflaged Cate, so the only way I'd find her was to listen for the sound of her contagious cackle.

My internal struggles about where I was devoting my time were magnified when it was my family that had to give. I wanted to be there for my kids the way my mom and dad were for me: to take them to the park, to school, to the doctor. The reality was the babysitter was doing more with the kids than I was, especially the fun stuff. It was unlike the way I was raised, and that pang of guilt never went away. Even though my mother worked when I was growing up, it didn't seem as if she did. I never thought about her as a working mom, or that my dad was home a lot. It's just how it was.

My parents arranged it so one of them was always there for us, which was an impressive feat before the days of corporate compassion. As a nurse, my mom was able to be home during the day, working the 3:00 to 11:00 p.m. shift, while my dad as an insurance adjuster made his own schedule—an early concept I'd later perfect. My dad got in around the time my mom left, after she had done all the errands and housework. On the days my mom worked, all my dad had to do was make dinner, shuttle us where we needed to go, and keep tabs on what we were doing. Everything else was already done.

Only in managing my own situation, did I understand how much my mother must have done to make it look seamless, because there's no way it could have been. I'm sure there were plenty of times my dad didn't keep up his end of the bargain the way he was apt to save someone else's ass, knowing my mom was competent enough to cover her own. On those occasions—and there were plenty of them—my mom would have to take on even more.

Rob's parents lived in town and the boys and I would often stop by on our stroller walks to say hello. I had gathered our things after a recent visit and lifted John into my arms. My mother-in-law asked if he had any words yet. "After all, he's nine months old."

"No, nothing yet," I said when she plucked a plastic apple from a cornucopia decorating her entryway table. "A—p—p—l—e" she enunciated, John staring at her lips.

"Apple," he immediately said, the word perfectly rolling off his tongue.

"Yay, Johnny!" I said squeezing him, his face brightly smiling. And, yet, it was also a belly blow. I looked at Ryan who was running around the room with a toy plane in his outstretched hand. *Why didn't I help you sooner?*

As soon as I got home, I set the kids off to play and called Noelle. I went to tell her about John, but stopped. *I can't tell her he's talking already.* Stuttering my way I said, "Uh, hi…I'm kind of…

well, I'm wishing I started speech therapy earlier with Ry." And then I started to cry. "I'm such a bad mother."

"Oh, Ange, you gotta stop that. I'm not sure where this is coming from, but you have to push those thoughts away. I had them, too, when Cate was born. I thought it was something I did when I was pregnant—that it was me."

"You have to know that's not true."

"Yeah, but so do you."

⟞⟋

Once in a while, I'd be in a total jam, swamped with work and knowing I had to go to Stepping Stones, which was almost a four-hour block of time between the commute and the class. As good as Linda was at covering for me, sometimes I just couldn't swing it, and I was left to figure out what to do. My dad called me every day and inevitably I'd unload my stress on him. He'd bail me out the way he always did when I was a kid, saying, "Honey, I have some time tomorrow. I'll take Cate to her thing and you get your work done."

Knowing my dad, he probably didn't have the time, but that was of little consequence. He didn't care about being at work at any given time, regardless of what the protocol was. Family and friends came first to him, and we all knew it. I found I couldn't say no to my dad. If he didn't take her, Cate would miss class, and that wasn't an option. *She might miss something really important.*

It was quite an operation for my dad to take Cate to her class. He left his house by about 5:30 a.m., not for the distance but for his routine. He had stops for coffee, a buttered roll, the ATM, and the place he'd get the *NY Post*. My dad would get to my apartment at around 7:30 a.m., load Cate in her car seat improperly into the car, drive the hour-and-a-half wretched trip down the Garden State Parkway, and as he'd say, "Do the thing at Stepping Stones."

He'd arrive at Stepping Stones holding the infant carrier off balance in one hand and hiking his ever-falling-down pants up with the other, I'm sure saying what he always said about the car seat, "Jesus, these things weigh a goddamn ton." If it were Tuesday, he'd join the mother's support group—a horrific thought. If it was a Thursday, he'd be with Cate during therapies—another horrific thought.

My dad never understood what the therapies were about. "It's a load of bullshit, Noelle," he'd tell me, having gone ahead and done them anyway. He usually had to prod Cate to participate, which was something to witness, because the two of them were stubborn as mules and already at odds because of it. There were some activities Cate flat-out refused to do, so he'd lean in close to her and whisper in his most convincing way, "Come on kid, just do what they want, and then they'll leave ya the hell alone."

When they were done with class one afternoon, my dad brought Cate home and told me stories about his trip. He talked about the therapist, "You know the one with the accent, the beautiful face, and the really big can?" He continued as a smile crossed his face, "What if when she's bending over ya, she let one rip? You'd be knocked right out of that room." I could picture it, since the therapists were always on the floor with the parents and their babies. However, my laughter soon turned to panic. I had to face these people in a few days.

8

LISTENING

It Isn't Croup, Doc

Deep healing.
Deep listening.
Deep waiting.
Deep watching.
All of these become
a part of my night watch.

From "The Angel of Night," *Seven Sacred Pauses*,
by Macrina Wiederkehr

ate was a healthy toddler and I was relieved that the scary things I read in the Down syndrome book hadn't reared their ugly heads. Although Cate did have her share of lingering colds, I didn't have any real medical concerns for her. This isn't to say that I was totally at ease on the subject, because there was a part of my brain that was still preoccupied with the possibility of what might go wrong, you know, someday. But as we approached Cate's first birthday (a milestone for any baby), it seemed we had bypassed anything serious. As fate would have it, this was precisely when her cough arrived.

Cate at 1 year old: Picks up table food and feeds herself; sits by herself; not yet crawling; gets on all fours and rocks back and forth; says "da da" and "ba ba"; has some tactile sensitivities; doesn't like loud noises (at her first birthday party I ask guests to sing quietly); responds to simple verbal requests such as "give me," "clap your hands"; waves and responds to "bye-bye."

Tim and I had just gone to bed the night we first heard an unusual cough coming from the girls' bedroom. It had a harsh, barking pitch and was persistent. We rushed in to find Cate crunched up against the corner of the crib in her pink bunny sleeper uncontrollably coughing. Her eyes were closed, but her body was so restless that she seemed unable to catch her breath. I couldn't tell if she was awake or asleep. *But how could she sleep through this?* I lifted her up and rubbed her back while the spasm continued without reprieve.

"Cough, cough, cough, cough, cough, cough…"

"Oh my God, Tim, what do we do?"

"Cough, cough, cough, cough, cough, cough…"

"Tim, this can't be normal."

"Cough, cough, cough, cough, cough, cough—breathe."

And then another relentless spasm started in, and another—one right after the other for the rest of the night. Come the light of day, the cough disappeared, but that night it returned. Tim and I attempted every home remedy we could think of to try and soothe her: flipping her on her stomach, patting her back, giving her a bottle. Yet nothing we did made any difference, and again, the coughing continued all night. With Cate smiling and well on exam the next morning, our pediatrician thought it was croup and gave us the protocol for dealing with it.

As most parents with a croupy baby know, the alternatives are to either bring the child into a hot, steamy bathroom or take her outside into the cold air. It was one of those medical treatments I was never sure of, like whether to put ice or heat on a pulled muscle. The nightly negotiating between Tim and me would begin as Cate's coughing did. One would start, "I'll get up," and the other would immediately counter, "No, no. I'll get up." We'd still be laying there after this exchange, neither one of us even motioning to get out of bed, unable to bounce back from our all-nighters the way we did in college. Eventually, the coughing spasms would become so severe that one of us had to get up. If it was my turn, then it was a matter of deciding on the treatment: Did I want to sweat or freeze my tail off?

If I opted to sweat, I'd strip Cate down to her diaper and myself to a tank top and underwear, take Cate into the bathroom, turn the shower on to hot, and sit on the toilet seat. I'd hold her facing out on my lap with my arms wrapped around her belly. When steam clouds gathered about, she'd slide down my sweaty legs coughing her awful cough and I'd shimmy her back up. It was the only fun of it—the sweaty baby slide—for soon enough the hot steamy air would saturate and begin to rain moldy orange drops on my head and bare shoulders.

If I chose to freeze, I walked around the parking lot like a homeless person with Cate wrapped up in blankets, going back and forth, and back and forth. "It'll be okay," I'd say now and then, nuzzling my face next to hers inside the blankets to keep warm. She'd peek at me, never fussing, and somehow drift off to sleep while continuing to cough. Of the two remedies, I usually opted for the strip-down steam approach and Tim chose outdoor duty. Neither ever worked.

ℒ—

While Noelle spent her nights in search of a solution for Cate's cough, so I spent my days helping Ryan with his speech. He'd aged out of the Birth to Three program a few months ago, but the therapist thought it would be beneficial if we kept the exercises going for another six months until he started preschool in the fall. I'd just twisted a piece of Bubblicious in half and put it on the left side of his jaw. "Okay, honey. Let's count to twenty while you chew on that side. And then we'll do twenty on the other side."

I watched him chewing away when it hit me how ridiculous this all seemed. *I don't think this is going anywhere.* "You know what, Ry, that's good for today," I said. "Give me your gum."

"Dere you doe, Mommy."

I kissed him on the top of the head and put the gum in the garbage. I was tempted to do the same with the page of exercises, but instead stuffed the paper into the junk drawer in the kitchen. *I don't know, but I think it's something else.*

Noelle called that night, yawning when she said hello. "What's up?"

"You sound so tired. Any change with Cate's cough?"

"Nope. Should be starting up any minute now."

"Gosh, sometimes you wonder if these doctors and therapists really know what they're talking about."

"Believe me, Ange. I'm right there with ya."

Night after night, after week after week, after month after month of this cough, we knew it wasn't the croup. The croup goes away and her cough was showing no signs of improvement. I wasn't sure what was going on, but it seemed that Cate had become this chronically sick baby—a chronically only-at-night sick baby. Whenever Caroline wasn't feeling well, one of us would take her to the pediatrician, give her the medicine they prescribed, and she'd get better. It was easy. With Cate, the pediatrician didn't have the remedy, and I began to wonder if we should see someone else.

Not only were we worried about Cate; we were beginning to worry about ourselves, because Tim and I never slept. Despite what happened to Cate under the cover of night, we still had places to be and responsibilities to manage during the day. There was rarely time to catch up with a nap or to get to bed early. I found that familiar nervous energy creeping up on me, but I pushed it aside to go about my days. On those rare occasions I didn't have to work in the evening, I'd climb into bed knowing we'd be up most of the night. After a time, if Cate didn't happen to be coughing, my own anxiety made it difficult to fall asleep.

I'd lie there anticipating that the cough would start at any second, close my eyes to attempt rest, and say a nighttime prayer if I remembered to. Truthfully, I don't know that it was a prayer; maybe it was a wish. *Please let Cate sleep tonight.* The cough usually arrived, but the sleep—almost never. I was conscious about not always asking for God's help. I didn't want to become an ungrateful person who only asked for things and no longer offered any thanks in return. Who knows, my prayers probably just got jostled up with the million other thoughts in my head and never even made their way to God.

Nothing we were doing was helping Cate, so I decided it was time to find a doctor who could. Our pediatrician referred us to an ear, nose, and throat (ENT) doctor in a neighboring town. I finagled my way through their system to get an appointment in one week, rather than the eight weeks they proposed. So began my initiation into the world of specialized medicine.

~

I sat on my porch steps with a remote phone in my hand, dialing Noelle's number while watching my kids play in the backyard. "Good luck at your ENT visit with Cate tomorrow," I said after our hellos. "Can't wait to hear what he finds."

"Me, too. Hopefully he has a magic pill and we'll all be getting some sleep soon," she said and we laughed. "How are your boys?"

"They're boys. John's running around with Ryan out here in the yard." *What am I saying? Cate's not even walking yet.* "I'm so sorry, I shouldn't have told you that."

"Of course tell me. Please, Ange, let's not let it be like that."

"Okay, it's just…well, you know. I wish Cate was right there with John."

"She will be."

~

I hung up with Ange and let out a sigh. *Cate will walk. She'll run.* Quickly shifting my thoughts to our appointment with the ENT tomorrow, I rubbed my eyes, thinking how Tim and I were almost delirious at the prospect of a solution. That night we pulled out the video camera to tape what was happening so the doctor could observe the severity of the coughing spasms. We thought it would be the only way to convey exactly what was going on. I'd made enough useless trips to the pediatrician's office the morning after a bad night when Cate appeared fine and I appeared nuts. "Now, Mrs. Alix, the way she is presenting is the trademark of croup." *But do you have croup for six months?* This doctor needed to see our nighttime Madame Hyde and not the asymptomatic Dr. Jekyll so we could resolve this.

Caroline, Cate, and I went to the appointment, and I told the doctor I had a video so he could see what was going on first-hand. "Mrs. Alix, I don't need to watch your video," the doctor said when I handed him the tape. "It sounds to me as if you're not getting enough sleep if you're up videotaping your daughter in the middle of the night." I couldn't believe it. *No shit, I'm not sleeping. My child has this outrageous cough you need to see so I can get some sleep!* The doctor excused himself from the room for a minute and I decided to leave. I stood up and put Cate on my hip, took Caroline by the hand and left. If he wasn't going to listen to me, I wasn't going to listen to him.

My face flushed red as I walked through the waiting room and headed for the parking lot, making it from the doctor's office to the car without breaking my stride. I got us all buckled in and sat there for a minute in the driver's seat, tightly gripping the ring of car keys in my hand. *I can't believe I just did that.* I was shaking because I was so mad, shaking because I couldn't believe I'd walked out on a doctor. *When did I become this crazy person?* I really wasn't one for bucking authority. I felt like an idiot having gone through everything we had without any notion about where to go from here.

When the girls and I got home, I saw the light of the answering machine was blinking. I avoided it and called Ange instead, totally at a loss, "It was like *Invasion of the Body Snatchers.* I just left."

"I'd never have the guts to do that."

"But, Ange, I feel like I just walked out on Sister Gregory. What do I do now?"

"Deep breath. Call your pediatrician."

___

Noelle and I used to quiver just at the sight of Sister Gregory, the principal at St. Mary's where we went to grade school. She epitomized the very word authority with an aura about her that left no doubt that she was in charge. I can still see her patrolling the halls with perfect posture—spine straight, nose slightly elevated, shoulders thrown back. Her hair was tightly tucked into a chin-length veil, her polyester business-style clothing impeccably fitted and pressed. If a statue could walk, that was Sister Gregory. Her strict policies stretched far and wide from mandating that classes walk in complete silence in two lines—one for boys, one for girls—to banning girls from wearing colored nail polish.

Toward the end of eighth grade, Noelle and I got caught breaking that last rule and Sister Gregory had us to her office for punishment. She pulled a bottle of nail polish remover and a bag of cotton balls from a drawer saying, "I would have expected more from the two of you." We couldn't get the polish off quickly enough and avoided wearing it for years, having been traumatized by the whole experience.

Shifting from my memories to the present, I knew exactly how Noelle felt in that doctor's office. That burning sense in your gut for your child when you know something is going on. Noelle *was* a mother bear, the way Mr. Clifford had described her when Cate was born—cradling Cate then, defending her now. I never would have said it of myself before, but I, too, was beginning to feel the roar within.

___

The message on the answering machine was from my pediatrician's office saying the ENT had called right after I left to explain what happened. When I called and spoke to the pediatrician, she suggested I go back and have him examine Cate. With my tail between my legs I reluctantly made another appointment, cringing at the thought of the water cooler conversations about me that I imagined would ensue: "Yep, she'll be here next Monday.Watch your back for tire tracks." *I'm actually a nice person.*

On exam, the doctor recommended Cate have a fluoroscopy and X-rays of her airway. We were sent to Columbia Babies Hospital in Manhattan for the tests and I have to say, it was the quickest hospital experience of my life. The medical technicians wrapped Cate in a baby-sized white sleeve that was like a straightjacket, laid her on the X-ray table, and held her there. *Oh my God, Cate.* And just as quickly as I had the thought, she was back in my arms.

The radiologist didn't do exactly what was ordered, saying he saw enough from the X-rays that he didn't think any other procedure was necessary. After asking him what he would do, the doctor said that if it were his grandchild, he'd have her see a colleague of his at the hospital—a pediatric pulmonologist. I liked his approach, an approach that was specific to Cate. Instead of doing a test for the sake of it and leaving us off to potentially go down the wrong road, he directed us to a person who would have an answer. I made the spot decision to schedule an appointment with the doctor he recommended.

At the first meeting Tim and I had with the pediatric pulmonologist, we found ourselves in the hands of a great doctor. He spent the first half hour of our appointment listening to what we were describing and asked questions to better understand what was going on. He was excellent on all counts: well-educated, experienced, with a great bedside manner to boot. Instead of making assumptions, he gathered information to form a diagnosis, taking me right back to my test-taking days in law school. A law student is taught to gather all the facts before doing the analysis and making a conclusion. As we sat there talking and listening to one another, I knew, as I had at Stepping Stones, that we were in the right place. *I'm so glad we came here.*

The pulmonologist told us this wasn't the croup, it was just Cate. The doctor said she was experiencing this cough because she had Down syndrome, where her physiological makeup was a little different from the rest of us. He explained that the medical term for Down syndrome is trisomy 21 for good reason: There's an extra 21st chromosome on every gene of the body. This extra genetic material affects people in different ways from mental retardation, to vision problems, to heart defects, to small airways and ear canals, to autoimmune issues, to low muscle tone.

Although doctors know people with Down syndrome have some of these shared medical issues and traits, they don't know why one person can have a health problem completely different from the next person. He diagnosed Cate with tracheamalasia (a narrowing of her trachea), that when combined with her chronic colds and anatomical features of Down syndrome, manifested in this cough. The doctor prescribed a treatment plan and asked to see her back in a few months. Not only had we found an answer to our problem, but we also found a doctor we were confident in. It was as if we hit the lotto.

When we got home, I jotted the doctor's contact information into my address book and drew a big star next to his name. I was mindful not only of his expertise, but also his ability to listen where others had fallen short. Though I'd always been one for talking, this doctor showed me how important the skill of listening was. *It makes for a better doctor and just a better person—a person I'd like to be.* The appointment affirmed for me the value of listening to myself as well, to that maternal instinct that told me to see this doctor today. And while that instinct may not always be right, I needed to remember to pay attention to it.

9

CHOICES

Expecting Claire

I shift from light to dark, from fear to knowing,
from separate to whole and back again
a thousand times each day, but truth is patient.
It waits, undiminished by my circumstances,
not wavering even a fraction of a degree from reality.
Truth waits until I wake,
until I leave my forgetfulness behind,
until I gather all my courage and look inside...

"Truth is Infinite,"
From *Root to Bloom* by Danna Faulds

Even though we understood why Cate was coughing, she was still coughing, and that meant we were still not sleeping. Very honestly, after so many sleepless months I was a mess trying to keep up with the demands and pace of my life. I never acknowledged even for a moment how bad things were for me, how much I was struggling inside. I just kept plugging on ignoring the signs, but my anxiety got worse and eventually manifested into some seemingly real physical symptoms.

I had chest pain so acute I was convinced I had some kind of heart problem and needed to see a cardiologist. After a barrage of tests including an echocardiogram he found nothing. The chest pain subsided when I began having another sharp pain, this time in the right side of my stomach. Figuring I must have some kind of bleeding ulcer, I went to my primary care physician who said I was probably fine, but sent me for an ultrasound just to check. The test revealed a small mass near my gallbladder and so he scheduled further tests, among them a CAT scan. By the time I left his office, I was convinced I had cancer and wasn't going to live much longer.

In the midst of all of this was a long-planned and much-needed weekend away for Tim and me in Fort Lauderdale for a college friend's wedding. We welcomed the break and thoroughly enjoyed ourselves as we hadn't in what seemed like ages. It was a weekend of raucous drinking, laughing, and fun just like old times. I returned refreshed, liking my husband again, and ready to immerse myself back into my life.

I arrived for my CAT scan and the technician asked if I was pregnant. I told him I didn't think I was, but he asked me to go to the lab and get a blood test just to be sure. It was negative. The CAT scan revealed nothing, not even what had appeared on the ultrasound. As if my insides hadn't been photographed enough, my doctor requested a full GI series of abdominal X-rays. I completed those tests the following day, and they didn't reveal anything either. Whatever was on the ultrasound was probably not a big deal—a polyp, a pollywog, or my pride.

It was a couple of days later when I realized I was late. Filled with angst, I piled the kids in the car to buy a home pregnancy test. Since Tim and I were married, I'd purchased more than my share of those little sticks, each mad dash to the drugstore a hopeful one. This wasn't at all how I felt now as I tightly gripped the steering wheel.

ℰ

I had just put John down for his afternoon nap and plugged Ry into a PBS show. Eager for a diversion while I was cleaning up the kitchen from lunch, I dialed Noelle's number. Her phone rang seven or eight times…*Huh, that's odd at this time of day…*when the answering machine picked up with Noelle's voice: "Hi, you've reached the Alix's. Leave a message at the beep."

"Ciao, my Irish friend. Miss you. Call me."

ℰ

Cate at 18 months: Crawling; pulls to a stand and walks holding on to furniture; creeps up stairs; says "mama"; emerging ability to imitate sounds ("ha" for "hat"); beginning to use the sign for "more"; points with her thumb; beginning to spoon feed independently; beginning to hold a crayon with a tripod grasp and scribble spontaneously; can build a tower of two cubes; beginning to have functional play (brush a doll's hair); yells for attention.

When we returned home from the drug store, I sat Cate down on the living room carpet with a box of her toys and sent Caroline off to play. I headed for the bathroom and took the test.

Five minutes later, the faintest line in the plus window appeared. I could hardly see it, but it was there. I ran back and forth from the bathroom to the kitchen trying to get a better look under different sets of lights. There seemed to be a line there, but it was only the slightest hint of one. I read the directions on the box once, then twice, trying to figure out if it had to be a certain shade of pink to be right. I thought maybe my hormones were a little off, not yet conceding I might actually be pregnant. The directions offered no relief, no variance stating: "Barely pink means you're safe."

The same panic I had after delivering Cate visited me again. I couldn't believe what I was seeing and what it could mean. *I can't be pregnant.* I rolled the stick back and forth in my fingers, the line staring back at me from every angle, now distorted, as my eyes welled with tears. *This can't be happening.* I put the stick down, burying my face in my hands. I'd just exposed myself—my abdomen no less—to so much radiation. If I were pregnant when I had those tests, I knew it could be tragically harmful to a baby.

I was sobbing, completely shaken by the possibility of being pregnant under the circumstances. I called Tim, who was calm in the midst of my complete hysteria. I went on and on about how bad all that radiation must be for a fetus, because you don't even get dental X-rays when you're pregnant. As we spoke, I began to question how I could even be pregnant. "But, Tim, we're always careful." He and I reviewed the past month and there was a night in Fort Lauderdale that neither of us could remember.

After hanging up with Tim, I called my obstetrician. She listened to my story and expressed concern about the affect of direct radiation on a fetus so early in its development. My doctor suggested I come in for a pregnancy test and if it was positive go to a genetic counselor. I went to her office the next morning knowing this test would reveal the truth, and it did. I was pregnant, and my life that was already upside-down turned inside out.

～ℓ～

It was December and we'd just celebrated the boys' birthdays. Ryan was four and thriving in preschool, which he had started in the fall. It was a traditional program of learning by playing, making crafts, and making friends. Ryan still wasn't a big talker, but Rob often reminded me, "Neither am I," when I'd question it. All the while, John developed language effortlessly. Just two years old, he was already having conversations with me, and I'd never had one of those with Ry.

"Can I eat one?" John asked me of the chocolate chip cookies I'd just pulled from the oven.

"They need to cool, Cubbie."

"How long?"

"Let's give them a few minutes, okay."

"Why?"

"So they don't burn your tongue."

"Now?"

"Just about," I said breaking a cookie in half and blowing on it.

"Why do we have to wait, Mommy?"

I was amazed how naturally talking came to John without chewing gum or doing push-ups with his tongue. For the most part, though, I didn't seek out differences between my boys. With only two years separating them, I treated them more like twins than individuals, often dressing them in similar outfits, assuming they had common interests. They were boys and they were brothers. I thought one should be very much like the other. And yet they weren't. *Why is it that John has ten questions for every answer when Ryan doesn't?* I began to wonder if there was something else going on. Something that wasn't just physiological.

༄

In my heart, I knew I wanted another child, but this timing was all wrong. The definitive news I was pregnant set my mind in motion, rewinding the past few days, hearing the X-ray technician ask: "Are you pregnant?" and my immediate thought that I wasn't. *My God I was pregnant after all.* I pictured myself lying on my back without a heavy protective apron while test after test was performed on my abdomen. Fast forward nine months and in flooded images of what my life would be like with three children close in age, including a baby who might be disabled and Cate who might not even be walking yet.

Even though I hadn't known I was pregnant, I felt totally responsible for all of this—that my own anxiety was the likely cause of all my symptoms and the situation we now confronted. It was hard to fathom how I could have been so stupid and not recognize my symptoms were self-imposed and nothing more. *Why was I so quick to see a doctor and have those tests?* The thought that I had hurt my own baby—a baby who could have been perfectly healthy—tormented me every second of every minute of the coming days.

Tim and I arranged to meet a genetic counselor at Lenox Hill Hospital where I had delivered Caroline and Cate. We had to give a detailed family history and describe the events of the past two weeks. After listening to us and reading all the information we provided, the genetic counselor began to present the facts her data revealed. She described what the chances were that our baby would be born with a birth defect. Next she posed what those potential abnormalities would be, given the exposure to radiation in the first stages of development.

As we learned, a genetic counselor is basically a risk assessor who deals in probabilities based upon whatever collected data is out there. She explained the risks could range from a baby being born without a limb, to mental retardation, to a laundry list of various other physical problems. The risks of having a child with any of these birth defects seemed small because the percentage likelihood was so small. However, the genetic counselor kept reiterating there was no way to know with certainty what the effect of the radiation would be. The baby could be disabled in some way, or the baby could be perfectly fine.

Apart from the radiation risk, we wondered if we were also more likely to have another child with Down syndrome. The counselor told us that Cate did not have the "hereditary" form of trisomy 21 (if that's even the right way to say it). The likelihood of us having a second baby with the disability was very small, equivalent to the same risk as when we had Cate. This counselor couldn't tell us what to do or if anything was wrong with our baby with any degree of certainty. She spoke to us in terms of possibilities and percentages, all of which for Tim and me seemed more like formalized guesswork than real, hard facts.

While Tim drove us home, I started doing the math. There was the 3 to 5 percent risk for any couple of having a baby with a birth defect, and then the 5 to 10 percent risk from the radiation I had. In talking it through, Tim and I figured we were at about a 15 percent risk of having a baby with some kind of problem. The odds seemed good to us—an 85 percent chance that everything would be okay.

More than anything else on the ride home, the counselor's guarded words stayed with us: "There are no guarantees, there are no definitive answers here." It was a good thing to speak with this woman and understand more about what we were up against, even though in many ways the numbers were meaningless. After all, I had a baby with Down syndrome when I was twenty-nine and drank milk instead of wine and ate baby carrots instead of potato chips. So what did any of this really say?

My obstetrician was cautious with her tone and what she said when we spoke after my meeting with the genetic counselor. She never used the word abortion, but she did tell me there was the option to terminate the pregnancy. She never encouraged or discouraged me one way or the other. She just put the choice out there.

Though I wasn't surprised to hear the alternatives my obstetrician proposed, I guess I never let my mind go there, never let myself consider that as an option for me. *My God, I'm married and have two kids.* We thought learning about the risks of this pregnancy was to help us understand what we faced, not to help us figure out whether or not to have this baby.

I hung up the phone and looked at Cate who was sitting on the floor with her legs splayed apart and the soles of her feet touching one another. She giggled while dumping all the VCR tapes from a basket onto the hardwood floor. Caroline was lying on her belly next to Cate, her long skinny legs accentuated by the striped leggings she wore. She was coloring and singing along with the *Blues Clues* show on TV.

What if this baby is severely handicapped? I'll always blame myself. Then again, maybe the baby is okay. But if something is wrong, will I be able to handle it? What could it mean for Caroline and Cate?

I don't think I slept at all during the next couple of weeks with the voice of the genetic counselor ringing in my ears. "There are no guarantees." I wanted some direction, some guidance. Even though I knew terminating wasn't an option for me, it was out there, and every time I pushed the thought of it away, it found its way back into my head. I think Tim was in a similar place, but I don't know. He didn't or couldn't talk about it. He could only comment on the tangible things the genetic counselor told us instead of what I needed to talk about: my guilt, my conscience, the unknown.

I called my parents and held nothing back. They talked with me, never telling me what to do. Intuitively they seemed to understand that the only way for me to be at peace was to work this through myself. I had the sense that no matter what happened, they would stand by me. In separate conversations, my mom and dad both said they each had the feeling everything would be okay with the baby. It was a relief for me to hear because I wanted to believe that, too. I knew that whatever my decision, it was mine to live with forever.

I had the urge to call Ange right away, but I hardly knew where to begin. In my heart, I knew what she would do if she were in my shoes. I wasn't sure I could be completely open with her about all that I was thinking. Nothing was ever hidden between us, but I was embarrassed, maybe even ashamed. *Why can't I dial the phone?* A few days later, she called me.

"Hey, how are you? I've left a few messages. Everything okay?"

"I'm sorry, Ange," she said quietly, the tone of her voice lacking it's usual punch. "I've wanted to call you about something, but…"

"Is it Cate—is she okay?"

"No, no, no. It's not Cate. She's fine."

I sat down on the dining room chair next to me with concern for Noelle bubbling up inside. "It's me—you know you can tell me anything."

For the next hour Noelle talked and I listened. She didn't need to hear my opinion, to have me offer advice. She just needed to talk and say whatever it was she wanted to. And I needed to pay attention—to hear every word, to not judge, to simply be her friend.

There are certain things that are only between good friends. Things we keep locked inside, never to be shared with anyone else. Things that you don't have to qualify with a caveat: "I have to tell you something, but, please, don't tell a soul." Your friendship means more than that. This was one of those times for us. Feelings, thoughts, and worries forever sealed away.

One night after hours of lying in bed awake, I don't know why, but I decided to let it all go. I let go of the statistics and the possibilities and the what-ifs. I let go of the choice as if it wasn't mine to make. I woke up Tim and told him that we could do this. "We have to have this baby." I wasn't convinced the baby would be okay, but I knew we would be.

"That's how I feel, too," Tim agreed as he pulled me in and held me tightly. In that moment, the weight I had carried for so many days lifted, and I began to have faith that everything would be okay, even if the baby wasn't.

Scattered and tentative as my mind had been, it settled into a peaceful rhythm that night. I lay awake in Tim's arms and found myself smiling. *We are happy.* Despite our uncertainty when Cate was born and recent trouble with her health, we had a good life. I had trust in Tim and me, in our marriage. We were closer after having Cate, and whatever happened, there was strength in all the emotions we'd shared. No matter what the future was, I knew having this baby was how it was meant to be.

Cate at 22 months (December 18, 1998, Noelle's birthday):
Walks for the first time.

"Ange—Cate's walking!"

"Yaaaaaayyyyyy! Oh my gosh—best birthday present ever!"

"Totally, although maybe better yet, baby number three in a few months."

"At peace?"

"I am."

～

The months I was expecting this baby were strangely reminiscent of when I was pregnant with Cate. There was too little time to do everything. If it was a Thursday morning, I'd get Cate and Caroline fed, trying to leave by 7:30 a.m. to be at Stepping Stones on time, but not actually getting out the door until 8 a.m. or later. Seeing the traffic already backed up by a mile at the Bergen toll, I'd start passing out snacks to the kids, thinking: "What's the point? I'm already so late." But knowing we were already on our way, and not wanting Cate to miss anything, I'd just keep driving. My mind would then shift to work. *Linda, I hope you can cover for me until I get back.* I'd try and refocus when I'd get to Stepping Stones, making sure to pull the paci from Cate's mouth before we walked in the door and concentrate on therapies for the next hour.

Going against the girlfriend part of me, I wouldn't join everyone after class for coffee. "Ugh, I wish I could stay," I'd say craving that friendship time, but knowing I had none to spare. I'd meet Lisa, our babysitter, at our apartment and do the handoff to her, head to the bedroom (a.k.a., my office), take a deep breath, and pray that no one realized I was gone all morning. The next five hours were spent drafting agreements and fighting the computer with its archaic dial-up connection.

The 5 p.m. knock on the door from Lisa always came too soon. I'd make some semblance of dinner, do tubs and the nighttime routine, and sit back down to finish the drafting I hadn't completed earlier. Around midnight, I'd call it quits, only to get in and out of bed during the night to deal with Cate. And before it seemed possible, it was time to get up and do it all over again. With another baby on the way, and acknowledging how the stress and anxiety affected me with two kids, I began to wonder how I'd ever handle it with three.

With only a two-bedroom apartment, Tim and I knew we needed to move, and it would have to be outside the metro-New York area. The only way we could afford to stay was if I worked, and I just didn't think I could do that once the new baby came. It was déjà vu. I'd soon have to tell my firm that I was pregnant, moving, and quitting. *They're gonna think I'm such a flake.*

We considered towns within a two-hour radius of my parents. I needed the safety net of knowing they were only a short car ride away. With that Tim and I made a major life change, selecting a rural New England town just outside of Hartford, Connecticut. By the most fortunate of circumstances this was only about ten minutes from where Angela lived—life threw me a bone.

As you might imagine, our move wasn't in any way organized or easy. Tim accepted a new job, which not only involved the sacrifice of a significant pay cut, but also the need to begin immediately, which was hard on me. He stayed with his parents who lived in the area, working and house-hunting while I was on my own in New Jersey with the girls. I was still working, still doing Stepping Stones, and Cate was still coughing.

The best way to cope with temporarily being a single mom was to not worry about the baby—and I didn't, which was remarkable for me. This conscious release was a departure from my controlling ways. Even when I said my nighttime prayers, I didn't pray for the baby to be okay or for things to be different. I prayed for strength to handle life as it was, and life as it was going to be.

Before I knew it, my due date came and went and a week and half later, I was scheduled to be induced. It wasn't until Tim and I were driving to Lenox Hill Hospital that my fears about this baby resurfaced and I began to consider what the next day would bring. "Is our whole life going to change the way it did two years ago?" I asked, setting my hand on his knee.

"I was just thinking that, too." He took my hand and squeezed it until the traffic picked up and he needed to put both hands back on the wheel. We didn't mention our apprehension again, learning almost two days later the answer to the telling question I posed was no.

Claire was born healthy and beautiful. She was big at nearly ten pounds, with this huge Irish-Clifford head. When the doctor said we had a girl and that she was okay, I was relieved, happy, and most of all thankful for my children. For the gift of each of them and the way they came into my life. *To think I had a hand in any of it.* And secretly I was excited that Claire was a girl. Caroline would have a typical sister and Cate, sandwiched like peanut butter right between the two, would have another sister close in age.

10

CHAOS

The New Normal

I closed my eyes and waited,
trusting in some faithful teaching.
At first I heard only the clashing jangle
of my overextended and anxious life,
but the longer I was attentive
the more I noticed the steady heartbeat
of something strong, deep, and true.

Joyce Rupp
From *The Cosmic Dance*

It was the middle of July and Claire was two days old when we moved into our house in Simsbury, Connecticut. As we turned onto our street, everything seemed so green, so open, without the urban distractions of noise or traffic. We pulled into our driveway, and Caroline and Cate bounded out of the minivan to explore the house and yard with my mom following quickly after them.

"Cate, you need to stop and wait for me," I could hear her say when I opened my door. Caroline was way ahead and didn't look back to check on Cate who tripped as soon as she got going. Cate never took the extra second to be careful. When she began walking at Stepping Stones (running, actually), the physical therapists warned us that she might regress to crawling. But that didn't happen with Cate—she ran and she never stopped.

I gingerly stepped out of the car and snuggled my face right up against Claire's, her pale blue eyes smiling even then. "We're home," I whispered to her before lifting her out of the car seat. When I turned around, it was as if I were seeing this place for the first time, not remembering we had a pretty grape arbor or a narrow brook that curved its way along our property. Not to sound corny, but the birds were chirping and the air smelled like fresh-cut grass. *This is nice.*

Tim had been working on the house to get it ready for us and was anxious to show me everything he'd done: installing a hardwood floor, gutting the kitchen, painting a couple of rooms. I followed him around with Claire in my arms, not paying attention to the updates he was so proud of and instead focusing on the colonial blue décor, the shaggy rust carpets, and the metallic wallpaper in the bathrooms. *I gotta sit down.*

Tim continued on his tour, not realizing that I'd ditched him. I could hear him talking as if I were still right behind him, his voice echoing off the walls because we didn't have much furniture. "See how I got the wood floor to line up from the kitchen to the dining room?...Uh, Noelle?...Noelle?" He came back to find me sitting on the couch with Claire in my lap. "Yeah, it looks good, but holy crap there's so much we need to redo. And what are those UFO-looking lights on the deck?"

"Would you just relax? That's just cosmetic stuff. Rome wasn't built in a day, and you've lived here for what, three minutes? We'll get to it." *I know, I know.*

Tim was right; I needed to be patient. It would take time to make it ours. Anyway, this move wasn't just about a house. And I guess that's what hit me while I sat on the couch: all that was ahead, when it felt like so much was already behind us. But as I thought about it, I wasn't starting off here totally by myself. I had Ange only ten minutes away—my built-in security blanket.

I was thrilled to have my best-friend-of-life just over a mountain and through the woods. Her move to the town next to mine meant the world to both of us. "What are the odds on us living ten minutes apart again?" I asked when she called to tell me that she and the girls were in their new home safe and sound.

"You're gonna be so sick of me, Ange."

All at once it was like old times having Noelle nearby as she instantly added a spark of spontaneity and humor to my calculated, more serious life. For the next few days, she called me panicking about why they chose to live in the country instead of an urban town. Noelle was a city-girl at heart even though we were raised in the middle of nowhere (the coolest store was a Jacques C. Penney forty minutes away). She never imagined her house in Simsbury with its big yard and babbling brook would attract the wildlife it did.

With her first call she protested about the deer roaming in her yard, "I gotta call someone to see if it's possible to spray for ticks. I'm worried we're gonna get Lyme disease." The following day it was a coyote that tormented her. "Ange, I think it's got mange.

It's nasty looking and just lying in the yard," she said, "I'm afraid to go outside." Another creature sighting had her phoning me late one evening, well past my 10 p.m. bedtime. I jumped out of bed; my heart racing because I assumed it was my mother about some family crisis.

"Hello!" I said and then heard Noelle whisper, "What's low to the ground, walks on all fours, has a wide back, and grunts?" All I could think of was a wild pig.

"Maybe, but I called my dad and he thinks it's a baby bear."

"What does Tim think?"

"He told me to stop guessing and go see what it is."

"Shouldn't he do that?"

"Tell me about it. What the heck was I thinking moving here?"

"I don't know, but I'm glad you did."

                         ~

Cate at 2½: Walks and runs with a fast gait; goes up and down a small slide independently; avoids ride-on toys; uses a combination of natural gestures, facial/ body language, and voice to communicate needs, wants, and ideas; beginning to imitate a vertical stroke for writing; note from her therapist: "There are many times when Cate has had enough with sitting and attending to task and needs more time to move around."

My mom stayed with us that first week, wanting to give me the chance to rest with Claire and settle in. I put her on what I liked to call "Cate duty." Cate was two and a half and full of bad stuff, always racing off somewhere and into everything. Hardly the placid child with a glazed look I had envisioned. I knew my mom would have preferred to care for Claire rather than act as Cate's bodyguard, but I needed her help with Cate. The baby didn't move and Cate never stopped.

My mom jumped right in the way she did after Caroline and Cate were born and easily managed all of it without any direction from me. She unpacked the kitchen, made dinners, and looked after us, especially me. I watched her efficiently maneuver about from my spot on the postpartum donut cushion and pictured myself doing the same thing for my girls one day. Feeling that same mother-daughter connection to reach out, to protect, to care for your children no matter how old they are. *Except I probably won't do as good a job as she does.* My mom made it look simple, so I figured I could easily handle it, too, once she left. But when her car pulled out of the driveway, I realized otherwise and couldn't stop crying. She was on her way to Virginia to help my sister who had just delivered her third baby as well.

Complain though I did those first few days without my mom, much of the unpacking was done. The furniture and bigger items easily found space here, and it was just a matter of finding places for the little stuff. I came across Ange's baby card when I was sifting through a pile of important papers and sat down on my bed to read it. I pulled open the drawer to my bedside table, but hesitated putting it away. Her card didn't belong there any more.

Maybe I was past those fears her note calmed, or perhaps it was the comfort I felt in having Ange nearby. I wasn't really sure, but I didn't need to have it next to me the way I used to. I still wanted to keep her note safe, to know where it was. So I went downstairs clutching the card to my chest, carefully placing it inside a keepsake box I stored in a small drawer of my secretary desk. This was one of those growing moments you recognize the instant it happens, such as accepting your diploma or putting a ring on your husband's finger. All at once I'd found a permanent home for my family and the words that carried me here.

❧

Soon enough Noelle started calling me with questions about doctors, bakeries, and furniture stores in town. More often than not she called just to say hi. We fell into the routine where her calls began with a story about Cate, and my calls to her with a "Hey, how's it going?" which was like opening a can of worms. Even with this consistent format, every call was unlike the one before it, a carnival ride of laughter and concerns, of joy and disbelief, of sharing and listening.

"Did I tell you Cate was drawing with sidewalk chalk in the driveway today totally nude?"

"That's not so bad."

"It is when you're meeting the next door neighbor for the first time."

The proximity between us was the breath of air our friendship needed, and it satisfied my desire to keep up the promise I made to her when Cate was born. It was one thing to be there for Noelle in spirit, and quite another to be there for her in person. To have her here, to see her face, to share our days was a gift and we both knew it.

❧

Tim and I treated this move with every hope it would be our last. Overall, we did anticipate it would be a great thing for us, a place we could really call home. We had our whole family in mind when searching for a house, wanting a good school system for all the girls, along with a progressive special education program for Cate. Simsbury was a town offering full inclusion where special education students learned in the same classroom as regular education students. It seemed an attractive model, but what did I know?

Despite my hopes, there was a doubting feeling that crept in sometimes as I made my way about Simsbury. This was a wealthy town, with not much, if any, diversity. Among the prestigious bumper stickers from universities, travel teams, and vacation spots, I imagined one reading: "It's hard to be average in Simsbury." I wondered if we would have the same warm feeling about this neighborhood I had about mine as a child.

I grew up on a cul-de-sac where everyone moved in about the same time, most having come from New York City to the country. It was a neighborhood where you could walk into anyone's house at any time of day, where people sat out in the cul-de-sac each night in a circle, where you went swimming in each other's above-ground pools, where everybody knew your business. Almost all of those same families still live there. I wanted that for myself, for my girls here in Simsbury.

A few days after my mom left, I was outside in my backyard and saw an older woman walking at a determined pace to try to step over the brook that bordered my yard. She stopped short and motioned to me with both hands to come her way. Her face had a million wrinkles as it came into my view, evidence of much living (it could be me some day). I liked her instantly even before she thrust out her hand and opened her mouth.

"Hiya, Noelle, I'm Audrey Winslow," she said in a hoarse, Linda-ish way. "We're backyard neighbors here."

"Nice to meet you, Audrey, but how did you know my name?"

"I met Tim a few times and wondered when the hell you were moving in." *What a curmudgeon. My dad's gonna love her.* I helped her cross the brook by way of an old plank and brought her inside to meet the girls. When I introduced Caroline to Audrey she said, "Jesus, that kid looks exactly like her father." And then

I motioned to introduce Cate who was leaning over the infant seat inspecting the new baby when Audrey interrupted, "That one's gonna give you a lot of trouble and a lot of love."

As fate would have it, Audrey was originally from Brooklyn and a retired special education teacher who had an adult daughter with special needs. Although we were separated in age by about forty years, I could tell already she was going to be my friend.

The kids and I often went to Noelle's house when Claire was a newborn, so Noelle wouldn't have to travel. We stopped by after naptime one August afternoon. It was one of those comfortable visits you have with an old friend that you don't often have with a new one. Where I felt I could linger all day. Where there was no pressure to keep the conversation going. Where I could be myself and talk about things I'd never reveal to a new friend at a playgroup, like being excited about this great bra I just found at Marshalls that actually gave me a shape, or how I just spent three hours cleaning my house and it was still a disaster. The time Noelle and I shared together was just so natural.

Our conversations would stop and start as we attempted to catch up with each other and keep an eye on the kids who were climbing on the play set, pulling toys out of the garage, and chasing each other around the yard. When Caroline suggested frogging in the brook to Ryan and John, my nirvana hit a snag when I thought about the clean-up instead of the fun. "So you're going in the muddy water to catch frogs?"

"Would you just let them be kids," Noelle reprimanded while she dug through a box of rain boots she kept in her garage and pulled out two pairs for Ryan and John.

"Okay, but let me just grab the Purell from my purse. I think frogs carry salmonella."

"You're a lunatic."

The kids must have spent an hour in and out of the brook, trapping frogs in nets and dumping them in heavy plastic tubs Tim had salvaged from his renovation work. Despite being somewhat disgusted, I couldn't help but smile. "Remember how we used to play when we were little?"

"Yeah, nothing planned. I remember the long summers, packing lunches and going off all day to make forts in the woods."

"And remember my Barbie collection with all the vintage dolls and clothes from my older cousins."

"It was the best—you had the airplane and camper, too. I always wanted you to invite me over so I could play with them."

When the kids were done frogging, I disinfected their hands and began packing the car. I reached out to hug Noelle goodbye, not wanting to leave.

"I'll never take this for granted," she said before letting go.

In order for me to keep an eye on Cate, Claire lived in her infant seat or strapped to my chest in the baby carrier, and Caroline was plugged into the TV more often than I would have liked. Even so, Cate seemed to be one step ahead of me. While I knew life would be busy with three kids and Cate as a toddler, I kind of thought I would figure it out, that our new life in the country would take on an easy rhythm once I got us into a routine.

No such luck, however, since Cate only occupied herself for a minute before moving on to the next activity—activities that were dangerous, required a major clean-up, or needed my constant supervision. Claire would usually get her bottle either back-handed by Caroline who was watching TV, or in my arms while I followed Cate around. I looked forward to Claire's middle-of-the-night feeding because it was peaceful, quiet, and just the two of us.

To complicate matters, this was a two-story home so the stairs were a new obstacle for Cate since we'd always lived on one floor. She became obsessed with mastering the stairs on her own. However, lacking the skill and better judgment to wait for me, she tumbled down them at least once a day. (I did have gates; they just didn't stop her.) As if Caroline thought I couldn't hear the godforsaken crash and thump, she'd alert me, never moving from her spot in front of the TV: "Mommy, I think Cate just fell down the stairs." I'd race to the bottom of the stairs to find Cate in the exact position she landed in, like David Letterman stuck to the wall in his Velcro suit.

When she wasn't attempting the stairs, Cate was trying to steal pacifiers from Claire. Even though we finally heeded the words of the speech pathologist and broke Cate from the pacifier months before, she never gave up her perpetual quest for one. Cate would bend over Claire when she was in her infant seat or car seat and feel around for a pacifier behind her back or under her bottom. When Cate found one, I'd hear her giggle and then quick footsteps as she made her escape down the hallway and away from me. Her pilfering ways later earned her the name Sticky because she was so damn good at it.

Once when Claire was still a newborn and propped in her car seat, we found a half-eaten lemon on her chest—a fair trade in Cate's mind for a good paci. I found Claire sticking out her tongue trying to get a lick of that lemon which was strategically placed just out of reach on her chest. Ultimately, Cate won and we bought a set of pacifiers just for her. Even though it was a step backwards for Cate, we hoped it would save Claire's life.

❧

It was not only the giving of friendship to Noelle that energized me; it was the receiving, too. I had forgotten that friendship was symbiotic: what one person needed the other willingly gave. Not only did Noelle need my friendship, I needed hers just as much. I didn't have a best friend in town before Noelle moved in. For all the women I'd come to know, there wasn't anyone I called just because, to rant about silly things, to reminisce.

"Remember that last summer in college before senior year when it was just you, me, and Brian hanging out together?" I asked her one day out of the blue.

"Yeah, we were like the Three Stooges. None of us had anybody else," Noelle said as she got into a laughing fit, trying to ask me about the day we rented canoes at Fahnestock State Park. "Remember how Brian really needed to get back to shore because there was something bad about the mayo on the sandwich he ate, and I couldn't row straight?"

I laughed, remembering the trip, but not the incident. I told her the only thing that was really clear about that summer was when Brian did get a girlfriend and we were all hanging out in the den at my parents' old house where I grew up. "Brian was lying on the floor and she was sitting next to him and for some reason she was pushing on his stomach and he kept telling her to stop but she didn't, and he farted."

Noelle was crying at this point, recalling a similar incident with her dad. "My mom had those cushy chairs he couldn't get out of and one Easter he rocked himself back and forth about ten times to get the momentum to stand. When my dad finally did get himself up, he let one go. We still call it the Easter Massacre."

I dropped the phone with laughter, not having heard the story before. But knowing her dad and those chairs, I could picture it as clearly as if I were there.

~

I would try and venture out with the three girls every day in some small measure fulfilling my need to escape the house. I learned early on, I needed a set procedure to get us all into the minivan or someone wouldn't make it in. I found out the hard way I had to buckle in Cate first. When I buckled in Claire first, Cate escaped running full speed down the street. "CAROLINE, DON'T MOVE!" I yelled to Caroline who was left standing alone in the driveway.

For all of the fun stops the four of us made, there were a few I dreaded. The grocery store was one of them, because it was truly an impossible endeavor. I'd have Claire in the infant carrier attached to my chest and Cate and Caroline in a side-by-side seated basket. If it took me longer than a second to pull something off a shelf, Cate would manage to squeeze herself out of the cart harness like Houdini and take off in the store.

The rescue and recovery were always the same. I'd quickly unbuckle Caroline and take her by the hand, leave my basket, and chase down Cate who was racing through the store laughing, with a huge smile on her face. She wouldn't run anywhere in particular, just as far away from me as she could get. *When is she going to stop this?* I used to need a nap when we came home, in fact, we all went in for a least an hour.

When we didn't have errands or appointments that required us to get in the car, I attempted to walk every day as I had in Manhattan and New Jersey. But now it would have to be just around the neighborhood, without coffee shops or bakeries to stop for indulgences. It seemed every time I got us dressed and out the door, we'd only get to the end of the driveway and have to go back inside for some crisis: a forgotten sippy cup; an emergency diaper change; a Band-Aid for a skinned knee.

One day when we actually made it past our driveway, I met my neighbor Steve who was walking his dog. I stopped to introduce myself, providing Cate the perfect opportunity to take off down the street. As usual, she was running and not looking ahead. I yelled at her to come back but she didn't listen. She never listened. "Sometimes her feet are faster than her brain," I jokingly said to him, both of us watching her peel away.

"Oh, does she have Down syndrome?" he asked, taking what I said the wrong way. I paused, realizing I hadn't introduced her in my typical "This is my daughter Cate who has Down syndrome" fashion. This may have been the first time I saw my daughter for who she was—just Cate—without having to explain about her disability first. I was about to answer Steve, when four-year-old Caroline piped in, "You know I have a little bit of Down syndrome, too."

"Actually Caroline, you don't," I said trying to get back to the conversation. But, she immediately reassured me, "Yes, Mommy, I have a little." Caroline wouldn't let it go. I turned to Steve kind of embarrassed and then looked at Caroline saying, "Cate has Down syndrome, but you and Claire don't. It just means that it takes your sister a little bit longer to do things. That's all."

Caroline must have heard the term Down syndrome hundreds of times in our home, but never understood what it meant and why it applied to Cate. This was the big moment I pined over when Cate was born, when I wondered how I would explain to Caroline that her sister had Down syndrome. Yet, here it was right out in the open for the neighbors to witness. The big life talk I'd thought about for years. It was totally normal—not a big deal at all.

ℓ—

Noelle was the person I thought of when there was something I needed to share or when I needed an honest answer. Hers was the comforting voice on the other end of the phone that wouldn't chastise me for how I'd react to a certain situation. "There's no right or wrong way to feel," she'd say emphatically. "Cut yourself some slack." And I'd push the worry away.

At the same time, she was just the person to give me a little tough love when I needed it, including the evening I was out bargain shopping and wound up with my first speeding ticket while driving our fifteen-year-old Volvo station wagon.

"Why don't you just go to a real store? You'd save yourself two hundred bucks on the ticket and get something you don't have to return."

While she was probably right, there was nothing quite like the thrill of a deal, especially when the original price tag was still dangling from the sleeve as proof to my husband of a bargain. "Rob, see how much money I saved?"

For as often as our conversations were about the minutiae of life ("Ange, what's up with the infestation of lady bugs in my house? I hate to vacuum them up, but one just flew out of my hair at the gym."), we also talked about private thoughts, secret worries, deeper things.

"I don't think our family moving to Simsbury was by coincidence," Noelle told me, when I drove her to the service station one day to pick up her car.

"That makes two of us," I said believing every word.

ℓ—

I used to think getting out of the house was difficult when we first moved in, but it became more trying as the months passed. I'd get everything ready to leave in the foyer—packing the diaper bag and snacks, collecting everyone's shoes, loading Claire into her car seat, tracking down Caroline, and capturing Cate—only to find that one of each pair of shoes was missing.

The first few times it happened, I went back upstairs thinking maybe I just grabbed one of each pair of shoes. Of course the other shoe wasn't in the closet where it belonged. *Is this what they mean by the early onset of Alzheimer's?* Every time we were ready to go, the shoes would disappear. After a couple of days of this, I knew it wasn't me.

I asked Caroline about the shoes and could tell by her blank stare she had no idea. Then, I interrogated the culprit: "Cate, where are the shoes? Show Mommy where the shoes are. Please, pleeaase, show Mommy where the shoes are." Cate didn't talk (she only had a few words), but I knew she understood what I was saying. She was never able to show me where she hid the shoes. It was up to me to find them.

Shoe-hunting set me back at least an hour every day. I'd find shoes stuffed in drawers and in the garbage, tucked in bags inside of Caroline's backpack, and placed in the refrigerator on a shelf as if they were produce. Maybe she thought her game—or whatever this was—was funny, but I didn't. I had this use-every-second mentality that I carried over from my life as a working mom. To drop everything and search for shoes was not how I did things.

Eventually the shoe-hiding stopped, to be replaced for months by another random act. In slipping a foot into one of my clogs (the shoe-of-choice for a size 5 triple-E foot), I felt something wet and squishy. At first I thought it was a dead animal and immediately pulled my foot out. Summoning the courage to check what it was, I reached a hand into the clog and yanked out half of a chewed lemon.

And, so it went. One of her antics might last a few months and then she'd be on to the next. After the food-in-the-shoes deal had run its course, she began dumping the contents of dresser drawers into one huge pile in the middle of her bedroom. Tim and I soon came to call these activities Cate's jobs because she had to do them every day. I began to expect the unexpected from her, since there was no way to predict what she might do next. As frustrating as the chaos was to cope with, it would make me laugh out loud a couple of times a day.

～ℓ～

Before long, our friendship grew closer than it had ever been. As our conversations evolved, we began to really appreciate what it meant as women in our thirties to have in each other a lifelong friend. Our memories of the past, our experiences in all the years gone by were exactly what united us in a way we shared with no one else.

"It's just the best to talk with you, Ange. There's no prelude necessary."

"Yeah, you already know I'm a worrywart, an overthinker, a self-doubter…Remind me why I'm your friend again."

"Because God knows it's harder to be my friend than yours."

Just as I would think I hadn't heard from her in a while the phone would ring and I'd hear her voice. Or, I'd call her and she'd say, "Oh, Ange, I was just thinking about you." This pull to connect became a necessary part of our lives, as much as running errands and making dinner. So without planning or pinkie swears, Noelle and I began talking on the phone every day.

More often than not, a crying child, the pediatrician on call-waiting, or a neighbor at the door would interrupt our calls. We never said goodbye in these instances; it was always one of us telling the other, "I'll call you later." These words offered an unspoken promise of what our friendship had become: If I don't get back to you today, we'll talk tomorrow.

～

Cate's behavior set her apart from Caroline—from any other child I knew. Her jobs weren't activities that most parents would consider typical of a toddler. Angela never called with news that John was stuffing garbage in her shoes. Whenever I was on the brink of losing my sanity, I'd call her for assurances that this nonsense would end, "She's not always going to do this, right?"

"Could be a phase, but I don't know. It's probably just what she does."

"Yeah, but does anybody else's kid do these things?"

"Not anybody I know."

Despite hours in thought about Cate's jobs (someone like me is never free from obsessive thinking), I couldn't say for sure why she behaved the way she did. I suppose it could have been the extra genetic material on the 21st chromosome, but I couldn't help but think it was a different kind of genetics at play. Cate was so much like my dad, and up until now all the chaos I experienced in my life usually revolved around him. Whenever I talked to my parents about her latest jobs, my dad would always say, "That kid's a screwball." *Yeah, Dad, just like you.*

It happened that many of Cate's jobs went undetected where we didn't plug her as the source. After months of Tim wearing his oldest ties to work every day, I finally asked him what the deal was. "Are you saving your good ties for some special occasion, or just wanting to look like an '80s throwback?"

"Actually I don't know where they are."

"Who loses a whole rack of ties?"

At each birthday, Father's Day, and Christmas, I made it a point to get him one or two decent ties to replenish his supply.

A few years later, when we were clearing the den to repaint it, I found all of Tim's ties stashed in the corner behind the play kitchen.

As Cate's jobs changed and diversified, I began adapting to her ways rather than railing against them. This piece of Cate wasn't something I could control or change. Perhaps it was a phase as Ange suggested, or it may have been just Cate. My organized days gave way to the chaos, which offered up a bit of laughter and kept me guessing. Though I still had my daily to-do list (always will), Cate forced me—as the cliché says—to stop and smell the roses in spite of it.

11

FRAGILITY

A Christmas Present

> *Some ask the world*
> *and are diminished in the receiving of it.*
> *You gave me only this small pool*
> *that the more I drink from,*
> *the more overflows me with sourceless light.*

"Gift," *Collected Poems, 1945-1990,* **by R.S. Thomas**

The fall after we moved in, it was one cold after another for the girls, though Cate never got over hers. They all simply folded into one cold that lasted for months. There were many conversations with the pediatrician's office about what antibiotic was she on, when did she finish it, did such-and-such antibiotic work the last time. The same conversation was repeated a week later when I'd bring her back. I was told to keep a journal about

Cate's illnesses, medicines, this, that, and the other, but I never did.

Most appointments I'd have to start my story from scratch, and honestly, I couldn't remember everything. I'd give my rendition week after week, "Cate just got off an antibiotic and seems to have developed a new cold…Yeah, I think there were a couple of days when she seemed a little better…Uh-ha, well this does seem like a new cold, but I can't say for sure…I think she was on Zithromax last time, but it didn't work that well…Maybe it was Augmentin that worked better… Actually, I don't really know what worked."

Cate rarely improved after whatever medicine she was given and many times seemed even more junky, a term I used often to describe how she sounded. Despite being chronically plagued by these colds, which frequently turned to respiratory infections, Cate's energy level didn't seem to be affected. She was always the same Cate, getting up at an ungodly hour after waking up five times a night to play, full of mischief and energy. Being sick was normal for her, so how she acted wasn't a gauge of how sick she was.

It was about a week before Christmas and Cate was junky as usual. My mom and dad came to celebrate my birthday, which was always an excuse to kick off the holidays a little early. Within less than an hour's time that evening, Cate's health deteriorated from wrestling with Caroline to lying on the floor in front of the TV, her breathing quick and shallow, and her body hot to the touch and somewhat limp. My mom, who isn't an alarmist, thought I should call the pediatrician's office. The on-call doctor recommended we go to the emergency room at a nearby children's hospital. It was a hospital we'd never been to and knew nothing about.

When Tim and I got to the emergency room with Cate,

they immediately triaged her. Cate's oxygen level was in the low 80s—anything below 90 requires oxygen and a hospital stay. She also had these petechiae (little broken blood vessels that looked like red dots) all over her chest. I tried to explain to the doctor that these weren't unusual for Cate. She'd had them before and they'd just come and go. Still, he was concerned and recommended a spinal tap to rule out meningitis.

Meningitis, what the heck is he talking about? Don't people die from that? I thought she might just have a fever. Isn't a spinal tap when they stick that huge needle in your back? Does this guy know what he's doing? Is this even a good hospital?

Many questions swirled in my brain and out of my mouth came one or two coherent thoughts, "Wait a minute I'm not sure this is even the right hospital for us. Maybe I should call my pediatrician and ask if we should take Cate to New York or Boston." But the attending doctor quickly squashed that plan: "You don't have time for that." I fell silent and my quick-breathing panicky feeling returned. *She was fine just a couple of hours ago, playing with Caroline and watching Barney...*

While the staff prepared to do the spinal tap, I made the emergency room doctor insane with questions, including one about his competency (he looked like he'd just hit puberty). "Is there someone maybe more experienced who does this all the time who might assist?"

"Ma'am," the poor guy answered, "I do this all the time." Nurses and other ER staff held Cate down as she silently lay on her side in the shape of the letter "c." I couldn't watch and turned my head into Tim's chest when the doctor bent down to draw the fluid.

"Darn, I didn't get it. Let's try again," he said all at once.

Just please let this be over. Don't let my neurosis shake his confidence.

The second time, he got the needle in the right spot and the fluid he drained was clear. "Thankfully, Mr. and Mrs. Alix, this isn't meningitis," he told us, but he cautioned, "Your daughter is still very sick." *He's really concerned. Why wasn't I as worried when I brought her in? I knew she had to be seen, but I thought she just needed a new antibiotic.*

I called my parents and told them that Cate was being admitted and my mom was collected as always. "Noelle, it's the best place for her." My second phone call was to Ange. I told her where I was and what was happening, and I just cried. She listened and asked if she could come down. "No, it's late. They're doing all these tests and we don't have a room yet. I'll call you later."

I hung up the kitchen phone on its wall mounting and turned to Ryan and John who were still awake and at the table having a bedtime snack. They were giddy with exhaustion from a full day, attempting to swallow spoonfuls of Cheerios and milk from their bowls despite contagious belly laughs. *What if this was one of them?* I kissed one and then the other on the crook of the nose and studied their joyful faces: Ryan blinking just his left eye the way he did when he was tired; John pursing his lips being silly, "Hey, Ryan, look at me." *Every moment is a gift.*

I went upstairs to our bedroom to find Rob paying bills and told him about Noelle's call. "I need to go and be with her," I said, looking for my car keys and grabbing the pair of jeans draped over the end of our bed. "Can you put the kids to sleep?"

"Hang on a second," he said. "I know how much you want to go, but you might be in the way tonight. Plus, I don't really want you alone downtown in a parking garage at night. I'm sure Tim is with her."

I knew he was right, his voice of reason redirecting my emotional impulse. I cupped my hands over my teary eyes, feeling utterly helpless and did the only thing I could. *Please God, protect Cate.*

———

After we were settled in a room, a pulmonologist examined Cate and told us she had double viral pneumonia along with a respiratory virus called RSV. He explained that newborns and preemies were especially susceptible to RSV and when older children got it, the virus usually manifested as a cold. Cate was almost three years old now, but, the doctor explained, "Children with Down syndrome have compromised immune systems, smaller airways..." *I know, I know, I know all this. Just tell me she's going to be okay.* "...So it's a tougher combination of illnesses for her to fight."

The doctor also told us RSV and viral pneumonia need to run their course, and although she was being treated with IV antibiotics and oxygen, it would probably get worse before it got better. He continued to explain how only a very small percentage of children progress to the point where they need to go to the ICU to be put on a respirator to help them breathe.

"Cate won't fall in that percentage, right? She'll be fine, right?"

But he couldn't give me the confirmation I was looking for. "Mrs. Alix, we need to wait and see."

I was frightened. Cate lay in the hospital bed unlike the boisterous child I knew, without the strength to move and having such trouble breathing. Seeing her tiny body through the clear plastic of an oxygen tent, I was reminded of the moment I first saw her through the nursery room glass. It was a time that seemed so distant if even possible in my recollection as I fixed my gaze on her: then my child whom I didn't know, now my daughter whom I loved more than life.

I told Tim to go home at some point in the middle of the night. There was only one couch in the room and I couldn't leave Cate. People were in and out all night so it was a relief when the sun came out and I could stop trying to fall asleep. I called Tim to check in at home and was about to call Ange when the phone rang.

⟋

Noelle answered in a near whisper, and spoke in a decidedly slow manner. I almost didn't recognize her voice. She explained the diagnosis and how serious this was. "No one will tell me if Cate will be okay."

"I'll be there in about an hour."

"No, I'm okay, really."

"I'm coming anyway."

I finished dressing and was leaving my room to move the kids along, when I paused at my bedroom dresser and opened the top drawer. I pulled out a box of religious mementos that was stuffed underneath my jewelry, finding the wooden rosary ring I'd put there months ago. Looking at the ring in my open hand, there was a sense in me, certain and strong, that I should take this to Noelle. I slipped it into my pants pocket and went about my morning, getting the kids to school and gathering a few things for Cate and Noelle to lift their spirits.

I drove to the hospital with my care packages and thought about how to share the rosary ring with Noelle, hoping she'd accept it. This wasn't a frivolous thing I could give her along with the rest of what I'd gathered. ("Hey, I picked up a *People Magazine* for you. Oh, and a rosary.") Though we'd rarely talked about faith explicitly, there was something in all the years that made me feel I could.

On arriving at the hospital, I slowly opened the door to Cate's room and peaked inside. The lights were off and Noelle was propped up in a chair next to Cate who lay ever still under an oxygen tent. We looked at each other, smiling half smiles while I tiptoed across the room and set my things down on the beige vinyl couch.

Noelle quietly got up and we hugged each other as if holding on for dear life.

Everything I'd held at bay the past twenty-four hours came pouring out: the exhaustion, the tears, the fears. "She's going to be okay, right?" I asked, since this was what troubled me most. I knew Angela wouldn't lie. She couldn't, not now.

"Cate's very sick, but she's strong," she said, the two of us still clutching each other.

Outside of Tim and my family, Angela was the only other person I needed then. She brought me a change of clothes, a coffee, a bagel, and a trashy magazine, encouraging me to take a few minutes to eat and get dressed and she would look after Cate. After I changed and brushed my teeth, we spent some time talking and sitting together while Cate faded in and out of sleep. Afraid as I was, somehow it was peaceful just the three of us there.

After a time, I stood up and threaded an arm through the sleeve of my winter coat. "I don't think Cate should have too long a visit today," I said quietly. "I'll be back tomorrow." Before saying goodbye, I pulled the rosary ring from my pants pocket. "I want you to borrow this," I said setting the ring in Noelle's hand and closing her fingers over it. "It's small enough so no one will see it."

"I don't need anything. Really, I'll be okay."

"Please," I said. "You need something to hold onto."

◦~

I reluctantly took what Ange had given me. Her saying "borrow" not "have" struck me. *It must be important to her.* I hugged her and thanked her for being here, for everything. I wanted to thank her, too, for being my friend, but I don't know if I did.

With Cate asleep, I sat down on the couch and opened my hand to see what Ange had placed there. It was a small elastic ring of ten brown wooden beads and a cross. I put it on my middle finger and lay the cross against my palm, folded my hand shut, and started talking to God. I can't say if it was Ange's rosary ring that prompted me to talk to Him, rather than say a prayer I'd memorized long ago. It's just what I did.

◦~

The rosary ring was a gift from my parents, a memento from their travels in Germany. Their trip abroad was a pilgrimage of sorts, my mom searching for her family roots in the farmland town of Billerbeck. She found them at a cathedral there, learning this was where her father's family had worshipped years ago. She purchased the rosary ring from that church and beautifully wrapped it for me, the way she did all her gifts.

I guess part of me was hoping there might be a pretty piece of jewelry inside this lovely little box, but it was something sentimental, something religious, something my mother would give to me. "It's small so you can wear it anytime," she encouraged me. "Some people are even using these rings during their daily commutes." I did appreciate this gift; the idea of how prayer could be part of a busy life. My mom never pushed her faith on me, but liked to offer gentle reminders it was there. To make sure it was there inside me, too.

I'd recently made a commitment to pray more, which was something I'd left behind. As is the case with many such plans, I started strong and then met with the difficulty of actually keeping to it. The rosary ring sat for a long time in the basket next to my bed, a basket overflowing with unfulfilled resolutions: the book club book to be read the month it was assigned, back issues of magazines to be thumbed through, the breast self-exam card to be followed, the journal to be filled with memories. After dusting the rosary ring off for the umpteenth time, I tucked it away in my dresser drawer and made the vow to use it some day.

Tim and I were together for only about an hour a day at the hospital when we did what we called, the switch. We found ourselves in this pattern where we would take turns sleeping at the hospital, while the other was at home with Caroline and Claire. During the day, it was a juggling act trying to find a place to drop off the girls, Tim trying to go to work, not go to work, and very honestly not getting the "take whatever time you need, I understand" words he needed to hear from his boss. Since I wasn't working, Tim's job had great significance. He felt tremendous pressure to be at two places at once—and so did I.

I missed Caroline and Claire when I was at the hospital and when I was at home, all I thought about was Cate. One day while on my home shift, I made the point of getting Caroline and Claire to the doctor because they both sounded awful. Turns out, they both had bronchitis and probably RSV as well. It seemed incomprehensible how a bad cold for Caroline and Claire might become a life-threatening illness for Cate.

Tim and I continued the switch into a second week as Christmas was fast approaching. It didn't feel at all like the holidays for us, though the hospital was decorated and Santa and his elves came to visit the children with bags filled with gifts. Our house reflected our focus since we only had a half-decorated Christmas tree visible through our bay window. It was distinctly dark, with little sign of festivity.

The doctor was accurate when he said Cate would get worse before she got better. She was on oxygen and IV medication, and received around-the-clock breathing treatments and chest PT (a regime of gentle pounding on her chest to help move the mucous she couldn't). Despite these efforts, Cate's health continued to deteriorate. On December 23rd, her doctors talked to us about moving her up to the ICU where she would be placed on a respirator to help her breathe. The rare scenario presented to us when we first arrived was our likely next step.

I sat on the bed next to Cate, slowly stroking her forehead with my hand. She was impossibly small while she lay motionless in the middle of the large hospital bed, an oxygen tube in her nose, a paci in her mouth, and a stuffed Barney doll under her arm that she kept petting with her thumb. When Cate would awaken, she'd look around by moving her eyes without having the strength to turn her head. Every now and then, she'd raise her hand to see the red light of the pulsox monitor, which was taped to her right forefinger. I gripped the rosary ring. *Please hear me.*

⁓

I called to tell my mom about Cate's downturn, to ask for her prayers. In my heart, I hoped she would take extra care with this request. I'd always thought this was more her job than my own, that her prayers were better than mine. She'd spent so much of her life cultivating a relationship with God when I was only a novice, the way I occasionally dusted it off and more often stashed it in drawers. *God will really listen to you, Mom.*

I mentioned to her the feeling I had about the rosary ring she'd given me when I first visited Noelle, unclear what exactly had happened at my dresser that morning. In the same top-of-mind way my mom could tell me how to make a German roast with spaetzle and gravy, she instantly said, "It was your guardian angel coming to help you." Her confidence gave me strength and a new perspective about the way God worked. In the silence that followed, I contemplated the power of my own faith. *Perhaps He was helping me help Noelle.*

"Thanks, Mom," I said, not simply to acknowledge her understanding in this instance, but for sharing her faith with me all along so I could share it now with my friend.

My parents had been back and forth from New York a bunch of times to help, and on Christmas Eve while my dad was home with Caroline and Claire, my mom came to relieve me at the hospital. I wanted to go to the toy store for Caroline and Claire to have a Christmas morning. I could have cared less about Christmas at that point, but Caroline was four years old and excited. I didn't want to disappoint her.

I returned to the hospital in the late afternoon with the most fearful anticipation that they may have already moved Cate to the ICU. I slowly opened the door picturing the empty bed I'd find, but instead saw Cate still lying there and my mom who looked up from the book she was reading to her. With a smile she said, "The doctor was just in and said he heard a minor improvement. He's going to wait before moving her to the ICU, thinking her illness may have peaked yesterday and could be turning for the better."

I dropped my purse and car keys on the floor and started to cry. It was one of those good cries I couldn't stop. I hugged my mom hard and lay down next to Cate kissing her cheeks, wanting to be as close to her as I could possibly get. I thanked God probably a hundred times knowing I had a debt to pay to Him, vowing to always remember the gratefulness I felt at this moment.

With an improvement in Cate's health by Christmas morning, we knew the doctor's prognosis was right. She didn't have to go to the ICU and was now in the recovery phase of this illness. We spent Christmas Day in the hospital and it was the best Christmas I ever had. I held Claire most of the day, let Caroline cruise around the hall in a wheelchair, ate cafeteria food, and talked with Tim and my parents about nothing in particular.

When Cate was finally discharged a little over a week later, there were two things I wanted to do. The first thing was to give Ange her rosary ring back, but that would have to wait a day or two. Happily, the second thing I could do immediately. I asked Tim to wait for me out front with the car so I could stop in at the ER to apologize and thank the young doctor who did the spinal tap on Cate.

"Honey, you should always do what feels right," my dad's familiar words nudged me along the corridors, "If ya love 'em, let 'em know. If ya did something stupid, say you're sorry."

By chance the doctor was there. He told me that he appreciated my coming by but that I didn't need to apologize, that he would have reacted the same way if it were his child. He smiled before being pulled away by a new crisis—someone else's daughter to save. Amidst the commotion, I sensed how perceptive my dad was.

That night, I climbed into bed next to Tim for the first time in a while. With a clear mind and everyone under one roof, my devotions began once again with thank you prayers instead of asking ones. It wasn't long into my prayers when I had a thought, "Tim, do you think Cate getting better on Christmas Eve was coincidence or a sign from God?" By his response I could tell his mind was more on sleep than conversation, "I guess you could think of it as a sign if you want."

"You know, I kind of do," I said, with the sense that God had given me a gift that day of all days. The gift of my daughter Cate, again.

Cate at 3: Calls herself by name ("ca"); uses one-or two-word phrases: "see," "whas dat," "me me" (help me); loves Barney; follows simple Simon Says directions ("touch your ears," "touch your eyes," "touch your nose"); matches basic shapes and colors; walks and runs with a wide leg base and toes pointed outward; still falls and trips a lot; prefers to go down stairs on her stomach; can kick a ball, but can't catch one.

Not long after Cate was discharged from the hospital, I stopped by Noelle's house for a quick visit to check in on her and Cate. On my way out the door, Noelle said, "Don't go yet." I followed her into the living room, where she stopped to open a small drawer in her secretary desk. From the drawer she pulled a pretty floral box, and carefully lifted the lid. She took out my rosary ring and with surprise said, "Oh, but wait." She picked up a card and looked at it for a minute. But then she set the card down and put the rosary ring on her middle finger, folding her hand in half to grip the cross. "I wore this every second of every day for two weeks," she explained, unfolding her hand to take off the ring, which she placed in my palm. "It made me feel safe."

I was happy to see that it was worn in places, no longer as new as it once was, the way leather boots grow more attractive with age. I knew in running my fingers over the rosary ring that it was the buoy that helped lift Noelle through, and part of the miracle that made Cate well.

Noelle put her hand on my forearm, while picking up the card that also had come from her special box. "Remember this?" she asked. With tears in her eyes, she handed me a baby card. "I never told you what your note did for me back then. Your words carried me through some hard days." I didn't recognize the card in scanning the well-worn white cover, "A Baby Girl…" lettered in raised pink calligraphy across the top.

On opening it, I saw my handwriting and all the memories of that time returned. Of the call from Carolyn about Cate and how I felt, of the hours I spent figuring out what to say to Noelle. "I can't believe you kept this."

"Oh my God, kept it? I read your card four or five times a day."

"You did?"

"Yeah I did—and every time I read it I felt better. I had that same feeling about your rosary ring. I've always trusted you."

I swallowed hard, unable to speak.

"Ange, please know I could never, not ever, repay you for all you've given me."

"But you've given me just as much."

"Come on, we both know that's not true."

Oh, but it is.

We laughed and threw our arms around each other, neither one wanting to let go, when Noelle saved us from getting too serious. "Now get the hell outta here, Angela Guadagno Martin," she said, stepping back to reveal her smiling face. "I'll call ya later."

12

LOST

Roll With It, Baby

Your children are not your children.
They are the sons and daughters of Life's longing for itself.
They come through you but not from you,
and though they are with you, yet they belong not to you.
You may give them your love, but not your thoughts,
for they have their own thoughts.
You may house their bodies, but not their souls,
for their souls dwell in the house of tomorrow,
which you cannot visit, not even in your dreams.

"On Children," ***The Prophet*** **by Kahlil Gibran**

I t was true that Noelle had given me as much; she just didn't
know it. It was the same thing she'd always given me, what
she continues to give me—that piece of her that's not naturally

in me. Noelle and I had this great complement of attributes that strengthened our friendship because it allowed us to prod each other along. Where I helped Noelle walk the straight and narrow, she pulled me out of my shell.

When we were seniors in high school, I'd be content to stay home and watch TV with my parents on a Friday night. This wasn't because I wanted to, but because that was easier for me—easier than going out and feeling uncomfortable in the middle of a crowd. This choice would make Noelle crazy because she didn't have a shy bone in her body and probably knew even then what she tells me still, "Being shy is never a good thing."

I guess you could say I was confidently insecure as a teenager: confident in my own abilities, but insecure about my weaknesses. I understood what it took to be a good student, to work hard at anything (I earned my private pilot's license before my high school diploma). But the whole social scene was another story—a network I didn't know how to navigate. Did hard work, persistence, and integrity get you a date with a cute guy? *Yeah, maybe when you're thirty.*

All of this came effortlessly to Noelle, who would insist that I go with her to the latest big party. I knew there would be tons of boys there, and while most girls saw this as the reason to go, it's what made me reluctant. I think Noelle intuitively knew this about me so she'd force me to go and tell me it would be fun. She'd call and tell me she was picking me up. "Okay, no excuses. I'll be right there," she'd say and quickly hang up so I couldn't back down.

I'd hear her Nova coming down the hill in my neighborhood about an hour later (precisely on time for Noelle), knowing it was loaded with girls. I'd get butterflies in my stomach while I tried to straighten my hair and add a bonus layer of cover-up to my acne. Half the time I'd attempt to wimp out when Noelle arrived, "Ah, Noelle..." But she was too smart for that lead. "Get in the car.

C'mon we're going," she'd order, and then plead, "It won't be the same without you."

◦—

No sooner had we gotten past the Christmas crisis, than our life settled back to its status quo, our different kind of normal that teetered somewhere on the edge between balance and utter mayhem. Only a few days after our return from the hospital came a call from a partner I used to work for. This woman was my mentor, so when I initially heard her voice, panic set in. *Oh my God, what mistake did she uncover?* Immediately I shifted my brain from mother to lawyer, the familiar sense of insecurity returning as I prepared to defend my actions, whatever they were.

Instead she explained that she had joined another large law firm that was opening a New York office and was charged with building a finance practice there. She went on to tell me this firm was progressive when it came to alternative work arrangements, and yadda, yadda, yadda. "Noelle, just come down and interview. What do you have to lose?"

Long story short, Tim's job in Connecticut wasn't the fit we hoped it might be. As hard as it was for me to believe, I was about to become a three-day-a-week lawyer, working from my Connecticut home for the New York office of a Texas law firm. *Yee haw!*

Once that was squared away (not an easy task emotionally or logistically), I received another phone call regarding an issue that I knew was coming but had avoided. This one was from the town special education director to discuss Cate's enrollment in the preschool program offered by the school district. I knew that early intervention would end when Cate turned three and that the school system would take over. With Cate's February birthday, it meant that she would be starting preschool in the middle of the year.

I hoped we might bypass the system by explaining that Cate just got out of the hospital. "Couldn't she start preschool in the fall and keep the early intervention services going until then?"

While this woman was sympathetic to my case, she couldn't accommodate the request. There wasn't any shopping around for alternatives, no Monte Hall to offer us two more doors to check behind. How I wished to throw on an emergency brake. *Isn't there a sweet program two mornings a week in a church basement she could go to next year?*

Beyond these anxieties, it hardly seemed the time to think about public education for Cate—to think of her as a student. She was still a baby in many ways, not yet potty-trained, needing constant supervision, still drinking from a sippy cup. She only talked a little bit and it was more like baby speak ("Whas dat?") when most kids her age were holding conversations. Caroline had seemed so much older when she went to preschool.

Though I felt backed into a corner, having fewer choices was probably better for me anyway because I don't like to shop around. Take my approach to fashion: Go to a favorite clothing store. Try on an outfit. Ignore the price tag. Buy it and leave. It's the antithesis of Angela who can't pay "retail," and Tim who tells me about the $4 bathing suit he got at Job Lot, paying the price by getting fat man's rash at the beach the first time he wore it.

Despite Cate's being more toddler than preschooler, we were encouraged not only to send her to school, but also to use van transportation to get her there. A resource teacher explained to me by phone, "It'll save you a trip, and the kids like it." I initially declined, thinking the idea was ludicrous. (*You don't put three year olds on buses... Cate still falls asleep in her car seat... She can*

slither out through the straps no matter how tight you make them...)
And it's hard to admit, but I hated the picture in my mind of
the short handicapped buses and the idea that my daughter
would be on one.

I just wanted life to go on with no big things to think about
and no big decisions to make, but that's not how life presents
itself most times. As I'd learned many times with the "do I go
back to work" choice, I needed to make the decision about preschool and move on. Cate would go to the town preschool, take
the bus in the morning, and I would pick her up after school.
Okay, a compromise. And a compromise is exactly what my life
became now that I was back to work with a new babysitter in
our home a few days a week, Cate starting preschool, Caroline
in preschool, and Claire along for the ride. I was spinning all
my dishes as best I could.

With these changes there was one constant, which didn't
serve the calming factor that a constant should: Cate's daily job.
Most of her work these days was concentrated in hiding and
wandering off. Cate would not merely be out of sight and, after
a bit of searching, turn up. Instead, she'd be lost in an "Oh my
God, Cate's completely gone" kind of way. The only consistent
thing about this new job, like all those that preceded it, was her
need to do it every single day.

There were times I didn't even know she was gone until
a sixth sense interrupted my thoughts and made me check on
her. I'd have what I thought were my eyes on her or be listening out for her, and I swear she'd evaporate. Poof, gone! Every
moment of every day, I was conscious of where she was and how
to keep her from getting lost, but she was dedicated to her job
and inevitably found holes in my fortress.

∾

Noelle and I intuitively were doing our best for our kids, but so often it didn't feel like enough. When Ryan started kindergarten the past fall, his teacher contacted us about his general comprehension in class, worried he might have a hearing problem. After ear tube surgery with an ENT in the spring, it didn't take long to realize the tubes weren't helping Ryan in school.

His kindergarten teacher talked about how she played a detective game with the kids. She whispered one new clue to each student every day and by the end of the week the children had to guess what she was hiding. "Thursday's clue is a giveaway," she'd explain. "Ryan just whispers the clue back to me." *What did this mean?*

I knew Ryan was bright the way he built complex gizmos out of legos, put intricate puzzles together, and drew with detail and accuracy. He was creative like me. We needed to understand what was going on because obviously there was a gap between Ryan's potential and his performance at school. In explaining the latest chapter in our saga to my mother she immediately said, "That's the sure sign of a learning disability."

We had Ryan tested just before summer vacation and the results revealed he did in fact have a learning disability—a receptive language learning disability. After almost three years, we finally had insight into what was going on. In a year-end meeting at school, we were told Ry's learning disability sometimes made written and verbal messages difficult for him to interpret. To clarify this statement I asked, "So Ryan doesn't always understand what he hears or reads?" Heads around the table bobbed up and down. "Well, how is he going to learn?"

The principal assured us Ryan would be okay. She explained that with our approval, he would be enrolled as a special education student and an individual education plan (IEP) drawn up with specific learning goals. "I can't believe it. At first it was just speech and now he's going to be in special ed?" I whispered to Rob while the principal continued her explanation.

He grabbed my forearm under the table and looked at me with misty eyes.

Although Rob and I had concerns about Ryan being a special education student, he needed the services and we wanted to be sure he'd get them. "I wish this weren't happening to him," I leaned in to tell Rob when we left the room.

"Me, too. But he'll do just fine," he said taking my hand when we walked out.

I called Noelle after the boys were asleep. "Why did I blindly go along for so many years?"

"Even if you could go back, I don't think the outcome would be any different," she said trying to ease my guilt. "This has nothing to do with what you did or didn't do."

"Maybe, but this should be resolved by now."

"I don't think so. Sometimes there's no one to blame. It's just as it is."

But I couldn't let it go at that. That summer we continued with our family read-alouds and worked on math. And looking ahead, I wanted to get hard-core strategies from his teacher next year to fix this once and for all. That way, Ryan would quickly close what I feared was an ever-widening gap with his peers. In short order he'd be like everybody else.

Tim and I came to know each store's code for a missing child (Code Pink, Code Adam, Code 11) having lost Cate in just about every store in town. Even when the two of us shopped together having discussed our man-to-man defense strategy in advance, she'd find a way to disappear. It was as if the two of us were discussing a big play on the ball field the way we'd set our plans.

"Okay, Tim, I've got Claire and Caroline, you have Cate. Just watch her, all right?" I'd be shopping as quickly as possible and before long I'd hear, "Shit, Noelle, I can't find her." We'd grab the other girls, ditch the cart, and begin our search. Mind you, we never thought someone took Cate. We knew she was merely escaping us and we were quick to tell store personnel who were frantically relaying all her physical statistics on walkie-talkies, treating these incidences as genuine child abductions.

Cate at 3½: Beginning to potty train; is helping dress herself and able to take off simple clothing such as socks, coat, and hat; uses the word "backpack," and finds her cubby herself at preschool; needs help putting her jacket on the hook; with verbal prompts, Cate can unzip her backpack, remove her lunch box, place it on the shelf, and go choose an activity to do.

For as many times as I'd lose her, I probably should have had my story straight, a recent photo in my wallet, a clear picture in my mind of what she was wearing that day, but I never did (journal-keeping, photo-stashing—who has time?). The moment of the escape always created a pressure situation, with me needing to call on my taxed mind and at the same time, think like Cate.

When we lost Cate one morning, Tim and I split up to start the search. He was carrying Claire and I had Caroline by the hand. I quickly connected with the store staff, "My daughter Cate is missing. She's wearing a yellow jacket and has Down syndrome." It turned out Claire had a yellow jacket on that day, too, so when a security person saw Tim jogging toward the entrance (our greatest fear was Cate alone in a parking lot), he was the prime suspect.

Tim continued on when they tried to stop him, "I've got to find my daughter," he said and the store's security team broke out. Meantime I found Cate and by the time I located Tim, he'd resolved the confusion. Once we were all locked safely in the car, Tim put the key in the ignition and before starting the engine turned to look at me. "Okay Noelle, just listen," he said taking a breath. "We've got to come up with a better game plan next time because I was almost arrested for abducting Claire."

Tim and I hardly had a complex about this because everyone lost Cate. After all, those were the rules: to be a family member or a friend, you had to lose Cate at least once. Most people had their own way of trying to contain her. My neighbor Ann put the house in lock-down whenever Cate came over. Anytime I'd drop off Cate to stay with her, the door would instantly close and lock with a firm click in front of me. From behind the door I'd hear Ann call out, "Okay, Noelle, bye!" Not to be left out, Ange lost her, too, and it was a bad one. But that's her story to tell.

I invited Noelle and the girls to go swimming with us at Winding Trails, a recreation park in the area, after Noelle called with her daily Cate-getting-lost story. I thought an afternoon at the beach would help her relax. At first Noelle hesitated, but I promised her it would be fun and I'd help her with the girls. "You need a break. It'll do you some good," I said as convincingly as I could. She reluctantly agreed, having already lost Cate that morning. Noelle's neighbor, Roger, had intercepted Cate, who was trucking up the street wearing her pajamas and Tim's work boots.

It was overcast so not many people were at Winding Trails, an easy day to keep track of everyone. After some swimming, the kids headed to the playscape and Caroline asked to go to the bathroom. "I'll watch the girls, you take Caroline," I said with every confidence. A few minutes later, I turned my head when I heard Noelle return and ask where the girls were. "They're right there at the bottom of the slide," I said and turned, pointing at the spot.

"Claire's there, but Cate isn't." In the instant it took for me to take my eyes off Cate to look at Noelle, she was gone. "She was just there a second ago."

I'd never lost a child the way I lost Cate that day. One minute watching her play and the next minute my heart set racing over where she might be. The worry about losing your own child is strong enough, but having lost my best friend's daughter was beyond terrifying. We were caught as if between two evils: on one side lay a wooded area and the other side a deep, dark lake.

Noelle and I canvassed the play area, scoping around in wide views. We then raced up and down the deserted beach, calling Cate's name, scanning the still water of the lake when a woman approached us. "Who are you looking for?" she asked in a serious tone.

"My daughter, Cate. She's three-and-a-half," Noelle said.

"Notify the lifeguards!" the woman yelled at Noelle, who looked at me and said, "I just need a minute to find her with my own eyes."

After a few more minutes I couldn't wait any longer and said, "It's time to tell a lifeguard." Noelle dropped to her knees and described Cate to the would-be rescuer, who radioed the news over loudspeakers across the park. Lifeguards began combing the beach, others were darting through the trees, and some had formed a line at the shore to search the cloudy water. I couldn't believe it had come to this.

Ten minutes later, a lifeguard appeared through the trees holding Cate by the hand. It was like the news stories you see about heroes bringing victims out of harm and into safety. For Noelle and for me, the sense of relief was overwhelming. She raced to hold Cate and I broke into tears apologizing for my incompetence, that the whole thing was my fault. Noelle assured me I wasn't to blame. Still I thought how different the day would have been had I not turned away. I gathered the rest of the kids and our stuff and headed to the car. I never asked Noelle to join us there again. It was an unspoken pact between us that Winding Trails was a place her family didn't go.

⎯⎯ ℰ ⎯⎯

They never seemed to lose Cate at school, so clearly they were doing something right. In fact, they were doing a lot right. Just as at Stepping Stones, the professionals in the school system showed us the way. Andrea Butler, the special needs director for the preschool was a constant source of support, my own private therapist of sorts. When I couldn't bear separating and refolding the same pile of clothes another day from Cate's lingering behavior of dumping drawers, I mentioned it to her and she suggested a home visit—an extraordinary outreach.

By this time I was used to exposing our family life and all its idiosyncrasies to strangers be they therapists, babysitters, or social workers. That said, it took a while for me to get used to receiving the unsolicited advice that came along with some of those visits.

"Ah, Mrs. Alix, you should let Cate get dressed on her own," or "Cate should be drinking from a regular cup by now."

Early on it was impossible for me to hear such suggestions without getting defensive. *I'm her mom; I know what's best for her.* I will say, however, it didn't take long to figure out that I probably didn't.

On balance, I'd gotten to a place where I did appreciate all the suggestions because they often saved my sanity, especially Andrea Butler's fix for the drawer dumping. It wasn't some sort of psychological voodoo, it was just a simple solution: a picture of a stop sign taped to each drawer—a visual clue for Cate to STOP. After the signs were "installed," I'd hear Cate go upstairs ready to begin work and say, "Top, noooo dum draws."

Unfortunately, there wasn't an easy answer to Cate's hiding and wandering off. We tried piggybacking off the last solution, posting pictures of stop signs on every outside door. But no such luck. She treated them more like yield signs: slow down, check for grown-ups, and go. Why they worked in one application and not another was one of the great mysteries about Cate, where logic and reason got lost along with her.

In any event, Cate's getting-lost wasn't just the focus of my life, but the main topic of conversation with Angela.

"I found Cate in the car this morning. How am I going to keep her alive and not completely squash her freedom?" I asked in a flurry, still winded over the whole search.

"Why don't you just lock the doors to the house?"

"Hello—of course we lock the doors, but we forget to relock them. We go in and out of the house however many times a day and we just forget."

Cate at 4: Potty-trained; knows some colors and shapes; beginning to identify family names in print when given a choice of two; can not yet count to ten; note from preschool teacher: "Cate is self confident and strong willed"; delayed in drawing and cutting skills; can imitate two-syllable words; can't jump with two feet; can throw a ball.

Cate's hiding and wandering off didn't end after a few months the way her other jobs did; it continued through her preschool years and beyond. For me, it was more of an era than a phase—an era of adrenalin rushes followed by waves of relief.

Fortunately this was Cate, so there were plenty of times when my worries turned to laughter, such as the day I decided to break with tradition and take a shower.

I readily admit to having few indulgences and given Cate's latest job, showering daily had become one of them. Early one summer night, when no one had to be anywhere, I decided to treat myself and jump in after telling Caroline to watch Cate: "No, *really* watch her."

Coming out of the shower, I put on one of Tim's T-shirts and was about to blow-dry my hair when it seemed too quiet. I asked Tim, who had just come in from work, where Cate was. "I think she's downstairs watching TV," he said throwing his keys and change into a catchall bowl. I went to check on her and she wasn't there. Then I asked Caroline who didn't have a clue.

Tim and I searched the house, calling her name, which meant nothing because Cate was famous for staying quiet when we were looking for her. We checked all the normal hiding spots—the dark corners in the closets, the spot behind the living room drapes, and in the tub behind the shower curtain—but she was nowhere to be found. Tim and I ran outside screaming her name when I heard, "Noelle, we've got her!"

Our neighbors from across the street brought Cate around from their backyard. She was holding two fistfuls of flowers she'd pulled up from their gardens. I ran to her and began bending over to pick her up when I stopped short. I was still in Tim's T-shirt and NO underwear. It was my anxiety nightmare coming true. You know, the one when you're running around your neighborhood completely naked. I took Cate by the hand and hesitated—afraid even to turn around because I didn't think the T-shirt was providing full coverage.

When Noelle called with her T-shirt story, I thought it would be months before she'd have another one that could top it. But only a few days later the phone rang and Noelle had a new winner.

"Ange, do you have a few minutes for a laugh."

"Of course."

"The girls and I were just up the street at a neighbor's house to pay her boys for mowing the lawn. I don't know the mom that well, but she's so nice. So we get chatting and Cate walks in her house. I was mortified, but the mom tells me, 'No, she's fine.' Guess where I found her?"

"I don't know, watching TV?"

"Close—she was naked between the sheets of this woman's bed, a remote in her hand, watching a cable news show."

"Unbelievable."

We hung up and I told my kids the story. Both of them started to laugh when Ry suddenly stopped. "Yeah, Mommy, but remember when you lost her at Winding Trails?" My stomach ached with the memory of it. Losing her had given me a new awareness I didn't have from my typical vantage point as a passive observer, simply listening on my end of the telephone receiver. My daily dose of Cate getting lost entailed waiting for the punch line and nothing more. I was immune to the worry because I knew the outcome. By the time Noelle called me, Cate would be lost and found. I never had the concern that swelled in me that afternoon, the idea that maybe we wouldn't find her.

Even though I knew Noelle lost Cate every day, I couldn't imagine how she did it. How she ended one day to face the same worry the next. I asked her about it once, and she told me in her upbeat way, "I like to think Cate keeps me on my toes, keeps me young."

About two summers later, I was bending over to clear off a picnic table at Winding Trails when someone goosed me on the butt. I shrieked and spun around wondering who would greet me in such a way and was stunned to see it was Noelle.

"Hola, amiga!" she said with a bright smile and open arms. "Bet you never guessed to see me here."

"You got that right," I said and we hugged each other.

"My neighbor, Lisa, invited us and it's such a beautiful day I couldn't say no. Anyway, it's been a while so I'm up for the challenge."

This hiding and wandering off business was all consuming for me in a day chock full with other things. Preschool became my saving grace, my respite care. With Caroline in kindergarten and Cate in preschool, I revised my work schedule to have Mondays and Fridays off with Claire, which I loved because I never had that with her. These long weekends gave me the chance I hadn't had in a while to just be a mom, when I didn't have to be on as a security guard, a lawyer, or anything special.

As it happened, preschool was only a 50/50 proposition for us. Cate was sent home often, either because she was sick or for her perpetual cough. I'd cringe every time the phone rang if it was before dismissal. "Ah, Mrs. Alix, I have Cate here with me," the nurse would say and I'd interrupt with assurances, "Really she's fine, it's just her airway." Unfortunately, that explanation never flew. "Still, Mrs. Alix, I think you should come get her," the nurse would say, squashing my defense. *Dangit, there goes my morning.*

So I found myself in this ironic state of wishing for one thing and getting the opposite. Whenever I needed Cate to be at school, she would wind up back home and when she was home, I couldn't keep her there. Although there were plenty of funny getting-lost episodes, there were a few that weren't.

One afternoon I went to visit my friend, Jill, who had moved to a nearby neighborhood. Jill and I were talking in her downstairs den when I sent Caroline up to check on Cate who was playing in one of the kids' bedrooms. Caroline came down to say she couldn't find her. We began checking closets, showers and still nothing, when I heard Jill say, "The slider door in our dining room is open." *Oh my God, Cate's outside.* I started running around the yard calling out Cate's name. I told Jill to watch the girls and jumped in my car and drove around the neighborhood, screaming Cate's name out the window and still nothing.

I sped back to Jill's and through my tears told her to call 911. There were so many wooded areas near her house and a main road nearby. Within what seemed like seconds, I saw a police car. I described Cate and the officer radioed all the details and ordered me to wait at home. But, I couldn't go home. I had to look for her, too.

I don't even know what ground I covered, making turn after turn and crying so hard I could barely see the road in front of me...*What if she's on the main road? She could be hit by a car. What if she's lost in the woods? What if she's scared? She's never been missing for this long...* I really had no idea what to do other than drive, pressing every person I saw into service, praying with every ounce of me that Cate would pop into view.

It was probably thirty minutes, though it seemed like hours, when I met up with one of the police cruisers searching for Cate. The officer said he just received word someone found her and another police officer was picking her up and bringing her home. My body collapsed over the steering wheel...*Thank you, God...*I caught my breath, drew my hands in to wipe my face, and headed home.

When I pulled up to our house, there were three police cars and Cate was in the back seat of one of them, looking out of the window appearing to be fine. This scene didn't quite register at first (it might happen when your teenager is eighteen and in trouble, not as a child because you lost her). I flew out of my car hysterically crying and she hugged me thinking I was hurt. "S'Mommy s'okay?"

A contractor working in the neighborhood found her walking along the road (not the main one) and dialed 911. It turns out she was near our street, but almost a mile from my friend Jill's house. Who knows how she ever got to where she was with no one spotting her; there were so many people searching. I went inside and dropped next to Cate on the den couch and held her tightly. "Stick, do you know how much I love you," I said, hugging her even harder. Spontaneously my mind began retracing the steps leading up to her disappearance. *How could I have lost her like this?*

Before that day was over, Tim located a chime system on the Internet that would alert us when a door opened or closed in our house. To monitor her elsewhere, we researched a GPS tracking device, though it didn't suit our situation. Tim said it was made for people with Alzheimer's disease, which will be me someday since all my brainpower will be used up second-guessing Cate.

That night over a glass of wine, Tim and I talked about what happened and, worse yet, what could have happened. We both knew hindsight was so easy with her and clairvoyance impossible. "This time she was okay, Tim, but she could have been hit by a car, or still be lost."

"Yeah, but we found her and she's okay."

I couldn't let it go at that, attempting to tap into Cate's psyche: "Why did she leave? Where was she going? What route did she take with no one seeing her?"

"Noelle, we'll probably never figure it out. It's just Cate. Let it be."

"I know, I know," I answered, after sucking down the last bit of wine in my glass.

"C'mon," Tim said, motioning his head to the stairs. "Let's put this day down." Instead of tidying up, I left our glasses on the counter and slipped under Tim's outstretched arm. As we headed up to bed, Tim stopped short to leave me in the foyer and went back through the house and locked all the doors.

13

TRUST

Giving Her Wings

Finish every day and be done with it.
You have done what you could.
Some blunders and absurdities, no doubt crept in.
Forget them as soon as you can, tomorrow is a new day;
Begin it well and serenely, with too high a spirit
to be cumbered with your old nonsense.

Ralph Waldo Emerson

I t was an afternoon in the spring of Cate's second year in pre-school when "Town of Simsbury" flashed on my caller ID. Unlike most people who probably treat calls from school with the urgency of a 911 responder, I often had about a three-second delay in answering. Usually by about the fourth ring, however, my conscience would get the better of me and I'd pick up the receiver.

This time it was the school office about scheduling a date for Cate's annual PPT (planning and placement team) meeting to discuss our plans for next year. It seemed a world away since the only pressing thing for me was the present moment. I knew a major discussion point of the meeting would be Cate's readiness—or in my estimation, her lack of readiness—for kindergarten. But I quickly pushed that thought out of my mind.

Unlike the early years with Cate when I couldn't stop thinking about the future, now I wished to avoid it entirely. I'd reach a point where I was at ease with her program and the people, and then—bam—we'd have to move on. It never seemed I could linger in my latest comfort zone. We always had to press forward because you have to—that's the thing about life. And, yet, change with Cate was never easy for me.

It was a familiar group that gathered a few weeks later for the PPT, a group of people I'd come to know and respect. I liked to think of them as Cate's posse and my own personal advisory board. We said our hellos and squeezed ourselves into miniature chairs at a low-set table. I was reminded of my parent therapy sessions at Stepping Stones as I shifted in my seat to find a comfortable position, getting butterflies in my stomach with the thought that I already had to contemplate grammar school for Cate. *Wasn't I just deciding on her preschool program?*

Our assembled group started right in on the advantages of sending Cate to kindergarten, but for the life of me I couldn't imagine how I'd be able to do that. "She only speaks in two-word sentences," I implored. Still a few of them encouraged me along: "Cate's progress will always lag behind her peers. Better to keep her with children she knows, children in her age group." *I guess that makes sense.*

On the flip side, there were others who suggested an extra year of preschool to give Cate the chance to mature: "It might make a difference when she gets to middle school." *Middle school?*

I pictured Cate in a regular middle school classroom along with typical kids, learning what? Earth science and algebra? I had no idea how this thing called inclusion worked.

I thought over the meeting while I drove home, so much information and so many opinions to sort out. Who knew that sending Cate to kindergarten would involve deliberation, that there would be pros and cons, different schools of thought, that whatever the choice, it might impact her future. There wasn't a definitive recommendation from anyone. No one was going to cite some precedent and tell me what to do.

Many hard truths surfaced as well, but the hardest truth of all was that Cate was always going to be behind her peers in school. Of course this wasn't breaking news, but to hear it out loud, to have it said so plainly, to have Cate already differentiated from the crowd at the age of five was crushing. Cate wouldn't make the same academic strides as kids her age, or her sisters. She was different from the average child.

The last time she was compared with her peers was at Stepping Stones, where everyone had Down syndrome. There wasn't a significant contrast between Cate and her classmates, nor in their ability to master the basics: drinking, crawling, walking, etc. We were always told our kids would get there—they'd get there differently, but they'd get there. Now I had no idea how far *there* was for Cate and when I should set her on her way.

Keeping Cate in preschool was an option, and I kind of liked it. Frankly, this was my first choice, though it was more to my benefit than hers—a comfortable decision, but probably not the right one. I could coast a bit, instead of being bombarded with new problems, new transitions. But what was good for me wasn't necessarily what was good for Cate, or any of my girls for that matter. Life was all about change.

⟡

Ryan was in the last quarter of first grade, and I was grateful. I was ready to move forward as I joked with Noelle that it was more like college than elementary school, its expectations for reading and writing so far above where Ryan was. He had an energetic young teacher in Miss Anderson, but she readily admitted at the beginning of the year that she'd never taught a child with Ryan's learning disability. "I'll read everything I can on the subject," she said earnestly. "We'll work together."

Homework began in November with a bound packet of material that led off with a cover letter specifying eight goals. I disobeyed point number four every night: "Parental involvement is that of facilitator, a gentle guide, not a teacher, providing hopefully a genuine bond with this experience." I had to be a teacher because it seemed Ryan needed me to be one. He couldn't do his homework without guidance, prompting, explanation.

I used to think that being a mother was teacher enough, providing the life lessons I instinctively offered: take turns, always try your best, be a good friend. But you give your children what they need even if it's not what you expect. I tried to make homework meaningful one-on-one time, but it was incredibly stressful for me. I shared my worries with Noelle one night when I called her after the kids had gone to bed, "Is school always going to be this hard for him?"

"Honestly, it probably will. But then again, other things will come easily to him that won't be easy for other kids."

Ryan's weekly homework included a reading schedule and two journal entries, which underscored "details, details, details" in drawing and writing. Thank goodness for the illustration piece.

This was his own work and by far his strength as he drew colorful intricate pictures of the stories he read and the words I helped him find.

Still I couldn't wait for second grade since I'd heard from friends that it was a fun year. With the curriculum of reptiles and amphibians, it would be more of a hands-on learning experience. *This will be a better environment for Ryan.* It appeared from early on that this was how he learned—by seeing, touching, and doing.

"Be sure to take care of the class tree frog and gecko, Speedy and Jade, during one of the breaks next year," suggested my friend, Amy, who had an older son. All you have to do is feed them crickets, plug in a heat lamp, and mist the tank with water."

"Where do you get crickets?" I wondered aloud after hanging up the phone when it came to me: *I bet Ryan knows.*

I struggled with the kindergarten decision for the next couple of weeks. I'd be leaning one way only to question myself when advice to the contrary suggested otherwise. "If we keep Cate in preschool another year, it gives her more time for her speech to improve," one of her teachers reasoned.

Then Rita, the speech therapist who came to our house, offered her opinion: "Another year isn't going to make a big difference, Noelle. Cate's always going to struggle with her speech."

As with everything with Cate, I had no personal experience to draw on, which made sifting through the options that much tougher. I would have loved to talk with a mom in my situation, someone with a child a year or two older than Cate who could tell me what kindergarten would be like for her. But, Cate wasn't just a first for me. She was one of the first children with Down syndrome to attend our local elementary school. There wasn't a precedent for reference. Cate was new territory for all of us.

Beyond this it wasn't just the issue of sending her to school. There was a litany of questions in my head that were either unresolved or yet to be asked: *I don't think she can use the bathroom on her own. Will someone go in with her? How will that look to the other kids? Will anyone understand what she says? She doesn't even know the concept of what a letter is. How will she find her way from the bus to the classroom? What if she escapes at school?"* But then again, I'd probably have the same questions next year.

To be honest, there was this nagging notion I'd harbored since Stepping Stones that was contributing to my indecisiveness—that Cate reach my ivy-league benchmark for her of being a high-functioning person with Down syndrome. *Would starting her in school now crush any hopes of this, or is kindergarten exactly what she needs?* I thought the person Cate would be someday hung in the balance with this decision, and that was why I had such trouble making it.

Each time I asked Tim what he thought, he would give me his typical boomerang answer, "I'm not sure, what do you think?"

"I have no clue. That's why I'm asking you."

I had Audrey over on my back deck for a glass of wine and wanted to hear her perspective about Cate and kindergarten, capitalizing on her experience in special education as well as her style of not beating around the bush. And more than anything, I respected her opinion as an older woman because she had lived. She was wise when I was still learning, still just finding my way.

"C'mon Noelle, it's not a life or death decision here," she said, pouring herself another glass of wine. "It's just kindergarten, for Christ's sake."

"But Aud, if I start her in school now and she isn't ready, she might be even further behind the other kids than she's already gonna be."

Audrey set her glass on the table and leaned in close to let me have it. "Jesus, what the hell are you doing here? Don't make this a big deal. Cate's always going to have Down syndrome. She'll be fine. That kid's with it." Then she clinked her glass to mine and took a swig. With that I decided to send Cate to kindergarten.

But this decision quickly prompted another. "Great choice," Andrea Butler (stop signs) said when I called with the news. "So will she take the van, or do you think we should talk about her riding the bus?" *Whoa, horsee!* "Andrea, I can barely imagine her going to kindergarten, let alone how she could ride the regular bus without a car seat or an aid."

From my vantage point, it seemed the most prudent choices were the ones that offered progress with the least amount of risk. *Okay, Cate will go to kindergarten, but she'll ride the special ed bus.* Even though I still didn't like the stigma of a minibus, it was better than the alternative: Cate by herself on the big yellow bus doing God knows what.

All the decisions revolving around Cate seemed hard, or maybe I just made them hard. What's the old saying about making a mountain out of a molehill? My obsessive brain was working overtime, all the time about her. I thought every change with Cate was monumental, but they weren't. I suppose it's easy to say that now with perspective on my side.

Cate was in her final week of preschool, though I hardly knew where the time went. My dad drove up with his basset hound, Boomer, for Cate's last show-and-share. She loved Boomer and we thought a live presentation would be fun for Cate and her class. Cate dragged the dog around the room, peering over the top of her fingerprint-smudged eyeglasses that sat too low on her nose, telling everyone about, "Boomer s'long, s'long ears."

Meanwhile, my dad was embarrassing me in regular fashion, explaining to the other parents why the dog smelled so badly.

Cate at 5: Recognizes the numbers one to five; right hand dominant but will still switch to her left; when drawing a person, draws face with legs and arms attached to the head; has hard time buttoning; sings the alphabet song with the class; when looking at a picture, can describe it as "brown bear" or "big bear"; can jump; can't hop on one foot.

"If you happen to notice that nasty odor, it's the necrotic tissue in the folds of Boomer's skin that gets infected and oozes." *Oh my God, Dad, stop talking.* Just as I was about to intercede, Cate's teacher politely said, "Thank you, Mr. Clifford. That's very interesting." I took her cue to gather my band of characters and get the heck out of there. Although the last thing I wanted to do was leave this comfortable place, I'd made the decision for Cate to go and I needed to do the same.

Andrea Butler assisted with Cate's transition to kindergarten, encouraging me with a phone call over the summer to put her on the big yellow bus for the first day of school. "You're incredible to be thinking about Cate on vacation," I said, caught out of the blue while getting the kids into swimsuits for an afternoon at the town pool. "Let's assume Cate's ready and give her the chance. I'll ride the bus and observe, see how she does," Andrea told me enthusiastically. "Don't underestimate your daughter, Noelle."

Honestly, in some respects, I never underestimated Cate. She accomplished more bad stuff by 5:00 a.m. than most people do in a year. It was the idea of raising the bar for her, to set my expectations at a level I didn't think she was ready for, to have confidence in the advice, and to jump yet again into the unknown.

———

It was the first full day of kindergarten for John and I'd slept through the alarm. By the time I heard Rob in the shower, I only had half an hour to get the kids on the bus. Immediately jumping into my routine, I was determined the kids would not be late even if I was. My perfectionist side wasn't about to blemish John's record with having him arrive tardy on his first day of kindergarten.

I sent John upstairs to get himself together and hugged Ryan, wishing him the best for a great first day. I practically pushed him out the door to the waiting bus and waved goodbye until it turned the corner. John walked downstairs ready to go. I fixed his hair while he zipped up his backpack. I couldn't look him in the eye. There wasn't time for a whole lot of whoopla or emotion or saying what I wanted to. We had to get to school.

I dressed and met him outside by the tree in our front yard where I quickly snapped a picture despite the rain. His smile was a best effort, trying to cover up his nerves. We made it to school through the first-day traffic jam and made a dash for the nearest door. He and I arrived in the kindergarten wing just when the morning bell sounded. John Martin was on time.

There wouldn't be an outdoor welcoming ceremony with the weather that day, so the hallway was tightly packed with parents and children, readying themselves for goodbyes. John and I were the last to enter this madness, and thank goodness for it. We found ourselves just outside the door of his classroom. His new teacher, Kathy Fischer, appeared in the doorway when we were taking off our raincoats.

"Good morning everyone," she said with a glowing smile and bent down to greet John. Kathy shook his hand and motioned for him to enter the classroom. John looked up at me, his expression saying it all: "This is the big moment?" I hugged and kissed him even though he avoided my affections, his brave little face holding its composure. Without looking back, John walked into his classroom. A wave of excitement and longing rose up in me.

I headed for the school cafeteria, passing other parents bidding their adieus, to attend a kindergarten orientation meeting when I unfolded my wet raincoat to find John's nestled inside. The vice principal happened to see me holding his coat. "Let me take it to him, Mrs. Martin. Who is John's teacher?"

That's when this whole crazy morning hit me.

I cradled John's coat in mine, the way I'd cradled him for so many years. I needed to let him go, without dwelling on it so much. Good-hearted people at this school would be helping him find his way—they already were. And it would be okay. Noelle made this transition years earlier as all working mothers had to. My day of separation came the old-fashioned way, in kindergarten.

Making my way out of the school lobby, I was glad for the rain. I threw my coat over my head and walked off into the storm. I called Noelle as soon as I got home. "I just dropped off John at school, and I can't stop crying. Don't you miss Cate?" I said, wiping my face with a tissue.

"Yeah, but I'm weathered," she said laughing, and then quickly added, "I needed to send her to kindergarten, instead of letting my doubts hold her back."

"I think that's the hardest part—the letting go. I have to say, it's hitting me harder this time than it did with Ry."

"Well, John's your baby," Noelle said. "It's a new chapter for you."

"But where does my story go from here?"

"I have no idea, but you'll figure it out. And by the way, you don't have to decide today."

I hung up with Ange and sat in front of my work computer ready to go with my day, still mindful of the words Andrea Butler had told me this summer. *Don't underestimate your daughter, Noelle.* It seemed I had only made two work calls when I heard the bus make a turn for our street. I ran outside and squatted down on my knees to meet Cate who greeted me the same way she would every day since. She barreled down the stairs nearly falling flat on her face, dropped her backpack on the driveway, and ran to me with open arms. "Hiiiiiiiiiiiiii Mommeeeeeee!!!!!!" *Thank you, Andrea.*

The feeling I had wasn't so much conviction in taking leaps of faith, but contentment in knowing there were people I trusted to help me take them. Soon enough I'd learn how silly I was to have placed so much emphasis on this decision, to think that this would be a big change. Kindergarten wouldn't rock me. Something I never imagined happening would.

14

HEAVEN

Pop Pop and the Twin Towers

Life is short and we have not too much time
for gladdening the hearts of those who are traveling with us.
Oh, be swift to love! Make haste to be kind.

Henri-Frederic Amiel

Cate's sixth birthday was fast approaching, and it was difficult for me to believe she was growing up, halfway through kindergarten and old enough for a big-girl party with all her classmates. My dad called and asked if we were coming to New York to celebrate. I said I wasn't sure since I had a lot going on at work, but he encouraged me. "Aw, c'mon, honey, let me see Stick on her birthday."

As busy as I was, I couldn't say no—not to my dad. So we went for a short visit. There was nothing overly special about it.

It was just a nice weekend away. My dad took Caroline to the dump, which was an outing that could be fun only with him. Turning into the driveway, he called out to me from his truck's open window, "Hey, Caroline really joked me out. She asked if they had a gift shop at the dump. Isn't that a good one?"

Tim, the kids, and I climbed in the minivan to leave that Sunday night when Caroline pulled a coin from her pocket. "Pop Pop wants me to give this to Connor," she said referring to my sister Kim's oldest son.

I looked at her and said, "Okay, don't lose it." As we pulled away, my dad stood in the driveway the way he often did with one hand in his pants pocket and the other waving goodbye.

Little did I know it was the last time I would see him.

⁓

Catholics don't have to go to church on Ash Wednesday, but there is a draw for me to do so since the ashes are a symbol of a most basic truth: "Remember," the priest says when he crosses a thumbprint of burnt palm ash on my forehead, "you are dust, and to dust you shall return." Sometimes the reminders of how precious life is are subtle, but this day is right out there. We are all human and one day, each of us will die.

Noelle's voice was hardly audible over the phone that afternoon, the tears and gasps for air interrupting what she was trying to say.

"Ange," she said finally, wanting to share the news without saying the words, "my dad died."

Although I knew her father had a long history of liver disease, I was stunned. "As awful as this is, your dad won't have to suffer any more," I said as if from a prepared speech. "He's in heaven and finally at peace."

"But he wasn't suffering," she said defiantly. "We just saw him last weekend. He was fine."

Why had I jumped to such a pat answer, saying what I thought would comfort her and what in my soul I believed, without considering how traumatic this was for her? I was crushed to think my condolences had the opposite affect—that my faith had gotten in the way.

"I gotta go," Noelle said, talking more to herself than to me. The phone call ended abruptly in a way our phone calls never did.

Noelle loved her father as much as anyone in this world. How could I have failed her precisely when she needed me? Making her feel better was my job, part of the promise I made to her so many years ago. I called her right back, without any idea about what to say. "Hello," she said, and it was all I needed to hear.

"I'm so sorry. I can't believe he's gone."

And together we cried.

My dad had died suddenly of a heart arrhythmia, a result of his liver disease. It's impossible to put into words how you feel when someone you love so tremendously dies, the hole in your life, the depth of sadness you experience. I was not prepared for this unimaginable sorrow. How could I be? How could anybody be? God, I loved him so much. I was lost without him. "Where are you, Dad?" I kept asking, desperate to hear his voice, to feel his hugs, to know he was okay.

There was only silence in reply.

As unexpectedly as Cate entered my life, my dad left it. Where faith shored me up after she was born, it now left me completely. Faith was the string I held onto when I questioned what life would be like with Cate. Since then, it had become part of who I was, what I said, choices I made. Now, I wondered if there even was a God. I was falling with nothing to grasp onto, no dangling thread of faith to reach out for, no baby in my arms to snuggle up with and make me feel better. All I ever believed in came into question at once. *Was faith something we hold onto just to make sense out of this world?*

~

I left for Noelle's house a few hours later, intentionally leaving the car radio off to be alone with my thoughts. Making the initial climb up the mountain, which separates our two towns, Mr. Clifford's voice broke the silence: "Angela Gwa-dan-yo Martin. Tell her I'm okay, hah?"

There was no mistaking his New York accent or the way he punctuated the end of a sentence. His voice was audible and clear as if he'd spoken to me from the passenger seat. I listened intently beyond the hum of the engine for another message, for more news, though none came. *Just my imagination, I guess.* Although when I pulled into Noelle's driveway, I wondered how in the world I was going to tell her what happened. I had the feeling I was supposed to.

I walked in the front door and was met in the foyer by Tim who was crying. He immediately took me in his arms and said, "I'm so afraid I've lost Noelle, too. You know how close she was to her dad."

"Oh my gosh, I know."

I found Noelle limp and lost, sitting on a kitchen stool beside the island counter Tim had built a few years before. Her neck was bent back at an uncomfortable angle while she stared up at the ceiling. "Why don't I feel him?" she asked. "I don't feel him at all." I was speechless for a time, wanting to tell her what I heard in the car and not wanting to tell her just as much.

She started to cry when I took her in my arms. And then the words slipped out of my mouth the way water splashes from an overfull bucket. "Your dad's okay. He told me so." This release was affirming to me. Yet my words passed over Noelle like fluffy white clouds on a summer day. She didn't hear them, her eyes still fixed on some faraway place.

ॐ

I don't think I ever thought about dying before. Sure, I used to believe when you die you go to heaven, that blind faith all Catholics have. This was why Sister Gregory sat us in church to pray for the souls of the faithful departed once a month in elementary school. But I guess I never thought deeply about what it meant—that in dying you actually leave this earth to live somewhere else.

The idea of dying and going to heaven was something I said, but was it true? I was troubled and confused as I heard the voices of Father Larry, the cherubic nun, and Angela telling me to believe that everything happens for a reason. There was purpose, a plan. Faith was supposed to lift me up and alleviate my doubts, to help me take comfort that my dad was with God. *If my faith is true, I'd know he's in heaven, but I don't know that at all.* There was no solace in what I used to believe because I couldn't feel him near me. I couldn't hear his voice. There was only a void, and I began to question everything.

ॐ

Noelle said her father talked about his wake and funeral many times the way maudlin Irish Catholics do, not wanting the family to spend any money on a fancy casket or to make a fuss. He said a pine box, or better yet, a garbage can would do. If they wanted to go all out, he recommended sticking a flower in his ass. They tried to honor some of his wishes, but no such luck. Turned out pine caskets were expensive. Noelle's family did have Irish music playing at the wake and would have tapped a keg had the funeral home let them.

Since the church was being renovated, Mr. Clifford's funeral was held in the St. Mary's School gym, where we had spent much of our childhood. Somber as this was, I couldn't help but smile at the irreverence of the scene. His casket was wheeled up under a broken basketball hoop. The mechanical arm that raised and lowered the hoop was stuck at an odd angle (not quite up and not quite down) and encased with duct tape—Mr. Clifford's favorite household remedy.

At the end of the service we walked out of the gym along the pathway behind the school leading to the plot in the cemetery reserved for him. It was a path we'd walked countless times as children to go in and out for recess. We passed the graves of Mrs. Murphy, our friend Brian's mom who died of emphysema, and Bobby Lewis and his girlfriend, who died in a car accident when they were teenagers. Still, we seemed too young to be walking this path for this reason. The people we loved weren't supposed to die yet.

When the priest finished his final blessing at the burial site, we began saying our goodbyes. I bent down, kissed my hand, and touched the casket.

"I don't want to leave him alone," Mrs. Clifford said.

We stood there in that awkward moment of wanting to stay but needing to leave, when Noelle turned to me and whispered, "He isn't here."

And then she walked away.

⁓

My dad was gone and this was what scared me most. In the absence of faith there was the real possibility he was simply dead. That this was the end of his life forever—a life that meant everything to me. It was too devastating a thought to have. More than that, it squelched everything I ever knew, how I lived my life, how I was raising my girls. As uncertain as I was, I held on to this little piece of me that cried out, *No, God is real, heaven is real*...as hard as it was to fathom.

I needed a sign my dad was okay, to find some sort of proof my faith was true. I figured if I really paid attention, I'd probably see it. After all, if there was a God who created each one of us with a unique purpose—who took us to heaven after our journey here—wouldn't He let us know it was okay? I wanted to confirm that everything I'd been taught and believed up to now was correct. That God and heaven existed, that good prevailed over evil, that my Good Samaritan dad whom I loved and adored was okay and I'd see him again some day.

No sooner would I take notice of something and think it was a sign than I'd call Ange or my sister to hear what they thought, for their assurances I was right. One morning I called Ange to share my latest sign incident. "The girls and I were just at the bus stop, and while we were standing there, a morning dove flew down from the wires above the road and landed on my mailbox two feet from us," I said all at once.

"Oh no, you hate birds."

"I'm scared to death of birds. Anyway, this bird doesn't move and it's just staring at us. The girls want to pet it because it's so close and I'm thinking, 'Why is this bird not moving?' We're all entranced while it patiently sits there—the bird staring at us and us staring right back—and I think, *Dad, is that you?* But then I think I must be crazy to have these thoughts. I mean why would he come as a bird when he knows how much I hate them?"

"Maybe it was a way to get your attention."

"Well, the bus comes for the girls and I'm left just staring at this bird wondering if it's my father. Then I figure I *am* crazy, but I don't want to go because if it *is* my dad, I don't want him to leave—ever. Finally I wandered up the driveway lost in my thoughts and turned to see the bird one more time, but it was gone."

I took a deep breath at the close of my story and said, "I'm sure a normal person wouldn't think it was a sign—a stupid bird landing on a mailbox. I am crazy, aren't I?"

"I don't think so. With all my heart I believe there's a heaven and that your dad is there. If you think it was a sign from him, it probably was."

"It's so easy to say that, Ange, but do you honestly believe it? Have you really thought about what it means to die, that your body stays here and your spirit goes to heaven? That God plans this for all of us. That it's actually *real*?"

"Faith is to simply believe. It's not scientific. It can't be proven. It just is."

But it wasn't so simple for me. I was unable to close off my thoughts and take comfort in Ange's words—the words I heard my whole life and prayed aloud at mass in the Profession of Faith, "We look for the resurrection of the dead, and the life of the world to come." *The life of the world to come.* It was just too big to consider.

Then there was Audrey on whom I dumped my fears as well. I liked to think she belonged to the church of hard knocks and would tell it to me straight.

"Jesus, I don't know if there's a heaven. I want to think so, but shit, I don't know." So I kept up my round-the-clock surveillance for a concrete answer, my one, definitive sign I wouldn't doubt. That no one would have to evaluate and convince me of. That I would just believe in without question.

Please God, show me, I silently prayed as I searched in every random place, at every moment of the day. I looked through my office window at the tree my neighbors planted in memory of my dad, in the bathwater doing tubs with the girls, off my deck to Audrey putzing in her yard, in the kitchen while I breaded chicken at the counter. After a while I figured I was creating signs out of nothing. Everything was a sign, so none of them could be.

Cate at 6: Can recognize 25/26 upper case and lower case letters; learning to count to twenty by rote; working on telling time to the hour; can cut out a simple form with scissors (e.g. square); can write her first and last name in upper case letters (handwriting is difficult for her); drops and catches a playground ball; hops on one foot; can't jump backwards; can't zip independently; difficulty in responding to how and why questions.

St. Patrick's Day fell on a Saturday that year. My brother was living in New York City and we all met up for the parade, since it was tradition, and we were trying to carry on even though life was so sad. There were about twenty of us: my mom, grandma, aunts, uncles, and cousins. It was a beautiful day, cold but sunny.

James lived in a high-rise on the Upper East Side with a rooftop terrace. We gathered up there after it turned dark to see the skyline of the city and beams of light honoring the recent victims of the Twin Towers. I lifted Cate into my arms—this was not a place I could stomach in the midst of her escaping phase. As I held her on my hip that clear night, she pointed to the beams of light in the sky. "Pop Pop," she said.

A quiet overcame me when I looked into the lights, searching for my dad, wondering if Cate was able to discern something I could not. *Do you see him, Cate?* Perhaps this was the sign I was praying for, or simply another sign I created for myself. I didn't know for certain, but it was a moment that made me stop and breathe, and think maybe, just maybe, there was a heaven after all.

That peaceful moment was quickly replaced by chaos in the minivan only a short while later. We were all driving back to my mom's house in Wappingers Falls. James tagged along probably because he didn't want to be alone. He'd had too much to drink and was, well, there's no polite way to say it, farting in my car. Tim, usually the calm one in our family, was overcome by the smell. "Geez, James," he said, and rolled the windows all the way down.

By some odd twist of fate, they didn't go back up.

We were driving sixty miles an hour as if in an arctic wind tunnel. All the girls woke up crying from the cold, while my mother and I screamed at James for being so disgusting. Not to leave Tim out of the blame, I yelled at him about why the windows were broken in our basically new car. "How are we going to get home like this?"

Our first plan was for Tim to try to get the windows up. When that failed, we met my uncle off the highway (he was just a few exits behind us) and traded his two warm teenagers for my three shivering little girls. Everyone in our car braced for the trip home. We ended up laughing much of the way, white plumes of mist coming from our mouths every time we did. Between laughing fits, I wondered if this whole scene was my one true sign. After all, this sort of thing only happened when my dad was around.

The days, weeks, and months after my dad died were far worse than any other time in my life. I used to think the days following Cate's birth were the hardest days, but there was no comparison. When Cate was born, every sad feeling was followed by the internal resolve—*it's going to be okay*—even though I wasn't sure how I'd get there. Now, every breath was a heavy one.

The toughest time of day for me was just before dawn as my first waking thoughts were of my dad and that he had died. As I languished in this devastating awareness, I'd hear "Hello, Timothy!" in one of those digitized voices that fills in when a human cannot. This was the sound of Cate turning on the computer—the military equivalent of all hell breaking loose.

The whirlwind erupting downstairs forced me out of bed, for which I was grateful. My will alone was not enough. I cringed at the prospect of what I'd find while I made my way to Cate. It was likely she'd be in the den, frustrated that the computer wasn't working because she'd already jammed two discs into the drive at once, undecided whether to play Barbie Secret Agent or Dalmatian Chow Time. She'd hear my footsteps coming down the hallway, yelling to me as if it were two in the afternoon: "S'Mom, s'want a snack!"

Other mornings I'd meet her in the kitchen just when she was stealing cereal and sour worms from the pantry, turning my attention away from thoughts of my dad and onto her misbehavior. Rather than greet her with a big bear hug, I'd first wave a finger in the air and stare her down: "Cate—uh uh, put it back."

"S'Mom, s—a—y want crunch!" I'd continue to look at her for a moment without reply, scanning her mismatched outfit of a too-small T-shirt and low-slung pajama pants, which caught under her heels. A thick wedge of bare belly peeked out between them. Without shifting my gaze, I'd wonder how it was possible. *She's exactly like him.* Then, I'd give in on the crunch. "That's it, now go watch TV and no more snacks."

While Cate's antics distracted me from thoughts of my dad, she was also the very reminder of him. These images of my dad weren't subtle the way my invented signs were. Even from when she was very young, it was as though she channeled him: The way she dressed. The food she loved. The antics she pulled. Part of me loved the pieces of him I saw in her, while the other part of me missed him all the more.

My unease about the faith I'd lost permeated every aspect of my life. I continued to cope by filling up my days, which was easy to do with three kids and a job. I found safety in the busyness of my life. The more I piled on, the less I had to feel. Angela tried to cut through my stoic approach, to have me open up about how I was really feeling. "You don't want to continue living like this, do you?"

I knew I was a mess and still was unable to do anything about it. I couldn't pep-talk myself into positive change the way I usually could. What I was experiencing went beyond sadness and beyond grief, and I longed not to feel this way. I'd taken Ange's advice countless times before, but for some reason I couldn't break free and do so now. *Will I ever be happy again?*

I worried about Noelle as I witnessed her descend into depression, immersing herself in work and keeping up a miserable schedule so not to think about the truth. Noelle was thin and worn out, helping others through their grief while losing herself in the process. I didn't know what to do other than be her friend.

I wondered if my faith would be strong enough to carry us through her sadness, if our friendship would be strong enough to pull her out of the dark place where she was. It wasn't only that I worried about Noelle's state of mind, but in the most selfish way

I missed my friend. Every time I called hoping the upbeat, funny woman I knew and loved would pick up the phone, another very different, very sad person answered.

I tried to convince her there was a heaven, but part of me understood that she needed to discover it on her own. I'd always had a comfortable feeling about faith, as sure of God and the existence of heaven as the earth beneath my feet. While there were times I put faith on hold, I'd never questioned it. Some say that's blind; I say that's grace. The best I could do for my friend was reassure her of what I knew. To help her understand her dad was okay and she would be, too.

To say Angela was my friend was hardly adequate. There was something about her that sealed our friendship during this time: how she listened to me, the advice she offered, the words she used. Not only did she make me feel better whenever we spoke, but what she said made sense. In my mind her advice wasn't so much opinion as it was truth. My own personal Jiminy Cricket, ever-present to guide me through the shadows.

For months, she told me to make changes, "Take a leave of absence from work, or whatever it takes. You need to stop chasing after everyone and take care of yourself." While I knew she was right, that I needed to stop, I wasn't sure how. The drive to press on was far stronger than my ability to face what I should.

Come spring, about a year after my dad died, my fortress crumbled. I suffered three or four straight days of insomnia and was afraid I might have to be hospitalized for psychiatric treatment. That day my call to Angela was a desperate plea for answers: "What's happening to me?"

"I don't know, but our talking isn't enough anymore. I think you need to see a doctor."

The next day I made an appointment with my physician and cried in her office for an hour. It was a day that provoked necessary changes in my life. She handed me a prescription for medication and a number for a therapist. When Tim got home, I told him about what happened, and that I took a leave of absence from my job. He looked like a deer in headlights while he took it all in, not sure what to focus on first, though I imagine it was, "Holy crap, we just lost half our income!" He pulled me into his arms and hugged me deeply. "You're going to be fine."

Ever so slowly I began to heal, knowing full well I couldn't do it alone.

In time my friend returned, somehow renewed by the journey. We talked on the phone every day as we had for a while. But beyond the power of our friendship, I think much of her healing came from within, from taking one day at a time.

It was on one of our spontaneous walks around her neighborhood when I knew she'd reached the other side of mourning. Somewhere in the conversation she told me, "I still miss my dad enormously, and think about him probably twenty times a day. But now I smile when I do."

Ever since then I'd catch myself spontaneously thinking of Mr. Clifford. It was always that I'd picture him in heaven. He wasn't among the crowds, but instead chose to sit at the front gates with St. Peter. There he welcomed people as they arrived, setting them at ease the way he did with an irreverent joke and a crooked smile.

To this day it makes me feel better when I go to a funeral of someone close to me knowing that Mr. Clifford will be there to say hello. And you know it would be just like him to play hooky from his day job the way he must have that St. Patrick's Day, stealing away in the Twin Tower floodlights to say goodnight to his granddaughter.

Not long after my dad died, I began having dreams about him. I'd wake up happy and warm, as if I'd just seen him. In the beginning, it was always a quick visit with him saying, "Honey, I can't stay," and then he'd leave. The dreams were as real as life. It was his face, his voice, his smell. Maybe this was a sign I made up for myself that he was somewhere, that he was okay. Hard as I tried, I couldn't make myself dream about him. It just happened sometimes, and I loved when it did.

My dad was a storyteller and most times it was hard to say whether or not he was telling the truth. He'd often tell us about how he talked to his mother (who died before I was born), explaining that he didn't pray to her, but had genuine conversations with her. "She comes to me in my dreams," he'd say.

He told me this was how he knew about Cate when I first called from the hospital with his, "I know honey, it'll be okay" comment before hearing my news. My dad said his mother told him the night before Cate was born that the baby had Down syndrome. Soon enough, I began to think maybe my dreams weren't dreams at all. That as my grandmother came to my dad in his dreams, so he was coming to me in mine.

My dreams of him were strikingly similar in the way he'd come and then have to go. I'd be having a barbeque and someone would say, "Noelle, your dad's here." Excited at the news, I'd run over and talk to him, hug him. He'd say, "Ya know, honey, you have a lot of people here. Go be with your friends. I gotta go—I love ya." Another time, he'd drive by in a big Oldsmobile and I'd run over trying to hug him through the window. "Hi honey. How are the kids? I better get going." And I'd say, "Okay, 'bye Dad." I loved seeing him and was never upset he needed to leave.

In time, the visits from my dad lessened. Perhaps he knew he didn't have to come as often, that I was slowly moving on. Who knows, maybe they were just dreams. Eventually I realized that even though he was here for only a short time, I had the greatest gift of all: he was my dad. I consciously tried to focus on that and not worry so much about what I did or didn't believe and to live without regrets the way he did.

On those rare occasions when my dad does visit, I always wake up in the best mood. And so many nights, even as I write these words, I go to sleep praying he'll come.

15

PNEUMONIA

The End of a Control Freak

The days of waiting and wondering,
these are the hardest.
We want to mend, to help, to act,
but sometimes we can only be.
Our healing is found there.

Author Unknown

I was looking forward to spending time with my kids that summer without the outside pressure of work, to take a walk every day and get back to the simpler pleasures I remembered and longed for. Money was going to be tight with me not working, but I needed to find myself, to get past my grief, and return to the life I had with my family. While this life was by no means perfect, it was our life and it was happy.

Those first few months that summer were a refreshing kind of busy for me, where I wasn't strapped for time, needing to accomplish more than one person could. I was centered on being a mom and being with my kids, making dinner—just doing everyday things I honestly enjoyed. In stepping back, I realized how much time I'd spent the past year just treading water. And now I felt I was moving forward. Healing, I think.

I loved having nothing hanging over my head at night, not thinking about what I needed to do, what I didn't get done: Did I read that loan agreement closely enough? Did I respond to that e-mail looking for a precedent? Did I make those revisions to the opinion we discussed on the conference call today? The weight of my professional worries (real, perceived, or otherwise) was gone and I was able to go to sleep at night. No Ambien or Tylenol PM required.

That fall the school year began as usual, with me second-guessing our decision to promote Cate to the next grade. (New year, same questions.) *Maybe she should have repeated kindergarten instead of going to first grade. Would another year of letters and sounds have been better than putting her in a class with kids learning to read and write? Can she stay awake all day?* As it turned out, school became the last thing on my mind.

Come September, Cate's typical lingering cold immediately turned to pneumonia, and she was admitted to the hospital. When she seemed recovered, we sent her back to school and a few weeks later the same thing happened: Cate's "new" cold immediately turned to pneumonia, and she was again hospitalized. In November and again in December, Cate was in and out of the hospital—a pattern that was as unbelievable as it was concerning.

Although this string of hospitalizations was new, being in the hospital around Christmas was familiar territory for us. It was the third year in a row that we spent the holidays there. With this history, you'd think I'd have my act together by mid-December, but as Caroline aptly says, "We're only early by accident." Once again I did the midnight run to Toys "R" Us, this time two days before Christmas.

Cate was discharged on Christmas Eve that year and my mom was with us helping out. At about 4:00 p.m., my doorbell rang and two of my neighbors dropped off some potatoes and a casserole. "Oh my gosh, what are you guys doing? It's Christmas." A few more cars pulled up and one neighbor after another contributed a dish for a turkey dinner with all the trimmings.

It was hard for me to accept their kindness, knowing how busy they were, too, and feeling completely undeserving of it. I tried to tell everyone what the gesture meant to Tim and me, but they probably could never know. I wanted my thanks to stay with them as much as their generosity would stay with me.

There was so much emotion that Christmas Eve—Cate was home, she was safe and getting better, we were given the gift of our neighbors—but at around midnight all of these nice, squishy feelings ended abruptly when I discovered we were out of Scotch tape. Turns out we had no tape at all. We ravaged the house looking for masking tape, duct tape, packing tape, electrical tape—any adhesive material we could think of.

"How the heck do you not have any Scotch tape?" my mother asked. "It's like we're camping in this house."

After muttering a few choice words under my breath and searching the house, the only thing I found were dried up glue sticks in the kids' craft box.

Tim had the idea of reusing the tape from the air hockey box that housed the surprise gift that year. Who knew that for once, the big obnoxious Christmas gift that you question whether or not you should buy, that's going to take up too much space, that you convince yourself won't lose its novelty a week after Christmas, would be the gift we were so thankful for that night. Although when I lay my head down on the pillow (vowing repeatedly to Tim that I'd shop and wrap in August next year), it was the faces of my neighbors that I saw as I drifted off to sleep.

Cate at 7: Learning sight words; working on forming consonant sounds; identifying letters on the computer keyboard; can tell the month and the year on a calendar, but needs cueing for the date; can recognize pennies, dimes and nickels, but needs cueing to recognize quarters; practicing writing upper case letters; still learning to count to twenty by rote; can swim underwater.

By winter we found ourselves in the midst of this awful cycle of multiple pneumonias and almost monthly hospitalizations. Even after all these years of Cate's coughing, colds, and occasional hospitalizations, I never thought of her as having a real health problem. Up to this point, my concerns primarily focused on her academic and social challenges. Now everything else faded from view, and the minutiae I obsessed over left along with it. Her health was all I cared about.

For as many times as Cate got pneumonia, I was never prepared for it. She'd be wrestling with her sisters and an hour later, lying on my bed, breathing a little shallow, feeling a little too hot, acting too lethargic, too sleepy. I second-guessed myself constantly, since it was usually after our pediatrician's office hours when a doctor could make the call about whether or not she needed to go to the hospital.

I'd call a neighbor for her opinion, "Can you come over for a sec and take a peek at Cate?" Then I'd phone Ange, my mom, or Kim—whomever I could reach—for backup counsel. "You know, Cate doesn't seem right," I'd say to hear their consistent responses, "Don't think about it. Just take her in." Nevertheless I always questioned, was always on the fence about what to do. Apparently, I had as much trouble discerning pneumonia signs as signs from heaven.

Eventually when night came, I'd drop everything for the ER. Tim was usually still at work, so I'd call in a neighbor to stay with Caroline and Claire. However, on what came to be our last nighttime dash to the emergency room that year, Tim was home and wanted to drive us. I called my neighbor, Ann, the way I had so many times to see if she could stay with the girls. When her husband, John, answered I said, "Can Ann come up?" In the background I heard her say, "Pillow or no pillow?"

"Pillow," I said, wanting to say so much more.

This was about the seventh or eighth time we headed for the ER. Tim and I were more worn out by Cate's pneumonia episodes than nervous about her getting better. We knew she would. It was about one o'clock in the morning, and Tim, Cate, and I were waiting in a triage room for Cate to be admitted. We were sitting next to her bed in uncomfortable chairs; a TV monitor mounted high on a wall was flashing light over the dim room. Cate was in and out of sleep—her cough would wake her up and then she'd drift back off. We were starving and Tim went to find food while I stayed with Cate. I was so tired, but couldn't take my eyes off her. Tim returned in the midst of my vigil an hour later (yep, an hour later) with one snack-size bag of popcorn. "You've gotta be kidding me."

"It's 2 a.m., Noelle. This isn't New York City—nothing's open," Tim said defensively.

The transport guy came to get us, and we all got on the elevator, standing to either side of Cate, who was dry-heaving. I yelled at Tim to quick give me something in case she threw up and he tossed me the damn popcorn bag. "You're a jackass!" I yelled.

"What do you want from me? We're in an elevator." It escalated from there, with more inappropriate language flying and before long, the transport guy started laughing. Then we all did.

As we stepped off the elevator and walked to Cate's room, her nurse handed me some tissues and told me it would be all right. *If you only knew.*

I don't think I'll ever be prepared to take an emergency phone call from Noelle, though I've answered so many. I'm always steeped in my own agenda, usually immersed in a seemingly important task. Somehow the phone rings a little differently when it's urgent, echoing through the house at a higher pitch rather than its typical, annoying drone. It's almost that the phone is saying, "Hurry and pick up, hurry and pick up!"

Cate's year of pneumonia was before the age of caller ID, so all I had was my intuition to say when I should answer. I'd hear that urgent ring, immediately surmise, *you know Cate's been sick for a while, I bet that's Noelle calling,* and grab it. Noelle called me every time she took Cate to the hospital, be it on her way out the door, from the car on the way to the hospital, or from the emergency room. Calling me was more important to her than obeying the hospital rules banning cell phone use.

"Okay, I'm standing on top of a chair with my right arm in the air trying to get reception. I can't hear you, but I hope you can hear me."

Her calls were always a quick burst of information, similar to how we used to call each other from pay phones in Europe during our semester abroad in college when we had no money. Now she was trying to squeeze in a few critical words of explanation between quick gasps for air because she didn't have time. "I'm at the ER. Cate got very lethargic about an hour ago. You know how she's been sounding."

"Let me get the kids dinner and I'll be right there."

"No, it's too crazy. They haven't even done X-rays yet, and then we have to get up to a room. I'll call you later, okay?"

I always had a biting feeling of guilt when I said, "Okay, but call me as soon as you hear some news." When all I really wanted to do was drop what I was doing and be with her. But Noelle didn't want to interrupt my life; she just wanted me to know. I think there was security in that for both of us. Knowing I was there for Noelle made her feel better, and knowing where she was made me feel better, too.

Though the year of pneumonia seems unreal to me now, there was a normalcy to it. I suppose you get used to your life however it may be. Once we'd get through the whole admitting routine and settle into a room, I had to answer a set of standard questions from a resident who took Cate's health history very seriously, as she should. But for me it was the same set of questions I'd answered last month, and the month before that, and the month before that. "Yes, it was a full term pregnancy. I was twenty-nine when I had her. No, I didn't know she had Down syndrome before birth. No, she didn't have the heart defect. Yes, she goes to a typical school."

After the resident would leave, I'd call Tim who was usually home with Caroline and Claire, give him the update, and make a plan about the days ahead. He'd get up to the hospital as soon as he could, doing everything I asked, yet completely disregarding what I wanted him to bring for me. Without fail, he'd pack my oldest, ugliest clothes and the bras at the bottom of my drawer with no elasticity. "Look what I found, Noelle. You never wear this," he'd tell me one hospital visit after the next. What could I say in response? He was being nice and yet, every time I hugged him hello and took the bag of clothes he'd collected, I wondered: *Why did you have to get creative?*

Cate was usually admitted to the sixth floor, where she had her favorite room, her favorite food, and her favorite nurses. I actually think Cate liked being in the hospital. She could eat in her bed and watch TV all day without any hassles from me. It was probably more like a ritzy hotel to her with room service and so many of us like her manservants, attending to her every command.

With Cate too sick to do anything but rest during the first few days of her hospital stays, visits from friends and family were a welcome reprieve. It was how we came to meet a little girl named Sydney, who would go on to become Cate's best friend. Sydney was a classmate of Cate's and made an impromptu visit to see her one Sunday morning, tagging along with her mom who was a nurse practitioner in the ER.

There was a light knock on Cate's door and in walked this tiny girl with a petite voice to match her physique.

"Hi, Cate," she said, waving a hello with one hand and passing Cate a lemon sliced in two equal halves with the other. "Your favorite."

Cate smiled and Sydney climbed up in the hospital bed and lay down next to her. I smiled with the thought of how she reminded me of Ange with her pencil-thin frame and curly brown hair. Her mom asked if Sydney could stay and visit while she went to get some paperwork done. The two spent the day side by side, eating fries, watching Scooby Doo, giggling at the TV, and napping when their eyes got heavy. A day that began with me unaware this little girl even existed ended with me realizing Cate had a friend.

The nights at the hospital with Cate were never as good as the days. She got into coughing spasms where the nurses came rushing in, calling the residents and the respiratory therapists. It was the cough that had happened all the time at home since she was an infant, the one I'd been trying to explain to doctors for years. Their urgent reaction validated my concerns that I wasn't overreacting all those times.

At about day four when she was feeling better, Cate would start her business—pulling the probes off, trying to get up herself when she was still connected to an IV, bending the automatic bed into a taco shell. Then there were her escapes, which she timed to coincide with whenever I had to go to the bathroom. "Now, Cate, just stay there," I'd say. As soon as I closed the door to the bathroom in her room, I'd hear a cackle and the door to her hospital room slam shut. "Shit!" I'd say, almost killing myself pulling up my pants, trying to get out of the bathroom and get her.

I will say it was easier to find Cate in the hospital than in the neighborhood. Her trademark cough gave her away every time. Even the nurses found it unmistakable, referring to her by room number, "Is that 619 I hear?" It made me think of the character Jean Valjean from *Les Miserables*, prisoner number 24601. Maybe she felt like a prisoner by day four. God knows I did.

⟶

The intensity of Noelle's initial calls lightened as the year progressed. We knew Cate would be okay, that the pneumonias would pass, and she would go home. My concern was more for Noelle, how she was always in crisis mode and never had a chance to regroup for the next go-round. She often questioned her lack of preparedness, especially on the rare instance when Cate was taken from the pediatrician's office to the hospital by ambulance.

"When am I going to learn my lesson and squeeze in a shower when Cate's been sick for a while? You cannot believe the shade of brown my hair is."

"Finally a case where brunettes edge out blondes."

The next-day visits after Cate was admitted to the hospital became strangely familiar. The only thing that changed for us was the date. Before heading to the hospital I'd stop for Noelle's favorites: if it was morning, a bagel and a latte with extra milk; if it was afternoon, a malted from the ice cream shop in the parking garage.

I often didn't know what room Cate was in since that detail rarely found its way into our abbreviated talks. Intuitively I'd say "Six" in boarding the elevator whenever someone asked, "Floor?" (We called these swags—strategic wild-ass guesses—at the advertising agency where I used to work.) I'd turn the corner from the elevator and find my way to Cate's room by listening out for her cough. "Sorry it took me a while to get here. I wound up parking on the roof today," I said one morning when I put down Noelle's things and leaned in to kiss her cheek.

"How many times have I told you not to be a follower the way you go along with the traffic pattern? You've got to take that quick left and get a good, low spot."

Noelle never looked herself in the hospital, with little sleep and wearing her bottom-of-the-barrel outfits that Tim brought. But she'd be her old self whenever Cate came home, instantly refreshed by crossing the threshold. Her breakdown would come a few days later.

"Why can't I seem to cope when I get home?"

"You're doing everything the nurses did in the hospital—and they took shifts."

No matter how strong my case, Noelle would rarely cut herself the slack. About a week later she'd summon the resolve to feel differently, telling me, "I'm done feeling like this." That self-talk she used was a powerful thing.

Tim and I tried to make life as normal as possible for our family that year. We did the switch, trading off a sleepless night at the hospital for a day at home. We'd change shifts sometime after dinner with Caroline and Claire in tow. They liked seeing Cate every day, but they especially loved going to the cafeteria where I'd drop twenty bucks on fries, popcorn, soda, and dessert. Cate knew all the cafeteria staff, usually getting away with at least one free item and a bonus for her sisters, proving Caroline's theory: "It's great going places with Cate because you always get free stuff."

Our new routines were a group effort on the part of my girlfriends and neighbors. They took care of things at home— snowblowing my driveway after a storm, dropping off meals, getting the other girls on and off the bus. Audrey would make Jell-O in clear plastic shot cups. "You don't need to make us anything," I'd say opening the door as she'd march up my front steps. "Shut up, Noelle."

I wasn't comfortable accepting help. I wanted to do everything myself, but there was no way I could be in all the places I needed to be that year. I had to compromise on what I wanted to do versus what realistically I could do. I prioritized where I needed to be and chose that. There was no getting around it. Tim and I needed help, and that had to be okay.

I remember having pneumonia once as a teenager. My pediatrician labeled it walking pneumonia, because you felt sick, but not sick enough to rest. That's what made it so dangerous. I'd say my lungs were my weak spot as a child, and even as an adult I was still plagued with bronchitis once a year and soon enough would be diagnosed with asthma. With these experiences and being privy to so many of Cate's episodes, I immediately recognized the pneumonia signs in myself one night, when I lay on the couch with a fever, shallow breathing, and back pain.

I found myself thinking of Cate and connecting with her in a way I hadn't before while I watched the minutes tick by from 2 a.m. to 2:30 a.m. to 3:00 a.m. Up to now, I'd only understood Cate's plight in a sympathetic sense. It was quite something else to know what she was experiencing on the inside. How scary it was to suddenly breathe as if through a straw or a barrel of sand. *This is how Cate must feel all the time, and she can't articulate what's happening to her.*

When I was a child, my mother, who had an affinity for the American Indian, often shared this bit of folklore: "You can't truly understand someone until you walk a mile in her moccasins." How right she was.

Most of the year, Cate didn't go to school; she was either in the hospital or her doctors wanted her home to build up strength. If someone could have predicted this a few months back, I'd have thought it catastrophic to have Cate miss that much school. Yet at this point I didn't care if she ever went to school again. I didn't have any pressures about what she should be doing or learning the way I usually did. This isn't to say I was oblivious to all she was missing, but the only thing I cared about was her being okay.

The school arranged for a paraprofessional to come to our house for about an hour a day. Enter Mrs. P, or "P" as Cate called her. Having Mrs. P in for tutoring was more or less a way to patch up this broken year. We didn't think Cate would make much progress, but it was a good alternative to Scooby Doo.

Little by little, the contraptions they used at the hospital started coming into our home. The first thing to arrive was something called an IPPB (intermittent positive pressure breathing) machine, which was a super-charged nebulizer. Essentially it was a generator connected to a nebulizer unit, which had a hose and mouthpiece Cate used to breathe in her meds. The generator helped get the medicine more deeply into Cate's lungs. The IPPB machine required a certain rhythmic breathing and, surprisingly, Cate was good at it. The second machine to come home was a pulmonary vest that, luckily for me, arrived when Ange was over for a visit.

I stopped by Noelle's house late that spring, shortly after Cate came home from the hospital for what would be the last time. Cate was sitting between Noelle's legs on the floor doing an IPPB treatment in the den, watching a Disney movie over fogged eyeglasses that had slid down her nose. I sat on the floor to join them when the doorbell rang. I motioned to stand back up, but Noelle stopped me. "Sit with Cate, Ange. This must be the vest lady." A woman from a medical supply company came to drop off a motorized pulmonary vest for Cate and show Noelle how to use it.

This woman was not like those leisure-suit vacuum cleaner salesmen who used to go door-to-door in the '70s when we were kids. She was a respiratory therapist, highly skilled and knowledgeable about pulmonary issues and therapies. She sat right down on the floor with us. Before even showing us the machine, she took a plastic lung out of her bag and pulled it apart to reveal a cross-section of the inside. She showed us how mucous lodged in the fine bronchioles of Cate's lungs and how the vest would shake it out of her. This was fascinating to Noelle and me, as we sat next to each other on the floor, eyes fixated on the plastic lung. We could see what was wrong with Cate and how this machine would help her.

The vest lady carefully assembled the vest, hooking the tubes to the machine and the pint-sized vest. It resembled the jetpack from the old TV show, *Lost in Space*. She explained about the two dials on the face of the machine. One was for frequency—how intensely the vest would shake. The other was for pressure—how tightly the vest would squeeze Cate's chest. She talked about what numbers to set them at to start, and how to adjust them as Cate got comfortable using it. Noelle kept looking at me with wide "Holy shit, are you paying attention?" eyes.

Noelle thanked the vest lady for coming and after seeing her out began to sweat. "Okay, what numbers am I supposed to set this thing at? Crap, let me get a piece of paper." I explained it to Noelle who was furiously writing. "What would I have done if you weren't here?"

ᘓ

Although Cate couldn't stand the vest ("Hate the vest—hate it, hate it, hate it!"), it worked. It made her cough up what was stuck in her lungs. She'd wear it sitting on the floor in the den, legs spread in a 180° split, singing along to whatever movie she was watching, with her raspy voice vibrating as if she were being driven over ridged pavement. She had to be policed the whole time it was on, but inevitably the doorbell or phone would ring.

"Don't touch the machine," I'd yell as I dashed off. In returning to the room, I'd hear her fumble in a panic trying to get all the pieces to this $17,000 gizmo she disassembled back together again. (I'll spare you the insurance nightmare.)

Bringing the machines into our home was one component of a strategy to get Cate well. The pulmonologists gave us a preventive well-plan and a defensive sick-plan that incorporated a combination of oral medications and the machines to snap this relentless cycle. When Cate was sick the machines had to be done pretty much every two hours around the clock. People tell me the schedule was similar to breast-feeding a newborn. Once I finished the treatments, I had to start right up again. Payback, I guess, for formula-feeding my babies.

On one of our last hospital visits that year, the pulmonologist said there would come a time when they wouldn't need to see Cate at the hospital. It seemed a lofty goal, one I couldn't imagine reaching. Looking ahead was something I'd stopped doing; I was just taking each day as it came.

In thinking about it though, dealing with Cate's health could have been the whole purpose of my year off from work. I was forced to stop my frenetic pace because pneumonia prevented me from doing or thinking about much else. I was stuck either in my house or in the hospital, Cate healing and me healing. Who knows, maybe it was the medicine we both needed.

16

PATIENCE

Issue de Jour

Be patient with everyone,
but above all with yourself.
Do not be disheartened by your imperfections,
but always rise up with fresh courage.

Saint Francis de Sales

Rob and I walked into the PPT meeting at the end of Ryan's third grade year with our standard set of questions about his progress. First and foremost on our checklist: Is he closing the gap with his peers? The principal opened the meeting and began to talk about Ryan's limited growth during the year—even though his teacher raved with opposite news at his first two conferences, the way his teachers did at his first two conferences every year.

The principal explained how his teachers reviewed what would be best for Ryan. There was a little-publicized program at a neighboring elementary school they recommended. It offered the benefit of having both a regular and special education teacher in one class and two connecting rooms so that small-group instruction could occur alongside class time. Ryan wouldn't be pulled out, but taught with others who needed additional instruction as well.

"Why didn't you offer this program to us when Ryan was younger? I would have rather changed schools when he was in first grade," I said, tallying up what seemed to be an inordinate amount of wasted time.

"Our goal is to teach children in their neighborhood schools," she explained, adding how Ryan had reached the maximum number of service hours and there was nothing more they could do at this school. *Are we just a number at the deli counter?*

I stepped back from the conversation to listen, wondering if they really were doing what was best for Ryan, or were simply done trying. It was hard to gauge from the faces in the room, although Ry's third-grade teacher made an impassioned plea. She'd completed her student teaching in this two-classroom model and advised how great this would be for him. I took her at her word—it was all that I had.

I called Noelle when I got home, upset over this meeting. "I can't believe Ryan has to change schools. I feel so badly for him."

"I know, but he'll be okay. He's a kid. They bounce back quick."

"I just wish I could make things easier for him."

"But you can't protect him from the hard stuff, Ange. That's what will make him strong. Ya know, sometimes you see what people are dealing with and sometimes you don't, but none of us gets away unscathed. Just give him the tools he needs. You of all people can do that."

❧

It had been a few months since Cate was last hospitalized, and from all counts her health was improving. We had a fairly uneventful summer where her colds lingered, but didn't turn to pneumonia, so the whole preventive plan seemed to be working. There weren't any middle of the night dashes to the ER, no calls for Ann to drop her family and bring a pillow to care for mine, no update calls with Ange to let her know about Cate and where I was. I began to feel as if I could let my guard down a bit, that maybe Cate had turned a corner. Unknowingly so had I.

Life was slowly returning to the one I remembered, now that we were out of crisis mode. When September rolled around, we sent Cate to second grade even though she never really made it through first. Right or wrong, we sent her ahead because of the friendships she had with classmates. This time there was nothing to deliberate over. I simply did what felt right and moved on. *Okay, progress.*

There was this palpable feeling of calm that settled in our home and inside me. Without realizing it, I'd been living on edge this past year, subconsciously aware at any moment my day could turn on a dime. And a full year before that, I was constantly keeping busy to mask the grief over my dad. That impending sense of urgency about Cate and that need to overfill my days to numb the pain of my dad's death had subsided. Normalcy, by our definition, had filled its place.

I was beginning to have those typical school days again, getting all three girls out to the bus stop, having Cate ask the neighbor's chocolate lab, Dutch, to lick breakfast from her face. "Dushy, Dushy, Dushy. Kiss me, kiss me, kiss me." The only thing I cared about those mornings was getting Cate off to school. Well, that, and having her give me the lemon halves she swiped from the refrigerator before she got on the bus.

Food wasn't allowed on the school bus, which was something she got in trouble for all the time. But it was a losing effort. She'd quickly slip the lemons in her pockets and get by me, turning at the top of the bus stairs to lie: "S'mom I need them. S'my teacher said I could." The bus would drive off and I'd wave goodbye. There were so many academic things I could have worried over, but right now it only mattered that she was actually at school. If she happened to learn something—and not get caught with the lemons—that was a bonus.

Although Cate's health was still a big part of the picture, it wasn't center stage. I could get back to living, but as it happened, I did so in a new way. When the call came to discuss my return to work, the typical "How can I do this?" pit in my stomach wasn't there. I was pretty relaxed, confident enough to talk about what I needed to make this work. Having a few good months with Cate under my belt, I felt I could start back in some abbreviated capacity.

I had no idea how Cate's health would be. I figured she would be home on and off, stuck on her breathing treatments, and maybe we'd be heading back to the hospital again. No longer could I adapt my life to my job the way I had for so many years. It needed to be the other way around. My office agreed to a per diem arrangement where I would be on call, accepting work as my time allowed. I felt emotionally strong in a way I hadn't in a while—perhaps ever. Though the past year was the antithesis of the restful one I pictured, somehow I was the better for it.

Cate was hardly the model student when she was in school that year, giving her teachers loads of grief with her "it's my way or the highway" behavior. I don't remember talking with them about *what* she was learning. We just talked about how to get her to learn anything because her stubbornness would get in the way. At parent-teacher conferences, I'd hear about Cate's refusal to practice writing. "Uh, s'hard for me," she'd say without lifting a pencil. Same deal with reading. Her teacher would open Cate's "hard word book" with stickler words "of, is, what," while Cate purposefully kept her head turned in the opposite direction.

"Cate, let's look over here."

"I s—a—y, I'm lookin'."

"No, Cate, you're not. Look down at your book."

"Uuuhhhh, I AM!" she'd reply, her head still deliberately turned the other way.

Every afternoon Cate brought home a progress note that told me about her day. The notes were always an interesting read. I discovered how she was escaping math with a bathroom pass only to join a fifth grade gym class, and how she would leave the classroom undetected, sneak into the library, plop down in a corner, and pull out a book.

But, she quickly learned to skirt the system. When the girls came off the bus, I'd ask them how school was. Caroline and Claire always had a lot to say, but Cate answered with the same, "S'great day, s'Mom!" Lately, Cate wasn't always coming home with a note, so I assumed her aide Mrs. P didn't write one. I didn't catch on until the afternoon I was at school to pick up the girls and stopped in to ask Mrs. P if she could be sure to write a progress note every day so that I knew how Cate was doing.

"I already do," she said, and my eyes widened. It took me a minute to figure it out. *Cate's chucking the notes.* I looked over at Mrs. P, who by her expression just had the same thought. She turned to Cate and said, "If you get a note saying you had a bad day, I'm going to give it to Caroline."

"No way, Jaaaane!" Cate said, popping her head out of her hall locker, her hair disheveled, white shirt stained with ketchup, and purple skirt twisted sideways.

As the girls and I made our way out of school, my mind still in disbelief, I ran into Cate's teacher who asked if I'd heard about her forgery.

"What?" I said, nearly undone.

"Wait here a second," she said and headed to her classroom. The teacher returned soon after and handed me a pink PTO excuse form with a bunch of scribbling on it. "Cate told me you were picking her up early from school yesterday and said, 'See, I have a note.'"

Cate's name was written (well, kind of) on the first line, and then there was a bunch of scribbling in the comment section, followed by what looked like the letters "m-o-m" in the signature block on the crumpled paper. Within the span of five minutes, I had learned that not only did Cate know how to discard evidence, but how to commit forgery. Probably a double felony in most states.

Cate at 8: Writes her name using upper and lower case letters; draws people with bodies and extremities (they used to be a head with legs); can dribble a basketball; can ride a bike with very LARGE training wheels; can skip; doesn't demonstrate basic safety rules (e.g. does not look both ways before crossing a street, talks to strangers, runs with sharp objects); can provide a short sentence to describe an object; articulation is clearer at the word or short sentence level.

I passed the forged note to Caroline whose mouth hung open in surprise, as she would never have the idea to forge a note, much less carry it out. "Mommy, did Cate really think her teacher would believe you wrote that?" Without hesitation, I said, "Absolutely." I was more stunned at the premeditated planning:

How she must have taken the paper from the PTO pad at home, filled it out, and hid it from me all before leaving for school.

It was probably a great break for Cate's teachers when she was out sick, as there were still plenty of days I had to keep her home for breathing treatments. During these stretches, I found it harder than ever to parent Cate the way I wanted to. Her stubbornness about what she did or didn't want to do was as much of a problem at home as it was at school. I never wanted to be the kind of parent where the kids ruled the roost. I was one who believed that you don't negotiate with your kids, that you don't use bribery, that you shouldn't give in to whining.

There was rarely much trouble holding my ground with Caroline and Claire, but Cate broke me almost every time. My weakness wasn't because I felt the need to cut her some slack. It was because she never caved—not ever—be it about having sausages for breakfast, watching TV instead of doing her homework, or disconnecting the machines when she didn't feel like doing her treatments. It didn't matter what she was supposed to do. Rules were of little significance to Cate.

As the school year progressed, I found myself doing all the things that I thought I wouldn't do as a parent. I negotiated with her: "I'll let you have sausages if you sit for your vest first." I bribed her: "I'll take you to McDonalds for fries if you do good work for Mrs. P." I relinquished my parenting ideals because I was faced with an immovable creature. It was easier to succumb and get things done, even though this was exactly what a behaviorist I saw recently at a conference said not to do. I suppose that also meant I shouldn't drink four cups of coffee in the morning, but I do. There's the textbook ideal and then there's real life.

Ryan was in fourth grade and had made the change to his new school. The adjustment was hard for him, so when he again mentioned getting a puppy (he'd been asking since preschool), Rob and I gave it more serious thought. This would be a way to indulge in my need to do something for him. Plus he and John were growing up. If we were going to get a dog, now was a good time. We'd heard all the benefits of children having a dog, which at the time outweighed all advice to the contrary about how the mom winds up with most of the care.

Two neighbors strongly advised a trip to the local pound to adopt a pet, but after a number of visits online, I wasn't sure about what we'd inherit there. I naively assumed that purchasing a dog from a breeder would eliminate problems. We ultimately settled on a golden retriever from a breeder in southern Connecticut.

Noelle was planning to get a puppy, too, but took an easier route. She and the girls quickly settled on a breed—a basset hound, like Boomer—without consulting Tim, since there was little chance of him squashing their momentum. He often refers to himself as a monarch in their family—a figurehead without any real power.

And, no need for research on Noelle's part. She knew a woman in town who had just gotten a basset and asked her where to go. Noelle contacted the breeder the woman recommended and within a few days had the picture of her pup on the fridge.

I studied the picture as I waited for Noelle to wrap up a work call so we could take a walk together. The puppy's left eye was smaller than the right, and cloudy. "Isn't she the sweetest thing with that reddish fur?" Noelle asked in her leading way. "We're gonna name her Mabel."

Not wanting to burst her bubble, I reluctantly told her I thought the puppy might have glaucoma.

"Shit, Ange," she said as she pulled the picture from the refrigerator for a closer look. "Do you think I'm getting a reject dog?"

I evaded her question with some lame response because something did seem a little strange. "Contact the breeder. It's probably just the picture."

Noelle called me later that day with news from the breeder that the puppy had two different colored eyes—one brown, the other blue. There wasn't anything wrong with the puppy's eyes or vision. "It's a genetic abnormality the breeder sees on a rare occasion," Noelle explained. "What are the odds?"

"Well, it's definitely your dog."

"I know, but I'm kind of bummed, spending all this money and I still can't get a normal dog. It'll probably look like Cujo."

"Could you pick another puppy?" I said almost under my breath, feeling like we'd both come farther than this.

"I thought of that, too. But doesn't Caroline tell me, 'Mommy, you say it doesn't matter what someone looks like on the outside.'"

That spring Noelle and her family brought home Mabel as we did Dixie. They were fast friends. Dixie didn't mind Mabel's blue eye and Mabel didn't mind Dixie's hip dysplasia (a common genetic anomaly we discovered when she was spayed). Whenever we walked our puppies together, people would stop Noelle to alert her: "Did you know your puppy has two different colored eyes?" And, in the next breath they'd say of Dixie, "Oh, what a beautiful dog."

Like our kids, some differences were in plain view, while others hid below the surface. *How true it is of everyone.*

Cate was only admitted to the hospital once that year, which was excellent progress. On occasion at her doctor's request, I'd take her to the children's hospital for X-rays, just to make sure that the cold that was taking eight weeks to go away (and still sounded awful) wasn't, in fact, pneumonia. At one of these visits,

Cate made her rounds of all the injured people in the waiting room. She stood in front of the young man next to us who was cradling one arm in the other, pointed at him, and said in a loud voice, "Whas wrong with that s'guy?"

"He probably broke his arm," I explained with a hushed voice hoping she'd get the hint.

"Oh," she said, as loudly as ever, asking him, "S'you okay?" before moving onto the teenager next to him who had an ice pack around his knee. "Whas wrong with that s'man?"

She continued her inquisition down the line, "Oh, whas wrong with that s'lady?" she asked me about a young girl with her arm in a sling. "You feel better?" she asked her with concern. On she went, to the other twelve people in the room. Cate and I were finally called for our turn and as we walked across the waiting room, I noticed many of the people she interrogated were smiling.

Cate was still sick a few weeks after this set of X-rays. By this time she and I were, as Cate would say, "sick-a-the-vest, sick-a-the-machines," but still needing to stay in our dreaded routine. One afternoon when Tim came home early from work, I asked if he thought Cate seemed any better. He walked into the den, squatted next to her on the floor, and put one hand on her chest and the other on her back. "Hey, Cate."

"Hi, s'Daddy," she said in a raspy voice and then coughed a junky cough.

Tim stood up and said, "Well, I don't think she's any worse."

"Yeah, I know, but I think I'm gonna call pulmonary. This is taking forever," I said, picking up the telephone and dialing the number for the children's hospital by heart. After waiting a few minutes on hold (getting into a slightly better mood with the Billy Joel ballad that was playing through the receiver), I heard the medical assistant's voice, "Pulmonary, thanks for waiting."

I started right in on my dissertation of the past few months to hear the assistant say, "Dr. Kelly is covering today. I'll have her call you back shortly."

When the hospital's number came up on my caller ID, I expected a more urgent response from Dr. Kelly other than the calm one she gave. "Noelle, be patient. You know Cate. It's just going to take some time." I'd often heard that statement about Cate from her doctors, but this time it struck a chord. There was no need to tweak her sick plan, no need to make a visit. The only additional medicine Cate needed was time and my patience to give it to her. Taking Dr. Kelly's advice meant I couldn't make Cate well on my schedule, no matter how much I tried. And as I thought about it, this was true of almost everything with Cate. *She's going to get there on her own time.*

Ever since Cate was born, I'd heard these words from everyone who worked with us—the Stepping Stones staff, her teachers, and therapists—even Tim. *It'll take a little longer for Cate. But she'll get there.* It made sense to me now. With her health, Cate needed time and the right medications. With academic skills, she needed the academic foundations and practice. And with all things Cate, she needed patience from me—probably the toughest piece of the puzzle. There are people like Tim who are naturally patient and people like me who consciously have to work at it.

One night after Cate and I went to battle over the difference between a dime and a nickel, I had her put on her shoes and we headed out to Dunkin' Donuts. I sent her to the counter with some coins to buy donut holes. An adventure she relished and tried to finagle to her advantage.

"S'I have five shocklit holes?" she told the counter person.

"Ah, she'll have two chocolate holes, please."

"S'Mom, s—a—y five," she said as the counter person looked at me for direction.

Practical ways of teaching Cate worked better for me. Well, most of the time anyway. I let her pour her own orange juice in the mornings even though half of it might spill under the refrigerator. I let her dial the telephone even though it took her five tries to get it right. And I let her mix her own martinis, you know, to be sure she had down all of life's basic skills. (Kidding!)

In thinking about it, managing Cate's unending list of Down syndrome issues fell into place, too. Without any effort to pare down what to focus on, or make a spreadsheet about what to deal with when, I stepped back and let life deal the cards. More often than not, one thing surfaced every day that required immediate attention, and that's what I focused on—my issue de jour. The way restaurants had their daily soups, so I had my daily dose of Cate's stuff. I didn't have to choose what to think about. It chose me.

This isn't to say I didn't lose my patience, but day-by-day I became a more patient person. Maybe it was because Cate's health was more manageable now, or that I resolved my working situation, or that I was on Paxil, or that I realized so much of what I placed importance on was irrelevant. Who knows, it was probably a hodgepodge of them all. The source of my transformation wasn't as important as what I did with it.

Noelle and I embraced the changes we saw in each other, changes that we shared, changes that were unique to each one. But we also loved in each other our differences. Those that were exposed in plain view, those we'd uncovered in the past, and those still buried as if treasure yet to find. Even now when we come across something we don't have in common, the one of us having the revelation will immediately say, "I can't believe I didn't know that about you."

For instance, the way we kept our cars: Noelle's was a mess and mine was neat. While this was an obvious point of difference, what Noelle didn't realize was how I was able to keep my car in such good condition. She'd learn my secret in asking me to run an errand with her on the somber occasion of her father-in-law's funeral. (He died a few months after being diagnosed with pancreatic cancer.)

We were about to get in the procession of cars leaving the cemetery on our way to a reception for family and friends when Noelle decided she wanted to avoid the formalities and get all the grandkids milkshakes at McDonalds. "Tim's gonna go with his mom, so would you take us?" she asked me.

"Of course," I said opening the doors of my car so Noelle, Mrs. Clifford, the three girls, and I could pile in.

I dropped Noelle off at the door of McDonalds and waited longer than I expected to for her to return. I assumed it was because the lines were long until I saw her with an armful of bags and a tray of drinks. "Aren't we going to a luncheon?" I asked.

"I know, but the kids will like this better," Noelle said when she got into the car and started passing some of it out.

"Uh, okay, but no one can eat in my car," I said since my two-year-old car was still new to me.

"What—you don't eat in your car?" she blurted at me as she scrunched up her eyebrows. "There's something so wrong with you."

I envisioned a chocolate shake and greasy fries dumping on my light grey leather seats as Claire passed Cate her meal in the way back. "Don't spill anything in Ange's car," Noelle said with a goofy face, turning around to sit down in the passenger seat while the girls chuckled. She pulled a fry from her batch, turned to me and said, "You gotta lighten up."

"Yeah, Frangela. Lighten up," Cate said between slurps of her orange juice.

"Uh-ha," Claire joined in agreement.

"I know, guys. You're right. But I can't help myself."

"You care too much about everything," Noelle said, handing me a fry. "Ya know, it's your weakness, but then again, it's also what makes everybody love you."

We arrived at the church basement where the luncheon was being held, and Noelle handed out the shakes to her nieces when one of her sisters-in-law whispered to me, "The kids adore Noelle because she remembers what it's like to be one." I couldn't help but concur and was hopeful that this carefree side of her disposition would continue to rub off on me.

❧

Just as we had moved Cate to second grade without too much thought, so we put her in the second grade CCD class, even though she'd missed an entire year there as well. (CCD is short for Confraternity of Christian Doctrine.) What Cate truly understood about going to religious education class, and what, if anything, she was getting from it was something I was very unsure about.

For the most part, CCD was taught by volunteer parents, the only qualification being a desire to share your faith. Typically no one had a teacher's certificate, much less a degree in special education for the job. For all I knew, Cate chewed the nose pieces off her eyeglasses the whole time she sat there. But not having her go didn't sit well with me either.

In second grade, the Catholic Church offers children the sacraments of First Reconciliation (forgiveness for sins) and First

Holy Communion (receiving the body and blood of Christ). As notices of these events came home with Cate, I found myself questioning what she really understood about religion and God. *Does Cate have any idea who God is? That we believe in God, that we believe Jesus is God's son? Then again, do other second graders?* I never wondered if Caroline had enough knowledge to make the sacraments, blindly having her follow along with the rest of the pack.

It seemed to me that typical second graders could understand more than Cate probably did about such amorphous ideas. So I wondered if Cate should make a sacrament she knew little about. *Are sacraments reserved only for those who truly can master some basic understanding?* I began to focus on what religion and faith were for Cate, something I never really thought about before and something I bombarded Angela about. My issue de jour for November.

"Do you think Cate knows what a sin is?"

"Probably not," she said, not at all caught off guard. "You'll have to explain it with examples of bad things she's done. Just as you would with Caroline and Claire."

"Are throwing notes away on the bus, stealing food, and forgery really sins?"

"I think when you're young, yes, those little transgressions are sins. They're the imperfect things we do. Things that are perfectly human."

Ange and I talked a lot about Cate's awareness of God, and our other kids' awareness of God, of sin.

"Is there some church directive about when a person is intellectually ready to receive the sacraments?"

"Maybe, but I think you should just consider reconciliation as a blessing for Cate, rather than something she has to understand," Angela said in a heartfelt way. "Think of her receiving God's forgiveness simply by His grace to give it."

I immediately agreed with her words. *She's probably right. God wouldn't be caught up in rigid rules. It's the soul of the person—the spirit of the sacrament—that matters.*

I talked with Cate about being sorry for doing bad things, explaining that sometimes we all do bad things, and we need to be sorry to be forgiven by God. I talked about God and Jesus. Most times when I asked a question about Jesus her response was, "Whas dat guy s'name again?"

We practiced many times what sins she would tell the priest.

"Sorry s'for stealing pretzels. Sorry s'for stealing crunch. Sorry s'for yelling to Claire."

Cate and I arrived at our church the evening of the First Reconciliation service. After the opening prayers by the pastor, the children got up to speak to the priests who were situated in various spots throughout the church. This would be a face-to-face confession for Cate—a more open experience than when Ange and I were growing up and made our confession anonymously to the priest behind the screen of a confessional. I motioned to Cate to get into the line that was forming at the Sacristy. When it was her turn, we walked into the room together to see the priest sitting in a chair facing us. Cate immediately sat down in the empty chair across from him, crossing her legs Indian-style.

"Hi, I'm Noelle and this is my daughter, Cate," I said feeling a little nervous.

"A pleasure to meet you both," he said in a soothing, deep voice.

"I'm just wondering if I should stay," I thought out loud, which quickly spilled into a waterfall of thoughts and concerns: "You see, I'm not sure she understands what this is about, and you might not be able to understand what she's saying, and gosh,

I don't even know if she should be doing this. It was so different with my older daughter."

The priest stood up and put his hand on my shoulder, "It's okay, slow down. First, you should realize it's absolutely fine Cate is here, but know that she doesn't have to come. She has no sin. Cate will go to heaven." *No sin, how can that be? Didn't Sister Gregory say we're all born with original sin? Do other seven-year-olds have sin? Stop analyzing, but I have so much I want to ask him!*

This priest was visiting from another parish. He was wonderful with Cate and with me—kind, gentle, and real. He didn't remark when she made her sign of the cross backwards and listened while she began to say her sins. When Cate was done confessing, the priest said, "Cate, I'm going to give a penance to your mom."

So I prepared myself to say about three Hail Marys and an Our Father on Cate's behalf when he turned to me and said, "Your penance is to take your daughters out for ice cream and to hug them." I began crying, reminded of my dad, as he continued. "Noelle, you are never to forget that you were given a tremendous gift from God."

"I know," I said without letting a second lapse when I reached out and hugged him. "I know that. I promise I do."

We left the church and I found myself still crying over what I considered a perfect experience if one could ever exist. And it was more than this powerful moment of living faithfully the way my dad did—not in a formal manner, but with kindness, with compassion. I understood right then and there that this priest—this person—had not randomly come into my life.

17

PEACE

Water Shoes at the Ritz-Carlton

Do everything with a mind that lets go.
Do not expect any praise or reward.
If you let go a little, you will have a little peace.
If you let go a lot, you will have a lot of peace.
If you let go completely, you will know complete peace and freedom.
Your struggles with the world will have come to an end.

Achaan Chah
A Still Forest Pool, **by Jack Kornfield and Paul Breiter**

I was eager to get out of the house and visit my mom one weekend in late November of Cate's second-grade year. With Cate well and the holidays coming, I was worried we might not get another chance. We went to church while at my mom's, and when it neared the end of mass we stood up to get in line for communion, my mom first, then the girls, and finally me. I inched my way along after them, as another pew emptied in front of me and I found myself separated from Cate by about ten people. I saw my mother walking back from communion followed promptly by Caroline and Claire, but not Cate. A bell went off in my head.

A few people filed along after the girls, when finally I spied Cate. She was sauntering down the aisle, arms swinging at her side. I got back to the pew and looked at her suspiciously. She opened her mouth and there, on the tip of her tongue, sat a host. Caroline, who witnessed our exchange, was completely undone, "Mom! Cate didn't make her First Holy Communion yet!" I turned to Caroline and all I could say was, "Well, she did now." My mom and I looked at each other in disbelief because it was November 30th—my dad's birthday.

On my way home to Simsbury, I called Ange and told her about Cate's First Holy Communion.

"So much for debating about her being ready to receive the sacraments," she said, laughing.

I moved on to the next subject, filling her in on the big topic of conversation this past weekend about plans for a cruise vacation with my mom's side of the family. "It's something they've always half-heartedly talked about doing," I explained. "Ever since my dad died, there's this new wave of energy with them, that 'You never know what the future holds, so let's just do it!' kind of momentum. He would have liked this change of heart, but I have to say the whole idea puts a knot in my stomach."

It didn't make sense for Tim and me to even entertain the thought of a cruise vacation. First off, I didn't think I was a cruise kind of person. I pictured a lot of glitz being involved. That I'd have to invest in cruisewear like oversized Jackie O sunglasses, high heels, and a cover up for the pool instead of the bargain shades, flip-flops, and Tim's old T-shirt I was accustomed to wearing.

Then there were the logistical problems of a huge boat, the cost of the trip, pneumonia looming, and the greatest wild card of all: Cate. A rational person would pass on such an opportunity and yet there was an appeal to it for me. I hadn't done something impulsive like this since I visited Ange the second semester of our junior year when we studied abroad. I left Dublin for Ange's flat in London armed with only her address, a couple of friends, and a backpack. I had no money—no lie. It worked out thanks to Ange being true to herself (the upstanding, responsible one of our duo) even in another country. She took us in for a week, while I made her drink a few pints and have some fun. For us, an even exchange.

So I mentioned the details of the cruise to Ange, subconsciously thinking she would talk me out of it. I was surprised to hear her say, "You know, maybe you should go. Cate could always have this lung problem, but you won't always have this chance. Just take the machines, psyche yourself up, and go." With that—and after bouncing it off Tim over a few glasses of wine one night—we paid the extra for travel insurance and booked the trip.

The departure for our cruise was in sight and Cate was uncharacteristically well for January. My subconscious kept picturing her getting sick while on the cruise in the middle of the ocean, needing to be airlifted to some random hospital. But I blocked the images out, threw caution aside, and hoped Cate's good health would last for the next seven days.

We'd never taken a trip south during the winter, so Caroline and Claire—not to mention me—were almost giddy, throwing flip-flops and bathing suits into our luggage. Cate was on a packing rampage, the way she always was (and still is) about packing. She put all her belongings (I mean ALL her belongings)—pictures, snacks, pens, movies, tchotchkas from her dresser top, even the TV and VCR remotes—into gallon-size Ziploc bags. When she filled an entire box of Ziplocs with stuff, she went to the pantry for another, opting for sandwich-size baggies.

I was excited about going on this big vacation, but I was distracted as well. There was this angst in my heart about my Uncle John (my dad's brother, the cook). I had called my Aunt Anne a few days earlier to catch up when she said my Uncle John wasn't well. He suffered from liver disease, like my dad. I asked Tim if we could stop on the way to the airport so I could see him before we left.

My Uncle John was awake when we arrived, but very sick. I got to give him a hug and have a short visit. It was difficult for me to see him this way and then have to leave, to go away on this extravagant vacation, knowing how he was. We boarded the plane at New York's JFK airport as planned and without our knowing, my Uncle John died the next day. My Aunt Anne insisted that no one call to tell us while we were away on our trip. She wanted it that way.

To learn he died while I was on vacation was devastating news to come home to. One of my favorite people in the world was gone and the funeral happened without me. I was heartbroken that while we were away and having fun the other side of my family was grieving. While I understood my aunt's selfless decision to keep the news from us, I couldn't help but question what seemed like a whim on my part to take this trip in the first place.

It gave me some solace to know I would set aside the time to mourn with my Aunt Anne, to bring closure on a life that was essential to me. After all, this wasn't just the loss of an important person in my life, but of a unique relationship. My Aunt Anne and Uncle John were one of those rare couples who were genuinely in love with each other, still holding hands after forty years of marriage. Still calling each other boyfriend and girlfriend. So it wasn't just my Uncle John I would miss, but the two of them together.

"I'm a kite without a string," my Aunt Anne said when we spoke after my return. I wished I could tie her down and keep her with me for a while.

I was anxious for the chance to finally visit with my Aunt Anne a few months later over lunch, meeting at a restaurant halfway between our houses the way we often did. When I arrived, she was already sitting at a table, wearing a crisp navy pantsuit, with two flutes of champagne set at our places. It was her signature drink at our luncheons. "Seeing each other is an occasion to celebrate," she'd say at our hellos.

All I wanted to do this afternoon was wrap her in a big bear hug, to know how she was, how she felt, and if she was okay. My Aunt Anne never, in all the years I've loved her, let a conversation be about her. She only wanted to know how you were doing. In a refreshing turn she did open up to me that day, offering another pearl of wisdom to my ever-growing strand.

"At one point in my life, I would have said I was lucky for all the help I've had this past year, for the people I've met, for all they've given your Uncle John and me. But it isn't luck, Noelle," she said setting a napkin in her lap. "I now understand that God was making his presence known to me in the people who came for us." Again, faith pressed itself up against me.

She referenced a host of people who stepped in when my Uncle John was sick, from the visiting nurse and the physical therapist, to the man who brought communion to the house, and probably twenty more. I found myself in awe of her as we sat and talked. As sad as she was, there was still a peacefulness about her the way there always was—a saintly quality that emanated from her every pore. *Is it that I'm lucky to have my Aunt Anne in my life, or is this really God making himself known to me?*

Our conversation often turned to memories of my Uncle John, and how he expressed his love for us with food. "Remember how we used to visit you in the Bronx for Sunday brunch when I was little?"

My Aunt Anne smiled and said, "I do remember."

"The goody bag is my favorite memory of those trips. An Uncle John goody bag was the best." At the end of every visit, he'd fill a large brown grocery bag for each of us with our favorite foods from his pantry. My bag would overflow with Oreos, olives, sardines, and M&Ms.

"He'd always have it there for you, Kim, and James, so whenever you visited he'd be ready," my Aunt Anne said, looking back in her mind and at me at the same time.

"And remember when my dad would take all us kids camping and Uncle John would pack the food? He'd fill those white Styrofoam coolers to the brim with extravagant food, not camping food: expensive steaks, lox, champagne and strawberries, shrimp cocktail. When my dad forgot the utensils one year, we passed this enormous steak around for everyone to take bites. And my dad, who clearly didn't have the engineering gene Uncle John did, could never get the ten-man tent set up, so he'd just tie the corners to four tree limbs and call it done. To get in the tent, you had to jump through the door flaps, aiming for the center of the floor. Only Kim and I fit—everyone else had to sleep outside with the raccoons."

"They were the closest of brothers," my Aunt Anne said, and reached over and put her hand on mine. "I don't know if

I told you, but before Uncle John died your dad visited him in his dreams."

"He did? What did Uncle John say about it?"

"Well, your father apologized to John that it took a while before he was able to come. Apparently it was a difficult journey. Your dad said, 'Sorry it's been so long, John, but Jesus, I've had a helluva time getting here,'" my Aunt Anne said and laughed, becoming more serious as she finished her story. "I believe every word of it."

"I do, too." *I really do.* And then an idea came to me. "What if we promise each other to do the same thing? You know, that whoever dies first comes back to tell the other that she's okay, that there is a heaven. Please, Aunt Anne, promise?"

"I'll try, but remember it's not up to us," she said, wanting to make this promise and not let me down.

It was hard to leave her that day and my subconscious simply couldn't. As I turned my car for the highway, I thought of her statement about God making His presence known to her in the people she met. I began to wonder if this was true of my own experience. For if my Aunt Anne was right, I'd met God, befriended Him, and known Him all my life without even realizing it.

I drove along and began to string together the faces of all the people who came to mind: my family, Father Larry, the cherubic nun, Linda, Audrey, Ann, Aunt Anne, Angela. *Was there a higher purpose in their connection to me?* I called Ange right then, "I just wanted to say thank you."

"Thank me, for what?"

I couldn't tell her for what, because it was for everything. I explained to her about my dad's visit with my Uncle John, and the covenant I had just made with my Aunt Anne. I suggested she and I do the same thing. "So, remember, if you die before I do, make sure you come back and tell me you're okay no matter how hard it is or how long it takes. Okay, Ange? Promise?"

"Of course I will. I promise," she said. "But, you've got to promise me something, too."

"Anything, what?"

"If I do die first, please know that I want an open casket, to have Andrea Bocelli singing in the background, and for people to sob uncontrollably. It's the Italian way."

⟋∾⟍

Cate at 9: Can count to fifty (still has trouble articulating the numbers thirteen and fourteen, and thirty and forty); reads at an approximate mid-first grade level; very difficult for her to spell words from memory; can tell time to the half hour; has a broad sight word vocabulary; working on first-grade math concepts; plays soccer and basketball in the town recreation leagues.

With our fifteenth wedding anniversary upon us, Rob and I sat down with Ryan and John to watch our wedding video, which is something we hadn't done since before the kids were born. I was half eager, half reluctant to open this window to the past, much preferring my own memories to those on a screen. A tide of emotions washed over me when I saw my bridesmaids walking one after the other down the aisle.

Noelle came into view and I looked at her as if through a crystal ball. There she walked, eager and innocent, her blonde hair bouncing with curls rolled in with a curling iron, her face cheerful with a walk-down-the-aisle smile. My eyes became watery when I thought about all she didn't know about her future. That soon enough she would love her life, but first there would be Cate's unexpected birth, her father's untimely death. And needing to summon a new kind of strength to put one foot in front of the other to find her way.

I had a jumble of feelings for her that I can describe only by saying they made my heart ache. What I felt for her wasn't sorrow, nor was it fear, although perhaps it was a combination of the two. Just knowing what would happen in her life before she would find happiness made me pause. Seeing her for the fraction of time the camera recorded her face plainly revealed how far she'd come.

"God, Ange, I'd never go back to my twenties." Noelle said when we talked about it the next morning. "I've come too far and learned too damn much. Still, there are a few things I'd change if I could."

"Yeah, like what?"

"Well, for one, I wish my ass were a few inches higher, and second, I wish I still didn't get zits when I now have wrinkles."

"Oh, do you have wrinkles? I didn't notice."

It's funny how you don't see the little flaws in the friends, people, and pets you love in your life. Take Mabel for instance. She was our dog from the instant we brought her home—wacky blue eye and all. The only real flaw with the dog was the one I hadn't anticipated: the Cate factor. Caroline and Claire were pretty responsible looking after Mabel. And while Cate loved looking after her, too, it was her own brand of caring that made all the difference. Now it wasn't just Cate roaming the house in the wee hours of the morning. There were Cate and Mabel to contend with, the two of them as partners in crime.

Some mornings Cate might start with letting the dog out, literally opening the door for Mabel to escape like a wanton criminal. (We wound up with an electric fence the following spring.) Our saving grace was that Mabel was true to her basset hound breed. She'd not so much run off as stop, sniff, and run. Stop, sniff, and run. It usually wasn't too difficult to catch up with her.

Then, there were the mornings when I'd come downstairs and see food remnants plastered to Mabel's ears. One morning I picked off what looked like a bit of pastel-colored marshmallow. Inspecting the evidence, I asked Cate if Mabel ate anything. Cate replied, "I fed her."

"Fed her what?"

"S'lucky Charms and milk."

"Cate, she eats dog food!"

"S'Mom, duh, s'breakfast."

Since Cate was usually the first one up, she not only fed Mabel breakfast, but took her for a morning walk. I'd awake to the doorbell ringing at dawn, race down the stairs half-asleep to find Cate locked out of the house. She'd stand on the stoop with a leash in her hand and no dog in sight. "Where's Mabel, Cate?" I'd ask.

"S'Mom, Mabel s'a crazy dog."

I was immediately pressed into dog-hunting service. I'd traipse through the neighborhood shaking her container of dog food and calling out, "Mabel, come!" The sound of food was pretty much the only command she obeyed. (So much for the time and money spent on training sessions.) Ah, yes, and so surfaced my latest issue de jour: looking for Mabel one direction and Cate the other.

We decided to spend Father's Day in Wappingers Falls with my parents that June. It was the chance to blow off baseball games and steal away to my favorite place at my favorite time of year. We planned to attend an early mass at St. Mary's and then go out to breakfast afterward to celebrate my dad and the day.

We approached the church from behind, which was the opposite way we went growing up. Back then, Dad took pride in parking our green Country Squire station wagon with the fake wood paneling in a small auxiliary lot on Main Street. "Oh, there's plenty of room," he'd say scanning the lot with the same affinity with which Mr. Clifford sought out his obstructed pew. I squeezed my eyes shut every time Dad jimmied the car back and forth into a narrow space.

"That's the skill of learning to drive a crane truck when you're twelve," he'd say proudly throwing the car into park. The four of us would shimmy between our car and the one next to us and hustle off to mass.

I missed those childhood days as we took the turn for the spacious parking lot in back, but Mom and Dad had moved on, and so had I. On either side of the narrow road leading to the parking lot was St. Mary's Cemetery, and in driving by I spied a tombstone that wasn't there before. "CLIFFORD" was chiseled in capital remember-me letters on the light grey marble surface along with the silhouette of a shamrock just above the name. *Have I not been here since Noelle's dad died?* The shock over the passage of time was as great as the pull to skip mass and just visit with him for a while.

The church renovations were complete (no more mass in the gym), though I found myself critiquing the choices. Some changes seemed fitting, while others questionable, including the repainted apostles that lined the tops of the clerestory windows. The renderings had an unintentional cartoon quality, with eyes that appeared to stare right at you. "Scary aren't they?" my mom whispered.

"I never realized how lovely the old paintings were. Did they have to redo them?" I asked to my mom's shrug of a response.

The pews were filled with familiar faces, each one older but much the same. A few rows ahead of us were Mr. and Mrs. Reynolds, and the O'Neil family. Behind us sat Mrs. Moran, our former back-door neighbor whose husband recently died. She was a gardener despite her seasonal allergies. I remember my dad yelling, "God bless you!" twenty times in response to her twenty sneezes on spring evenings when we were out working in the yard. A cantor with a big stiff hairdo from the '80s approached the microphone for the processional hymn. I winced at the memory of the off-tune ballad that would come.

"I'd like to stop at Mr. Clifford's grave," I said to my family after mass when we were stepping up into our car. "Let's all go," Dad said to my disappointment. Much of this experience wasn't what I'd planned on: Going to church backwards, the spooky saints, the real prayers we'd say for Noelle's dad when really I just wanted to talk to him. We parked alongside the cemetery and I led our little band to the gravesite. I rushed ahead of the pack to talk to Mr. Clifford. "I know you're not here, but we're going to say some prayers for you anyway," I whispered before the others arrived.

My mom and dad led us in the regimented, purposeful prayers of remembrance: The Our Father, the Hail Mary, the Glory Be, and the prayer for the faithful departed. In reciting each prayer, I found a spiritual comfort in the words and a sense of respect in saying them aloud with my family. It was a moment of grace for a good man I missed, a good man I knew was in a better place.

I lingered at his grave for a while and watched everyone trek off to the car. It's easier to walk away this time. I bent down to touch his stone knowing that it wasn't because I'd moved on, but that deep within my being I'd come home. Noelle and I both had. What we'd learned from each other wasn't isolated to the present. It was entirely connected to what was right here: our parents, this place, our growing up years. All at once I understood very plainly. *It's not simply that we've changed, but that we remember.*

～๑～

"Happy Mudder's Day, s'Mom!" Cate said as she ran past my bedroom and down the stairs, even though Hallmark was officially celebrating Father's Day. For Cate, every day was Mother's Day including Father's Day when she delivered a slightly modified greeting to Tim, "Happy Mudder's Day, s'Dad!" Amidst her morning crush of activities that now included making breakfast, doing laundry, playing video games, and taking care of Mabel, she still found time to bring me breakfast in bed—even on Father's Day. It was the happy surprise to see what she concocted before witnessing the havoc she caused downstairs.

Cate was always sure to collect some of my favorite foods and cart them upstairs to me on a tray, each item carefully placed in a paper cup, nested inside one of those keep-your-beer-cold koozie cups. One morning it might be a cup of corn pops, two granny smith apples and milk. When she was short on time, her breakfasts-in-bed were abbreviated. Once I got a cup of Gorgonzola cheese, and another time a cup of salted cashews.

"S'breakfast s'Mom!" she'd say, thumping up the stairs, as I lay half-conscious in bed. It was never the same meal twice. That Father's Day morning, she brought up a cup filled with baby carrots, a water bottle filled to the brim, and a clementine.

"Thanks, Stick," I said reaching over and kissing her forearm. "It looks delicious."

Ange stopped by the following morning to go for a walk with the dogs. She asked how Tim and I were doing, having spent Father's Day without our dads.

"He had moments of sadness, but didn't say much. For me, it was fine. My dad hated all the bullshit over the holidays anyway."

"I bet he did."

"I think about him all the time, every day, holiday or not. Besides, Cate's my constant reminder of him."

"It's weird how she's just like him, isn't it?"

"So screwy, completely irreverent, that total disregard of social status. And my dad's friends were all over the lot from CEOs to the guys who sold him his brisket sandwich at the deli. He was an equal opportunity friend, just like Cate."

"I'll always remember him as being happy."

"He *was* happy. Nothing left unsaid, no unfinished relationships. You knew how much he loved you your whole life."

"I think God, in His mercy, just plucked him up and took him right to heaven."

"Well, except that he probably took a detour or two on the way. But, you're right, Ange. He wouldn't have done well to have a timetable. There's no way he would have gone through his sock drawers to pull all his paperwork together. Plus, he was emotionally squishy. God protected him from having to say goodbye to us."

It's not often that I work consecutive days at my office in Manhattan, but that summer I had a closing and was there for about five days, which was two days' more outfits than I owned. I was staying at the Ritz-Carlton on Central Park South, some pretty fancy digs for a girl like me. When I traveled into midtown lately, I usually felt misplaced—just a mom driving a minivan and still playing in this prestigious arena.

When the deal closed, I went back to the hotel room to get my stuff and change. I put on my army-green cargo capris and Mary Jane sneakers (actually, they're water shoes I think look stylish) and went down to the main desk to check out. Once there, I realized I left my cell phone and BlackBerry chargers in the room, so I asked the bellhop if I could go up and get them.

"No, Ma'am, I'll get them for you."

I plunked down in a generous red velvet chair and waited, people-watching the way I loved to do. Scanning the room, I realized I was the only person with blonde hair and freckles. Everyone else appeared to be a wealthy foreigner with beautiful, distinctive features and elegant attire.

I was fascinated by this crowd, each person looking to be completely unlike me, presumably leading lives on the extreme opposite end of the spectrum from my own. This group was worldly in the same telling ways I was entirely pedestrian, from their accents and hairstyles, to their luggage and jewelry—not to mention their shoes.

I immediately called Ange, "Okay, I'm sitting here in the lobby of the Ritz-Carlton among the lifestyles of the rich and famous thinking of that old *Sesame Street* song. You know, the one that goes: "One of these things doesn't belong.""

"Let me guess, you're wearing those silly water-shoe sneakers you think look chic."

"Holy Moley, you know me too well. Anyway, I'm calling to tell you how fun the people-watching is, feeling so damn content for no good reason. I wish you were here."

We met at Noelle's house a few days after her business trip to Manhattan to spend the afternoon together. I peeked into her office and found her the way I often do—still not quite ready to go. I sat down at her kitchen island and flipped open a magazine, then Noelle walked out of her office. She took a cleansing breath and said to me with a smile that lifted her whole face, "Let's go have some fun." Of course I knew this meant I had a few more minutes to read because she was still wearing her pajamas and robe.

We got into her car and Noelle gave me her usual schpiel about how she meant to shower but didn't quite get to it. "So what you see is what you get." Since she was driving, she had control of where we were going. "Let me stop for a coffee first and then there's a store I want to take you to."

Needless to say I knew we weren't headed for Marshalls. Instead she pulled up to a local boutique that neither of us was appropriately dressed to walk into. "Why are we going here?" I asked.

"Because you need real jeans and they've got the goods, Chiquita. My treat."

"Oh geez, that's not what today is about."

We began looking around when a saleswoman with a bright smile approached. "Do you ladies need any help?"

"Actually, we do," Noelle said. "We're looking for jeans for my friend."

"We're the place for jeans," she said excitedly, walking us to the back of the store. "What style do you like?"

Noelle quickly cut me off, telling the woman, "Low on the hips, boot-cut. Not too dark, not too light." It was all I could do to keep from laughing at her clear directive like, "Yes da'ling, show me this, that, and the other" while dressed in her standard uniform of this beat-up nubby fleece jacket, black Adidas track pants, and running sneakers.

The saleswoman pulled a pair of jeans off the shelf and then went for another brand hanging on a rack. "These are the hottest jeans," she said. "All the stars are wearing them."

Noelle and I laughed out loud in unison, her saying what we both were thinking: "Now we totally have to get them."

The saleswoman lifted a third pair from another rack and I headed to the dressing room, poking through my pile. "Noelle, these jeans the stars are wearing cost $165."

"Don't look at the price, just try them on."

I've never put on jeans like the first pair I tried. They fit everywhere: in the waist, in the hips, in the length. And they happened to be the least expensive of the bunch. "You've gotta try the rest of them on to be sure," Noelle said.

I slid off the jeans I was wearing to try another pair when Noelle threw a couple of layered T-shirts over my dressing room door.

"What's this?"

"Don't ask questions."

So, I tried the whole outfit on: the made-for-me jeans and the layered T-shirts. I walked out to the three-way mirror and Noelle said, "Holy crap, you look so good." And she was right. I felt good.

"Ange, it's way better to invest in a few things that you love, that you'll wear all the time than sales-rack stuff that's cheaper, or doesn't even fit you, that you'll end up returning anyway."

"You're right," I said almost shamefully—this was advice she'd given me many times before.

"It's okay to buy something that makes you feel great. And, brace yourself, you can even pay full price for it."

"Thanks, and just so you know, I'm paying today."

"For this fun, wasteful, splurge? No way, this one's on me."

18

DIFFERENT

The Fine Line Between Freedom and Fitting In

You spent the first half of your life becoming somebody.
Now you can work on becoming nobody, which is really somebody.
For when you become nobody there is no tension,
no pretense, no one trying to be anyone or anything.
The natural state of the mind shines through unobstructed—
and the natural state of the mind is pure love.

Ram Dass

I t's always a big day at the end of summer when the kids get
their letters in the mail saying who their teachers are for the
upcoming school year. Typically it results in a hundred phone
calls all over town to see who is in whose class. Rarely is it a
big shocker when it comes to Cate, however, since it's usually
planned well in advance who her teacher will be.

255

If I were to guess, Cate's fourth grade teacher was predetermined in kindergarten, when Rick Collins first met Cate. He always went out of his way to say hi to her and to include her in his class doughnut sale on Wednesdays. Mr. Collins was also one of the coaches in town who promoted all kids being given an equal footing when learning to play a sport. He held strong to his value that each child treat each classmate, each team member, and each adult with respect. Cate loved him, calling him simply, "s'Collins."

Collins made it clear to his fourth grade class that every student was to be treated equally. He made it a point to tell me that he wanted Cate to be a full-fledged member of the class. However, as much as he tried to treat Cate like his other students, providing discipline when she broke the rules and holding her accountable when he should, he didn't always treat her like the others.

Cate would call him a chicken and he'd say she was an angel. He arranged for her to leave the classroom once a week to help the school librarian check out books—a job he initiated for her. He told her she would be on his high school track team when she got to ninth grade. Bottom line was, Collins had a big heart and even though he tried not to treat her differently, Cate was different to him.

I agreed with Mr. Collins's philosophy that all kids should be treated on a level playing field. So I was surprised by my reaction when I ran into a child from Cate's class and her father at a basketball game. The dad asked how Cate liked school, and said his daughter was having a good year. But he went on to mention how his daughter was bothered that Mr. Collins didn't practice what he preached, that everyone in the class should be treated the same.

"What do you mean?" I asked, unsure about where this was going.

"She says that apparently Mr. Collins doesn't treat all the kids the same, that he gives Cate lots of extra attention, special rewards. So I told my daughter if it was really bothering her, maybe she should speak to Mr. Collins about it."

"You're absolutely right," I instantly agreed. "All the kids should be treated the same." And then just as quickly, words to the contrary came rushing out of my mouth. "Then again, maybe it's okay to be extra kind once in a while. Maybe it would be helpful to explain to your daughter how different school can be for Cate. That when you daughter speaks, or asks a question in class, that most people don't just walk away, or ignore her, because they can't understand what she's saying, but that this happens to Cate all the time. Or, that when she writes down her homework it's an effortless task, but for Cate to be able to write even a sentence may take ten minutes and requires much guidance. I don't know, maybe it's okay that she receives some extra attention. She has struggles that you and I and your daughter may never experience."

I headed for my car and started crying as I reached for the door, upset and embarrassed that I just unloaded on this guy, who meant no harm. After all, I did understand how his daughter felt. At the same time, I understood from my own vantage point how nice it was that Collins bent his own rules for Cate, giving her such joy. I guess I wanted it both ways. I wanted Cate to be treated like everyone else, but when she was treated differently out of kindness, I wanted that too.

October seemed to come earlier that year along with the annual invitation to Noelle's Halloween birthday party for her grandmother. She threw great parties and this one was no exception as it was an amalgam of her favorite things—family, friends, neighbors, kids, dogs, food, and music—mingled together at once.

Of course there was the last-minute dash to the furniture store a few days before the event for some binge decorating. Little did most of her guests know, while these inanimate objects sat speechless in her home, that there was a story behind how each one arrived just in time (central to the plot being how she dragged me around town to find them).

I knew most of the people there, some new folks mixed in with the usual cast of characters: Mrs. Clifford and her sisters, James along with his wife, Cathy, and their new baby, James Kevin. No one was sure how to introduce the baby, much like no one ever knew what to call his namesake, Mr. Clifford. "I call him Jake," Mrs. Clifford said endearingly to which James bellowed, "Ma, that's a whole other name. I call him J.K."

Noelle came into the kitchen with her hair in a ponytail—a dead giveaway to her shower, without time for primping. "Everyone showed up on time. I need that one-hour buffer," she said and frantically began pulling meat platters, a ziti pan, and salad after salad out of her fridge. "Do you think I have enough food?"

"You're insane," I said, poking a serving spoon into a pasta dish.

Her grandmother walked into the kitchen, setting her wine glass down on the counter. I leaned my elbows on the table, staring at her in amazement, for she looked the same after all these years. "You're incredible," I said.

"Yes, you are," Noelle agreed, overhearing my comment, and threw an arm around her, "Okay Nana, I've got a new hat for you and it's better than the last one." From the counter Noelle lifted a framed reminder photo of the previous year's party of her grandmother wearing a witch's hat with spiders precariously dangling off the brim. Her Nana laughed while Noelle presented her with a beautiful new pointed black hat, swirled with white tulle and dusted with purple glitter.

I stopped to say hello to Audrey who quickly cut me off. "So Noelle tells me you're making a go at freelance writing and went to a writer's conference in New Haven."

"Yeah, writing is something I've wanted to get back to, and the conference was energizing."

"I hear it was expensive. Was it worth that kind of dough?"

"Well, after plenty of Noelle therapy—yes. Her theory is that sometimes you've got to invest in yourself," I said.

Audrey nodded her head in agreement, having self-published a children's book a few years earlier. She asked if so and so was at the conference. "Just curious, because she's such a blowhard," she said and held up her wine glass. "A toast to you and, hey, pour me a refill."

After topping off Audrey's glass, Cate came up to me holding a piece of lined loose-leaf paper and a pencil and asked, "Frangela, how d'ya spell strawberry?" She put the paper on the counter, gripped her pencil, and looked up at me over the rims of her eyeglasses.

"S-t-r..." I began.

"Wait, wait, wait," she said. "Frangela, too fast."

"S—t—r—a—w—b—e—r—r"

"Already did 'r'!"

"I know, there are two 'rs.'"

"Oh, yeah, s'forgot."

"Y," I said, and she shuffled away, heading for the basement.

After milling about a bit, I loaded a plate of food and sat down at the kitchen table. Noelle sat down next to me a few minutes later. She swiped the lone olive from my pasta salad and tossed it in her mouth, chatting away with her guests. As more people gathered to get in on Noelle's conversation, I was struck by a familiar feeling.

"I have a big piece of Cate, but I don't have all of her," Noelle often tells me. "She isn't just mine. I share her with a lot of people."

I smiled watching Noelle laugh and talk with her company. *She isn't just my friend—and that's exactly how it should be.*

❧

One of the biggest violators of the "treat everyone the same" rule was my brother-in-law, Dave. Ever since he rerouted his business trip to meet Cate for the first time, he's had a unique relationship with her. He called a few times a week for "Sticky updates" (by now her pilfering nickname stuck). Dave wanted to know what kind of trouble she was getting into, and was driving her nuts with his continuous repertoire: "Stick, Stick, watcha doing? I've got my eyes on you, Stick. Did you defeat Jin Lu's army on that videogame I sent you yet?"

"I'll crush you, s'Dave," she'd often say to his barrage.

Lately when Dave made his weekly calls, Cate talked about Collins, "S'Dave, s'Collins tooks my class to the movies and fries." As far as I could tell, this was purposeful banter on her part. I think she knew it made Dave jealous that someone else was giving her good stuff.

"Sticky, I'm sick of hearing about Collins. Stick, Stick—who do you like better, me or Collins?"

"S'Collins!" she blurted out, laughing at her answer.

Dave didn't want anyone taking over his coveted spot as Cate's favorite. He thought he had secured that position by mailing her Sticky care packages filled with juice boxes, Smarties, Fun Dip and hot chips (what we in our house call the salt and vinegar potato chips). Whenever we visited my sister and Dave in Virginia, he'd be at the ready with his Sticky survival pack of movies, video games, lemons, and orange juice. But things were changing with Cate. She was growing up and her relationships with others were growing, too.

One day Cate received a package in the mail from Dave with a big gold mailing envelope taped on top. Written in magic marker on the envelope were the words, "Open first." She was out of her skin with excitement, ripping it open. Inside was a six-page power point presentation with pictures and simple text for Cate to read. The front cover had a picture of two boxers fighting with the title, "Collins v. Dave." The following pages contained questions with check-the-box answers.

First page: Who do you like better, Collins or Dave? Second page: If your answer is Collins, deliver the contents of this box to your local food pantry. Third page: If your answer is Dave, you're all right, Stick. Enjoy the box. The last page had the name "Collins" typed in block letters, stamped with a circle and diagonal line through it. Just as some parks had similar signs prohibiting dogs, so Dave was kicking Collins off his turf.

A few months later, I was emptying Cate's backpack and pulled out the power point presentation. Horrified, I tracked her down holding the papers in my hand and asked, "Why was this in your backpack?"

"S'I brought it in for show-and-share."

What must Collins be thinking? I never told him about the good-hearted rivalry my brother-in-law had with him. I had the urge to send an e-mail, but decided to let it be. How could I possibly explain this insanity?

Ryan was transitioning to middle school when I heard about a talk being sponsored in Simsbury by The Center for Non-Verbal Learning Disorders. The facility was hosting a child neuropsychologist from Holland who specialized in how to teach children with learning disabilities as well as those with intellectual disabilities. I mentioned it to Noelle, thinking she might also be interested. We couldn't figure out exactly what non-verbal in the name of the organization meant. It lacked definition in its vagueness, but the promise of some insight on the subject and a night out together was reason enough to give this a shot.

Noelle and I entered the foyer hoping for clarity as we scanned posters hanging on the wall and thumbed through marketing materials set on folding tables. "I'm not sure if this is for us," I whispered so parents milling about couldn't hear.

"Yeah, I have no idea," she said as perplexed as when we arrived, fanning through a three-ring binder of material. "I'm here because Cate can't read phonetically, so I'm thinking this means she fits into a non-verbal category."

Noelle bumped into an acquaintance while participants from the first session began to exit the meeting room. From her take, it sounded worthwhile and they had cookies, so we paid our admission and took seats. "Hopefully we do belong here," Noelle said, "because I'd much rather go out for a glass of wine."

The doctor spoke brilliantly, her brain instantly translating her thoughts from Dutch to English. "You have to speak at least four languages in Holland," she joked with ease. "It's more like a state than a country." After listening to this woman for ten minutes, I understood more about Ryan's learning disability than I had discovered in nearly ten years of trying.

She explained that there were "verbal learners," those who learn by listening. On the other end of the scale, "visual learners," such as Ryan, first process visual data. "They like to jump in and do things," she said. "That's why Ryan does his homework and builds things without first reading the directions," I told myself.

"He doesn't have a self-monitoring deficiency as suggested by his fifth grade teacher. It's simply who he is."

Up shot Noelle's hand, "Well, my daughter has Down syndrome and she's having trouble learning phonics. I always thought she was a visual learner, but now I'm thinking she might be verbal." The doctor explained that learning style has nothing to do with a person's disability. "I don't want to know the disability," she said candidly. "Tell me what kind of learner your child is, and we go from there."

"How do I know what kind of learner she is?" Noelle probed, looking for the elusive key.

"In Holland, all children are evaluated by a child neuropsychologist before entering kindergarten. The teachers then separate the students in three groups within their classrooms, modifying lessons and homework accordingly," the doctor explained. "Isn't that the case here?" The crowd erupted with a mixture of laughter and groans.

The workshop concluded, and as we walked to the car Noelle said, "I didn't understand one thing about that talk. Visual, verbal—how the heck do I know?"

"I thought she was fantastic. Now I see that the way Ryan learns is separate from his disability. It's his strength really, and we need to tap that."

"Right now I'm thinking there's something else I'd like to tap. How about that drink?"

As Cate grew up, there were times I couldn't take charge over certain situations when I would have wished to—to iron things out, to make things better for her. This was true of her friendships, a number of which suffered growing pains that year. I watched as the girls in Cate's class became more mature physically and socially, and how Cate often found herself on the fringe. She was still young and immature in many ways, still difficult to understand.

Cate at 10: Primarily uses sight words when reading; computer is a motivational tool for her; easily frustrated when she's not able to do something right away; requires assistance with fasteners and shoe tying; continued progress in skip counting and rote counting (but continued difficulty in reading and using the number thirteen); able to tell time to the nearest fifteen minutes; able to count dimes to a dollar, but still working on nickels and quarters to a dollar; enjoys telling stories, but not always easy for the listener to understand what she says.

At times her attempts at friendship went ignored ("Hi Hunter, Hi Hunter, Hi Hunter," she'd say to no response), and in other instances she was excluded, or perhaps that was just my perception. Once we ran into her classmates at a movie birthday party to which she hadn't been invited. My heart broke for her, though she never caught on. Instead she ran up to each of the kids, so excited to see them. *How will she feel the day she understands she's been left out?*

There was the sweetness of Cate (a quality I hope she always has) that became uncool for a time while her peers navigated the early preteen years. Where Cate might see friends at the grocery store or the pool, run up, and throw her arms around them, now only a few months later, it was no longer an acceptable greeting. It caused her friends embarrassment and separated her a little more from the crowd. I was very much torn between the idea of allowing Cate to be herself and the desire to have her fit in.

With our oldest kids almost teenagers, Ange and I often found ourselves reliving our middle school traumas. We recalled what it was like when we were left out, or just stood idly by when it happened to others. "Ange, remember how ostracized Kathy Brennan was, how we probably weren't nice to her?"

"We never teased her, but we ignored her. And that was just as bad."

"Makes me feel awful to think of it."

"Me, too—no one should feel excluded. We see that now as adults, but I guess we didn't have the maturity back then."

I always made the extra effort to have Cate's friends to the house, to enroll her in sports programs, to help her be active and social with children around her age. Turns out, I probably didn't need to do anything, because Cate developed friendships on her own without any of my help. (Looking back, I see that my lasting relationships were found, not forced.) Her closest friend was Sydney, the little girl who first visited Cate in the hospital during the year of pneumonia.

From the moment I met Syd, I knew she was something special, and perhaps she needed to be. Cate was different and maybe she needed a different kind of friend. When Cate returned to school after her string of pneumonias had ended, Syd began calling the house in her petite voice to ask, "Can Cate play?" Their friendship quickly grew with them often spending time together, and soon enough, Syd became a fixture in Cate's life and ours.

Every year since they'd met, Syd and Cate were intentionally placed in the same class. I was conscious that having this arrangement was wonderful for Cate, but worried this may not have been in Syd's best interest, or perhaps wasn't what Syd wanted. I mentioned my concern to her mother in passing. She assured me it was fine by her, but she would check with Syd. A few days after that conversation, Syd's mom called back and said that Sydney became very upset and teary when faced with the prospect of being separated from Cate, saying, "I have to be in Cate's class."

So Syd along with Cate had the good fortune of having Collins for a fourth grade teacher. With a penchant for nick-naming all his students (Cate being just "Cate"), Collins dubbed Sydney "Super Syd." It was a name that stuck with me because Syd wasn't nice to Cate the way some kids were (because you're supposed to be). Syd was nice to Cate because they were friends. They argued, they danced, they had sleepovers, and they put on shows. Their relationship was unique, and it was remarkable, and sometimes it came at a cost.

Syd and Cate were part of a pack of girls, but occasionally their close friendship caused Syd to be placed in a tough position. When a girl in the group had a boy-girl party the following year, Syd said she wasn't going to go and this girl asked if it was because Cate wasn't invited. Syd said no, but told this girl she could invite Cate. The response was, "Why would we invite a Down syndrome kid to a boy-girl party? But fine, I'll invite her if you'll come."

A few weeks later somehow the story about this party came up and Syd's eyes were watery as she told me about it. I loved little Syd and told her not to give it another thought. That Cate wasn't hurt by any of it because she didn't even know about the party. I worried that Syd felt she had to be Cate's protector. It was too much responsibility for a young girl. I simply told her, "Not everyone gets it the way you do and that's okay."

ॐ

Ellie Lewis caught my eye when I entered the one-room, red brick schoolhouse to pick up Ryan from his cartooning class that Saturday morning. "Ryan did excellent work today," she said, walking around the table that filled the center of the room, eyeing each student's work.

I was concerned this class was too hard for him, despite her encouragement of his drawing talent at a program the previous summer. The students in this class were a year or two older with more advanced drawing skills. School was difficult for Ryan—I didn't want this to be. "Do you think this is the right place for him?" I asked.

"Oh, most of these students have been coming for years. But Ryan will catch up quickly. Look at his work." We walked over to Ryan and Ellie flipped open his sketchpad to reveal the intricate drawing of a science fiction character he drew from a reference. "This is beautiful," she said, turning the page to an original sketch. "This one will make a wonderful character for our book, Ryan," she said to him as I listened, beaming, not so much with pride, but with happiness for him.

I motioned her away from the table to share my thoughts. "You know, Ellie, it seems we work so hard on what's hard for Ryan, and never on what he's good at," I said half apologizing. "He has a learning disability, but he also has this incredible artistic gift. It's time to focus on this, too."

"Absolutely, Mrs. Martin. Ryan will develop his skills by looking at things like an artist," she explained. "We see shapes." Ellie reached for a black-and-white reference photo of Muhammad Ali. "Everything is made of shapes," she said guiding her finger around the outside line of his body. "There are shapes within shapes, shapes on top of shapes," she continued, now tracing the softer muscles of Ali's arms. I began to see crescent moons.

As Ryan and I made our way out of the schoolhouse, I looked at him through a new set of eyes. *If only everyone could see the whole picture—the whole person—the way artists do. Each one of us somehow flawed, each one of us incredibly gifted.*

∼

Cate's social skills were her strength as she soon came to have the lingo and flip attitude of a fourth grader. She stormed out of the kitchen one day when I'd admonished her for stealing food, "Take a bath, s'Mom," she said under her breath, when she turned on a heel and stormed off to the den.

"What did you say?"

"Sorry, s'Mom."

"You're right you're sorry," I said in disbelief, but at the same time, I caught myself with a sense of motherly pride. She was right in there, saying what any preteen might.

She loved playing video games, and consequently she often hung out with boys of varying ages. Cate occasionally invited herself next door for an evening of PlayStation with my neighbor's teenage son, switching handsets with him if she wasn't doing well. "Sick uh that guy," she'd say after a time, blaming the game for her own failings.

On weekends, she'd have her classmate and friend, Justin, over and they would play video games for hours.

"Cate, you're toast," he said once in the heat of battle, rapping the buttons of his handset.

"Where's the toast?" she asked, confused but inspired by the food reference.

"S'Mom, Justin have dinner here?"

I asked Cate to set the table and they sat down next to each other, heaping spaghetti and meatballs onto their plates. When

Cate finished eating her meatballs, she leaned in and stole one from Justin, stabbing it with her fork and taking a bite.

"Cate, man, you're crazy," he said.

This relationship faded a bit along with some others (with the exception of Super Syd), and I found myself wondering where Cate fit in. I tried to foster relationships with children who had special needs, with marginal or no success.

"That kid s'like Mike," she'd say, equating each new child with a little friend of hers with Down syndrome. These children were somehow different to Cate, and she placed them into a distinct group—a group in which she didn't include herself. In Cate's mind, she was like everybody else.

Once while we were in the ENT's office for Caroline, I left Cate and Claire in the playroom to wait. I poked my head in when Caroline was called for her appointment to see that Cate was talking to a boy her age with Down syndrome. When Caroline's visit was over and the four of us left the office, I asked Cate if she had fun playing with the little boy.

"S'what s'matter with that kid. He talks like pthththth," she said, making blowing raspberry sounds.

Caroline true to her superhero powers of stating the obvious noted their similarity, "Cate, don't you think you're just like that boy?"

"S'what the heck, Caroline!" she scoffed and trucked ahead of us to the car to get the front seat.

As we made our way home and into the house, I was paralyzed by the idea that Cate had basically what amounted to one close friend. I propped up against the kitchen counter, envisioning her lonely one-friend future, and the phone rang. I picked up the receiver to hear Ange's voice and was instantly calmed. *Maybe one best friend is all she needs.*

Ryan and I walked into our hairdresser's shop for his appointment and peeked behind a partition that separated the waiting room from her station. "Hi, Ryan. I'm just finishing up with Olivia. Come around and have a seat," Ileana said and pointed to the opening behind us. "They're replacing that big window and I don't want you and your mom to get hurt."

We looked at the hole where a picture window used to be, and at the men who were lifting an awkward six-by-six piece of glass into place.

In turning the corner, I saw myself in Olivia who was sitting in Ileana's chair. She was a teenager who looked to be in about ninth grade, with lanky limbs and a huge mound of frizzy out-of-control hair.

Ileana was trimming the front of her hair while three gigantic clips reigned in the back of it. Then Ileana said, "Angela, I think you have hair sort of like Olivia's. How do you care for it?" This girl looked totally mortified, bending her head lower at the chin so I could barely see her face.

"Oh my goodness, my hair is exactly like yours. I bet you hate it, right?"

She peeked out from under the morass with her gorgeous green eyes and smiled with a few nods.

"I have to tell you that your hair is beautiful, you just don't know it yet. I used to hate my hair. It took me half my life to figure out how to deal with it, but I love it now—I love my hair," I affirmed at the top of my lungs in the middle of this beauty shop as Ryan slouched ever lower in his chair. "My girlfriends all say they wish they had hair like mine, but it wasn't always that way so I know exactly how you feel."

This poor girl blushed crimson. Little had she known her

dreaded haircut today would include having a raving lunatic put her on the spot. I could tell that she was reserved, that her hair probably made her think what I used to think of myself when I was a teenager: that I was ugly. I was on a crusade to save her. I wanted this girl to be asked to the prom because I wasn't, to have boyfriends because I didn't.

Did I blame my hair for my social misfortune? Maybe not exclusively, but no doubt it was in the mix. I think how a person feels about herself shines through in how she acts. My hair was different, so it made me feel different from just about every other girl who flipped her perfectly parted and feathered hair from side to side. My hair never moved. And a part, isn't that something you have in a play?

As any dysfunctional mother would, I projected my hair angst on my kids, moving them from barbershop to barbershop at the first sign of a bad haircut. John's hair was straight and easily cut into the latest style, while Ryan's hair—thick and wavy—was more challenging to manage. That said, both boys had had their share of miscuts, which seemed to bother me more than them. Though I eventually did find "the barber" in town, when Ryan decided he liked a longer style, friends directed me here, to Ileana. (Again the lesson: different kids, different needs.)

Ileana worked on Olivia as I explained my method. "Okay, so here's what you need to do," I said with the seriousness of a doctor explaining a prescription. "Wash your hair, then condition it. But don't wash the conditioner out. That's the secret. You take a wide-tooth comb and comb the conditioner through your hair, and you leave it in."

"Wow," Ileana said, "you've got this technique down."

"You just leave the conditioner in there?" the girl's mother asked.

"Yes, but there's more," I said, so happy to share my knowledge after years of trial and error, to squash my humiliation and shame from a childhood of being called names (fro, mushroom top, and fuzz head among the benign ones) that were still salt in the wound. "So just wrap your head in a towel for a few minutes then flip your hair upside down and scrunch some maximum hold gel in there. Not the stiff kind, but the kind that leaves your hair soft. And that's it. Don't blow-dry it. Don't comb it. Don't touch it, except to fluff it a little with your fingers as it air dries."

"This sounds great," the mother said looking at her daughter. "Let's try it this weekend. Only on the weekend, right?"

And I could see the two of them, mother and daughter speaking without a word passing between them. The mother understanding how risking a new hairdo had to happen only on a day off from school—a day away from her peers.

"Believe me, I know," I said, because I did.

I tried to make eye contact with Olivia, but she wouldn't look at me. She was primed with a scrunchy around her wrist ready to throw her hair in a ponytail the second she was out of here. I imagined she wanted to be done, to push back her hair and not think about it and how it made her feel.

"Remember, we're trying to give you a hairstyle by cutting it in long layers," Ileana said. "No ponytail. It looks beautiful just as it is."

"She's so fortunate to have her hair that length at this time in her life," I said to Ileana after they left. "It took me all four years of college to grow out my hair and it wasn't pretty. I tried everything—even hand cream—to tame it while it grew sideways instead of down."

"You're so passionate about this. Maybe you should write an article about it, or at least give me a cheat sheet for my drawer so I can give it to my customers."

"I'll definitely do that for you. After two decades of perfecting my method, I'm happy to share it."

"Okay, Ryan, your turn," she said waving him over. Ileana began spritzing and combing through Ryan's hair when she turned to me and said, "I think you were meant to come here today and meet Olivia."

"So do I," I said holding back yet another outburst, this time on the faith Noelle and I had come to have. *If I get into that story, she'll really think I'm nuts and kick me out of her shop. Then I'll be searching for a hairdresser all over again.*

<hr />

Cate cuddled up next to me in bed after bringing me my breakfast one morning, rubbing her feet together like a grasshopper the way she does.

"S'love you, s'Mom," she said.

"Me, too, Stick," I replied, kissing the top of her head. *I just love how you say what you think in the moment.* My mind replaying an incident that happened just the day before when I did the total opposite, saying something just to fit in with the group. I was at a social function in Manhattan with Tim and was in the vulnerable position of trying to keep pace with the crowd. I caved under social pressure instead of being myself.

A group of us were standing in a circle holding drinks and chitchatting about subjects I had little interest in. Another guest started talking to me about how he tried to visit a new museum once a month now that he lived in the city, when I chimed in, "I loved going to all the museums when I lived here." When in fact, I walked by the Guggenheim every day and never once had the desire to go inside.

I got sucked into fitting into the high-brow conversation,

when I was anything but, never readily admitting to people that I like to read *The New York Post* instead of the *Wall Street Journal*, *People Magazine* instead of *Newsweek*, and watching *Entertainment Tonight* instead of *CNN*. How I envied Cate while I lay there trying to get out of bed, knowing she would never do that.

Granted, Cate's "tell it like I see it" manner made living with her both challenging and wonderful. She spoke with the emotion of the moment: "S'beautiful face, s'Mom," she'd tell me on the rare occasions I put on make-up, or "S'love you, s'Mom," she'd say and kiss the top of my head as I bent down to help her dress. If she was tired of playing soccer, she walked off the field. "All done with that." When guests came to visit, she did what she wanted to do. "S'gonna play PlayStation in the s'basement."
She's always herself.

Day by day I began to see how Cate was influencing me—who I was, how I acted, choices I made. I found myself being more accepting, a lot less rigid, and a little less judgmental. At least I was trying anyway. There were even instances when I was in a group of parents whose children had special needs, who had all the same concerns as me, but I felt differently than they did. It was evident when the town's inclusion specialist, Deb Cervas, asked if I would present with her at a special education meeting.

"The presentation has an introduction by me, and then slides for a parent to share." Deb said. "No prep required, Noelle. Just add your personal commentary." I immediately accepted with the hopes of helping this woman who had worked countless hours on our behalf. But I was odd man out from the moment I opened my mouth. Feeling like such a fool, I called Ange from the car to tell her what happened.

"The first slide in my presentation read, 'The parent-professional relationship is like a marriage.' So to break the ice I said, 'Yeah, it is, but if the marriage doesn't work out, you could always get a divorce. And I guess the alternative for us is home schooling, which, I don't know about you, but in my house would result in a murder-suicide.'"

"Hilarious," Ange said with a hearty laugh.

"But, no one laughed. Not even a chuckle."

"You're kidding. Sounds like an intense group."

"Totally! But I get it—I get their seriousness about education. It can be such an uphill climb. How frustrated am I that Cate still reads the Super Stop & Shop sign as "Shop, Shop, Shop." But, my God, it's okay to laugh at ourselves, isn't it?"

19

COMPASSION

Be Yourself

We were born to make manifest the glory of God that is within us.
It is not just in some of us; it is in everyone.
And as we let our own light shine, we unconsciously
give other people permission to do the same.
As we are liberated from our own fear,
our presence automatically liberates others.

Marianne Williamson
From *A Return to Love*

My brother, James, called me early one fall morning and asked, "Noelle, what about Team Cate and the Buddy Walk this year. Where we gonna meet?" The Buddy Walk is an event established by the National Down Syndrome Society that takes place in locations all over the country and around the world to promote acceptance and inclusion of people with Down syndrome. The Buddy Walk we attended was held in Central Park every fall and it had become an annual tradition with our family.

With so much family history riding on our attending, it was hard for me to share with James that I was considering not going this year. "I don't think we're gonna make it," I said, unable to come up with a better excuse because for whatever reason I was exhausted, overcommitted, and just wasn't motivated to hike it down there this year.

"Jesus, Noelle, we've got to do the Buddy Walk," he said primed with the guilt-ridden plea: "You've gotta bring Sticky."

Truth be told, the Buddy Walk was a nice day in the city for everyone and we usually ended up at the Dinosaur Bar-B-Que on 125th St. in Harlem for dinner before returning home. I wondered if the emotional pull to go had become stronger for my family than it had for me. That aside, I decided to stop dragging my feet and go.

We found a parking spot on the street (Tim carries on my dad's tradition of never paying for parking) and before we left the car, I made the girls and Tim sit for my "no T-shirts" lecture since we already had about twenty Buddy Walk T-shirts. "The last thing we need is another T-shirt in our house," I said, and everyone griped at once.

"Wait a minute, can't I just get one?" begged Caroline, "Mine is too small."

"Yeah, and I use those as my work shirts," Tim implored. "The ones I have are all stained."

"Okay, fine, one T-shirt per person, but no pennants." Didn't we come home with about ten Buddy Walk T-shirts and a carload of the National Down Syndrome Society blue and gold pennants. We met up with my family on the Upper West Side, around 106th street, and made our way to the start of the walk, where a band was playing. The actor Chris Burke who played Corky from the old TV show *Life Goes On* was there (he's been there every year I have), along with a few celebrities who have a connection to the event.

I took notice of the other families gathering here who were exactly like us: The packmule fathers carrying all the stuff, the brothers and sisters off and running, headed for face painting stations and the carnival games. Pulling up the rear were the kids with Down syndrome, some of whom squatted down, refusing to walk while the mothers encouraged them to move along. "You need to get up," they said in hushed voices. "People are going to trip over you." I felt right at home.

Cate decided to sit on one of the big rocks at the start of the walk and wouldn't move. "All right, you guys just go," I said to my family, as they looked at me for direction. "I'm gonna hang out here." My mother was exasperated and said, "She comes all the way here and doesn't even do the walk." I shrugged my shoulders and shooed them off. Having no agenda or to-do list to fulfill, I lay back on the big rock next to Cate, loving the sun's warmth on my face. (Mind you, I was gripping the back of Cate's shirt so I wouldn't lose her in all of this nirvana.) I couldn't help but revel in my ease. *What a road well traveled.*

Cate was about eight months old when we first attended the Buddy Walk. I was overwhelmed on arriving at the park, as we were absorbed into this sea of people with Down syndrome. I'd never seen so many people with the disability in my life: babies, toddlers, teenagers, and adults. I was vulnerable and lost, yet thrust into the middle of what essentially was a celebration. It was oddly reminiscent of the walk we took to see Cate in the hospital nursery after she was born. I was at the Buddy Walk, but not really present, just looking at each family, at each person with Down syndrome. It seemed that everyone but me was laughing and happy that day. I asked Tim if he felt like he belonged, because I wasn't sure I did.

My mom tried her best to make that first Buddy Walk the uplifting day the Stepping Stones staff said it would be. "Oh, Noelle, there's Corky from that TV show. Look how phenomenal he is." Given my narrow mindset at the time, I didn't appreciate all that he'd accomplished. My only thought was that I wanted to be the one to hold Cate in the BabyBjörn, to keep her close to me. I hoped that one day all of this would be totally normal, that I wouldn't always feel uneasy. And now here I was. The Buddy Walk was the same, but I was different.

That Cate had Down syndrome was no longer apparent to me, no longer the I-think-about-it-all-the-time kind of thing it used to be. In my life, there was Caroline, Cate, and Claire—each her own unique person. From my post on the rock, I was just enjoying a moment with my daughter, Cate. I wound up talking with parents who had older children with Down syndrome. I was curious to hear their take on inclusion practices and sports, but really more for the conversation than looking for answers.

I called Ange from the car on I-84 on our way home, "Don't get me wrong, I love going to the Buddy Walk. It's just I don't have the emotional need to go the way I used to," I said, filling her in on the trip.

"That's the same thing you say about your Down syndrome mother's group. How you love to go, but don't need to go as much anymore."

"Yeah, I guess that's right. I love talking with all of the women over a glass of wine. I guess it's more laid back for me now, where before I had more purpose in going. Needing to ask for advice on the latest issue de jour. These days I find myself telling the other moms not to worry, that some phase will pass or morph into something else. None of us necessarily has the answers, but we can relate to each other. And that's probably the most important thing anyway."

"You may not have all the answers, but you've come a long way."

"We both have. Hey, I gotta go, but I'll call you later."

I flipped my cell phone closed and wondered what I would do if I didn't have Angela to talk to. Almost as if he could read my mind, Tim asked, "Do you tell Ange everything—like really everything?" I smiled at him and turned away, clutching the phone in my lap, ignoring the fighting that was occurring in the seats behind me.

"Caroline, please, can I s'watch your DVD player?" begged Cate.

"No. You don't even take care of your own stuff. You'll just drop food all over it," said Caroline, having the upper hand.

"S'mom," whined Cate looking to turn her fortune. But no amount of prodding could distract me from my thoughts, and I nearly laughed out loud thinking how right Tim was. Ange and I had probably covered every possible topic from heaven to hair. *God I hope she doesn't get tired of hearing from me, because I'll never get tired of calling her.*

I kept my promise to Judy Linden, the former director of religious education at our church, and returned that October as a CCD teacher after a year's hiatus. When she retired, she had encouraged me to help the church in this ministry after she left, knowing how passionately I felt about the subject, "We can't take just any warm body, you know. Kids see right through those without faith." I selected grade six, figuring it was the last year I could teach Ryan without his being mortified.

The middle school years were impressionable ones, and my experiences with Noelle made me want to share my faith more than I ever had. A statement Ryan's new principal gave at his sixth grade parent breakfast stuck with me as well, and I needed to do something with it. "I moved from high school to middle school because the kids are still young enough to be saved," he preached from his podium in the cafeteria.

In preparing the first lesson, my mindset was noticeably different than when I'd tackled this before. Typically, I'd pour over the teacher's manual, previewing the suggested material, noting the content of what needed to be taught, and trying to get as much into my lesson as possible. I was instinctively a pleaser that way. Never had I deviated from what was expected of me.

Feeling more confident in my faith than ever, I skipped the textbook and made a list of the lessons I wanted to teach the kids this year: live your faith every day; say thank you prayers before asking ones; every person matters; God doesn't make mistakes; each of us has a gift we are meant to share. This last item, being closest to my heart, was what I would teach them first. Yes, I was a rebel with a cause.

The children listened intently as I opened the class with the parable of the talents. It tells of a wealthy man who entrusts his fortune to three of his servants while he is away. He allocates his money according to the promise of each of these men: to one he gives three bags of gold, to another two, and to the last he gives one. The key here is he wants them to use the money (i.e. the gift) as best as each could, which two of them do. The third man with the single bag of gold was fearful of losing the money and chose to bury it. To hide the gift away and do nothing with it.

From the expressions on my student's faces, I could see that they'd never heard this story before. We talked about its underlying message: how God wishes us to use the gifts He gives us, large or small, to the fullest. I spontaneously used Cate as an example of a person with only a little to give. "My best friend has a daughter with Down syndrome," I began and then abruptly stopped...*Oh my goodness, I'm so wrong. It's the opposite...* "She helped me see life more clearly. What a tremendous gift she shared."

When I told Noelle about my experience, she said, "I have goose bumps. That's what you wrote in Cate's baby card all those years ago. 'She was born to give love, receive love and teach us all...'"

I told Noelle how embarrassed I was to have initially thought so little of Cate's gifts. *Everyone has much to share if only we open our hearts.*

It was about halfway through Cate's fourth grade year when I received a call from an inner-city high school teacher, asking if I'd speak to her child development class about Down syndrome. She got my name from her colleague who was a neighbor of mine. This teacher explained that part of the curriculum was developmental disabilities, and she thought having a parent as a guest speaker would be an interesting way to cover the topic. "Sure," I said without hesitation. *Now here's a subject I can speak on without much preparation.*

Driving to the high school the morning of the talk, I felt sick to my stomach with nerves. To be honest, whenever I speak in front of a group, I get the same queasy sensation even if it's just raising my hand in a meeting to ask a question. Adding to my anxiety was the prospect of engaging a group of teenagers. I knew this was the age every adult dreads communicating with, and here I'd bargained to do so for forty-five minutes straight.

I met the teacher in the office and she took me to a large room full of students who were at first very quiet. I sat on a stool at the front of the room, took a deep breath, and reminded myself that all I needed to do was just be me. I opened by saying that I was not a teacher, not a doctor, that I did happen to be a lawyer (taking as a compliment one teen's outburst, "Lady, you don't look like a lawyer"), but I was there solely as a mom—a mom of a child with Down syndrome. I explained Down syndrome in simple terms, sharing some of its recognizable characteristics.

"You'll notice people with Down syndrome kind of look alike, sort of short with a broad neck, and have distinctive almond-shaped eyes." I added mental retardation to this list, telling them, "I hate even saying this term out loud, because, well, I just hate to say it, and when I was your age, I'd use the R-word in jest. Thank goodness there's the new, more palatable phrase of *intellectually disabled*." I told them about Caroline and Claire (that I had two typical children), and then I transitioned to my experiences with Cate.

I started with the day she was born, and found myself recanting what up to now I had only revealed to a select few women. How I was twenty-nine years old, had a normal pregnancy with normal test results, and how my world fell apart in just one second when the delivery room doctor said he suspected my baby had trisomy 21—the clinical term for Down syndrome. I shared with these strangers my honest emotions at that time, the words flowing from my mouth without a filter: "These are feelings I'm kind of ashamed of today," I said and talked about the sadness I tried to snap out of whenever it descended on me back then. "I'm happy to report I'm not the person I was so many years ago."

I was just about to tell them about Cate when a student raised his hand and asked, "Why didn't you give the baby up for adoption?" *Adoption—what? I'd never considered that. Not ever.* I caught myself lost for a moment, thinking back to that time still so vivid in my memory. "Adoption was never even a thought for me. Cate was always my baby."

I was about to continue, but there were a few more hands in the air. And so went the next hour: a spontaneous question and answer session with me speaking openly with teenagers who were asking honest, politically incorrect questions. I loved their questions as much as I loved talking to them.

"Are you embarrassed by her?" was the next question.

"Never, ever by her," I said truthfully, "but, sometimes I get embarrassed for her. Like when she took off her shirt at a soccer game because she was hot, or when she had a bathroom accident when she was in third grade. But never, ever by her."

The student who asked the question pressed the issue, "C'mon, don't you get embarrassed when you go to the store with her and people stare?"

"Honestly, I'm not sure people stare. Well, when she was a baby I did think that, but it was just my own insecurity. People may take a second look at her now, but I don't pay much attention. Still I think you make a good point. I probably have been embarrassed by her thousands of times, but not because she has Down syndrome. It's just because whenever one of your kids does or says something inappropriate, you get embarrassed. Perhaps these moments happen more with Cate, since she usually says the things most of us keep private. For example, yesterday I stopped to say hello to an elderly neighbor who, well, had truly gigantic ears with massive amounts of hair growing out of them. Cate interrupted our conversation asking, 'What's the matter with that guy's ears?' Thank God he was almost deaf."

Up went a roar of laughter.

A few more examples came to mind. "There was also the time when she tagged along to Claire's swimming lesson. While the instructor was working with Claire at the other end of the pool, I watched Cate, who couldn't swim, inch toward the water, despite my yelling at her not to do so. When I got up to grab her, she leapt in and was just beyond reach so I had to jump in to save her. Mind you, I couldn't get out of the pool because I was in jeans and a white T-shirt. This happens to be my uniform, but it didn't serve me well that day."

The kids egged me on to tell one more.

"Believe me, I could tell Cate stories all day. I've got tons of them. But my favorite might be the sweet-sixteen party where Cate ate about five thousand Cheez Doodles. The DJ played the music where you get up and do the conga line. She joined the line, grabbing on to the person in front of her who had on the tightest white pants ever. The woman left the line and all you could see were two perfect orange doodle-dust handprints on her butt. We left shortly after that."

I waited a moment before continuing, scanning this roomful of totally engaged teenagers. *I could talk about Cate's crazy antics all day, but I gotta move on.* "Okay, so once and for all, yes, I do get embarrassed because of her and by the chaos that she may cause, but only because she's just Cate. I'm never embarrassed because she has Down syndrome."

"What about her sisters, are they embarrassed by her?" was the next question.

"Now, that's a tougher one," I said mulling this over for a minute. "I think sometimes, they have been—yes. Mostly because she's not the 'norm.' She doesn't pay attention to social protocols, like the way she sits in the last seat of the bus when everyone knows that's for the oldest kids. She doesn't care. That's where the fun is. To understand Cate you need to know that she's always this way. She always does what she wants.

"She refers to adults by last name only, so when she says goodbye to the principal, she says, 'See ya later Smith.' Instead of putting on shoes for school, she might wear socks with flip-flops, slipping them between her fourth and pinky toes. She's barged into her sisters' classrooms accusing them of stealing her lunch because she got turkey instead of ham. She tells Claire's friends that she's their friend, not Claire. She walks around in her nightgown with no undies when their friends sleep over, or worse, she may sleep totally naked. She runs over to high-five the players on Caroline's soccer team at the end of every game as if she helped them win. And Caroline hates it.

"But there have been times, too, when they've been embarrassed for her. Many times, when Cate was sitting in the back of the bus, the older kids would ask her to say bad words and do inappropriate things, like 'Cate, say lesbian' or 'Cate, lick the seat.' She said and did all these things, thinking she was being funny. Caroline told Cate each time to be quiet and ignore what the kids were saying. But Cate probably liked the attention and ignored Caroline.

"Cate got off the bus one afternoon saying, 'Hate those boys, hate 'em, hate 'em, hate 'em.' I had no idea what she was talking about. She quickly went off on a tangent, asking if she could have a lemon and started talking about going to the movie store. Caroline walked in with a red face and watery eyes. Tears streamed down her cheeks when she began to tell me what the kids were doing.

Caroline told me she just couldn't take it any more. She stood up and told them to shut up, and stop making fun of Cate. The kids Caroline yelled at were the cool kids on the bus, making it that much harder for her. It was a heartbreaking day for me, a day Caroline grew up a little, a day that probably didn't affect Cate at all."

I needed to shift away from this topic, so I said, "Okay, now I have a question for you. Do you think my other daughters are ever jealous of Cate?" Before they could reply I jumped in: "I never anticipated it, but yes, they do get jealous sometimes. In their words, 'Cate always gets her way because she's *special*.' Kindness is showered on Cate in ways I could never have imagined. She gets special gifts, freebies, and passes. She gets a prize for playing the arcade game even though she doesn't win. She gets the extra trophy at all of Caroline's sporting events. She doesn't get reprimanded by a store manager when she shoplifts. She cuts in line and nobody says anything.

"To be sure, it's not all hard on Caroline and Claire. They've learned to milk the system along with Cate. When they walk by the bakery at the grocery store they'll say, 'C'mon Cate, you wanna go get a cookie?' knowing full well they've got a good shot at getting a free one if they approach the counter with her. Same deal at the carnival: they'll walk up to a game with Cate by their side, hoping to play for free, and maybe get a prize out of it. Best of all was the special needs pass at Disney World when we went last summer. We called Cate 'The Wonka Ticket' as we stood in the fast pass lane at every ride. She even wound up with an Italian boyfriend there."

"An Italian boyfriend?" one kid said.

"Yeah, it was really hot the afternoon we toured Epcot. Cate was basically done and we were deciding whether or not to call it a day, when a street show started and everyone sat down. I wandered into an apothecary in search of air conditioning and Cate followed behind me. I lifted a bottle of perfume and saw her sitting at a wrought iron table, across from a young, handsome Disney employee with an Italian accent. He was holding her hands in his, talking to her, and listening to everything she had to say. I walked over and said, 'Oh, you've met my daughter, Cate.'"

With a suave accent he said, "I am Roberto, and this is my girlfriend, the beautiful Catie."

"He then took a strand of chunky Wilma Flintstone pearls off the display and put them on her. Cate was smiling and actually wore them, which was strange. She's usually psycho about having things on her. He talked to us for a few minutes more, mostly concentrating on Cate. In getting ready to leave, I motioned to take the pearls off Cate, stopping short when he said, 'No, those are for my girlfriend, Catie.' She still has the necklace in a dresser drawer."

I tried to figure out where this discussion was headed when there were more hands, more questions: Could Cate have children and if she could, would they be mentally retarded? Was I afraid to have more children? Could she get married? Will she drive a car? Does she have friends? Will she ever be able to live by herself? Do you wish she didn't have Down syndrome?

This last question I could answer with certainty. I told them that when I had Cate, I often wondered what she would look like if she didn't have Down syndrome. "In the beginning I saw Down syndrome in everything about Cate. In how she looked, in what she did, in what she couldn't do. And it was more than that. I wondered who she would be without Down syndrome. How time has changed me.

"I wish Cate didn't have to struggle with some of the medical stuff she does. Or that it didn't have to be so hard for her to do things that come easily to the rest of us. But having Down syndrome is who Cate is. They're not separate. If Cate didn't have Down syndrome, Cate wouldn't be Cate. And you know what? I wouldn't be who I am today. Tim, Caroline, and Claire—none of us would be. If Cate didn't have Down syndrome, I wouldn't be here talking to you today. Oh my gosh, you have to know: I wouldn't change a thing.

"Having Cate in my life, I see the goodness in people that I probably wouldn't have seen otherwise. I've met people I never would have met otherwise. She receives so much kindness and I'm so thankful when I see people go out of their way for her and how it makes Cate feel. These acts of kindness that are shown to Cate make me realize how we need to be this way with everyone. And you guys, I'm not just talking about people with disabilities.

"We need to treat each person in the same manner. That's what Cate does. She doesn't recognize one person being different from another. Being nice to Cate is easy for most of us because we perceive her as less than us. She's the underdog. But Cate doesn't do that to others. She treats everyone the same—from the principal, to the custodian, to the most popular student in school. Now whether that's with respect or disrespect on Cate's part is the real issue, but either way it's the same." The group laughed and with every eye still focused on me, I continued on.

"You guys, it's so nice to say hi to the kid in the wheelchair, to make him feel included. But you should extend that same friendship to everybody the way Cate does. This means being nice to anyone you perceive as different from you. Different because she's not in your group of friends. Different because he's a nerd and not a jock. Different because she doesn't wear the right clothes. Cate doesn't have the prejudgments we are burdened with, that make us act differently with different people.

"Cate has this wide group of people she knows, whom I now know. There's this girl at Dunkin' Donuts who has a million piercings, who greets Cate at 6 a.m. on Saturday mornings with 'Hey Cate, ya going for the strawberry frosted or the chocolate stick today?' This girl is awesome, but I wouldn't have made the effort to see that without her kindness to my daughter, without my daughter's interaction with her. It's all good. She taught me to get past the earrings in this girl's nose and tongue to see the whole person. I didn't teach Cate compassion, she taught it to me.

"You know those kids you don't even take notice of in the hallway because you assume they're nobody? By just saying hello to them as you pass their lockers you've made a difference. If you and a friend sit down with someone at lunch who is by himself, that kid will not feel ignored. I know you're looking at me thinking, 'Yeah right lady,' but I'm serious. Not only can you do these little things. They matter a lot." You could hear a pin drop in that room, so I made one more point.

"When I was your age, I guess you could say I was part of a popular crowd. Silly as it sounds, we had this place called Jock Lounge—I know, how ridiculous. It had bench seats lining either side of a hallway. And I remember sitting and talking there with my friends, and some of the guys making fun of the kids walking past us. On occasion I'm sure I laughed right along with them. God, I could kick myself. I didn't get it until I was older, but you can get it now. Here's your opportunity to be compassionate, to make a life better by doing simple, kind acts. Acts that require no effort on your part can have a long-lasting impact on someone else. I don't mean to sound preachy, but I know it. I get it now and I hope you do, too."

I had no idea my talk would head in this direction, but here I was in this stream of consciousness mode of saying out loud what I guess I had come to believe. So many conversations with Angela spilling over with this crowd before me, my stool in this random place turned pulpit. The bell rang signaling the end of class and after we finished a few kids came up to me without the prompting of an adult, "That was fun, Mrs. Alix. Thanks."

"I so enjoyed talking with you. Thanks for listening and I

hope you got something out of it, mostly that you all have this great easy gift you can give. To just be yourself with everyone."

I couldn't dial Ange's phone number quickly enough when I got into my car. "That talk was nothing like I expected. I wound up speaking more about my own life, my own understanding, my own happiness—everything we've talked about, Ange. And I think they really listened."

"What I would give to have been a fly on the wall. I bet you made quite an impression."

"I hope so, because it felt right to share it, to share all of it. Oh, no, there's a cop. I'll call you later." I pulled the phone away from my ear and heard Ange in a far-away voice say her Italian goodbye, "Ciao, amica."

◦◦◦

It was late in July and the second week of swimming lessons at Winding Trails for the kids. I pulled in to unload our stuff and saw that the car was cockeyed enough in the parking spot that I had to fix it. I sent the kids ahead so not to be late, set my bag in the spot next to me, and hopped into the car. In turning the key in the ignition, I saw a woman speeding at me in her electric wheelchair. I rolled down my window after rolling my eyes and said, "I know my bags are there. I'm just straightening out."

"No, no," this woman said with a slur, "I wanted to tell you. Your hair s'beautiful."

I put my foot on the brake, "You just made my day."

"S'natural?"

"Yes," I said, nodding.

"You rat," she said with a bright smile, and I laughed out loud.

"Watch out," I told her, "I'm just going to straighten out, and then I'd like to talk with you." I pulled back into my spot, when she said through my open window.

"S'not just your hair. You're beautiful."

"My gosh, thank you so much," I said and stepped out of the car.

"Uh, skinny, too! Metabolism?"

"Yes, but my mom says that's going to stop when I turn fifty."

"How old now?"

"I'm forty."

"S'not fun getting old. Lose taste. Get fat. Can't do things."

"But look at you," I said. "You're so pretty." And she was in the way she cared about herself, from the lovely blouse she wore, to her neatly pulled back hair, to her eyeglasses that hung from a strand of faux pearls. She smiled and said, "I love you," and reached her face up to mine with pursed lips. I bent down and we kissed each other on the cheek.

"I'm so happy to have a new friend," I said. "What's your name?"

"Marie."

"Oh, that's my middle name. My first name is Angela."

"Really?" she said beaming.

"I've got to catch up with my kids, but it was nice to meet you, Marie." I picked up my things, waved at her and turned for the lake. In crossing the parking lot and heading for the picnic area, I began to cry at the thought of how fortunate I was for this exchange. To be open to this woman and appreciative of what made her beautiful as much as she saw beauty in me.

I wondered in that walk to find my boys, how many Maries I'd passed by in my life without a thought, whom I'd blown quickly by with just a nod and a smile. I don't know why Marie had difficulty with her speech, or why she was in a wheelchair. It didn't matter.

All I felt was gratefulness in having met her now, at this time in my life, and how I hoped to see her again.

20

EXPECTATIONS

Girls in Skins and Eggs in Bodies

Let us be still an instant and
forget all things we ever learned,
all thoughts we had and every preconception
that we hold of what things mean and what their purpose is.
Let us remember not our own ideas
of what the world is for—we do not know.
Let every image held of everyone be loosened
from our minds and swept away.

From *A Course in Miracles*

The school bus has always been an issue for Cate, not a major one, but certainly a place where she's been known to get into trouble. It's where most kids learn there's no Santa Claus, where they probably hear their first swear words, and maybe even talk about the birds and the bees. The further you sit in the back, the more educated a child becomes. And in Cate's instance, the stronger the temptation was to misbehave.

Now that she was older, I thought she was past playing truth or dare (licking the seat, saying swears) and could return to sitting in her coveted spot in the back. I was also looking for ways to let her be more independent (my latest issue de jour) and it seemed like a great opportunity to move her in this direction. The privilege didn't last long, however, when she listened to some kid who suggested she open the emergency door. By the fifth day of fifth grade, Cate was indefinitely banished to the front seat. The one right behind the bus driver.

As had long been my routine, I emptied Cate's backpack after school a few weeks later looking for some shred of evidence about what she did that day. Amidst a few books and crumpled worksheets was a stack of papers held together with an oversized magnetic clip. It looked like typed lists, but with handwritten notes. *What is this? She must have taken it from the teacher or something.* I put the clipped stack in the pile of papers on the counter and forgot about it.

About a week or two later, I was talking with the other moms at the bus stop waiting for the kids to come home when we saw the school bus turn onto Cedar Mill Drive, a street we didn't think the driver should take.

"Oh, great," my neighbor Kristen said, "it's a month into school and this bus driver still doesn't know the route." I immediately had a flashback: *That stack of papers from Cate's backpack… With that huge magnetic clip…The handwritten notes next to columns of type… Oh my God, I think the bus route is on my kitchen counter!*

As soon as the kids got off the bus and I finished chatting with my neighbors, I went into the house to dig through the pile of papers in my kitchen. From it I pulled out the clipped stack and sure enough it was the route for Bus 58, which had now been in my possession for over a week. *Caaaate!*

On closer inspection of the cover page, there were a series of columns: one of times, one of streets and house numbers with reminder notes jotted down next to some of them: "Wait for mom at stop;" "No pm drop off;" "Large group." *What possessed her to steal the bus route?*

I picked up the phone to call Ange. It took a minute for her to stop laughing before I could ask what she thought Cate's motivation might be. "Do you think she took it because she steals everything? You know, it was just something to take? Or was she pissed off about sitting in the front seat and took it out of spite?"

"First off, you'll never figure her out. But for what it's worth, my money's on what's behind door number two."

That afternoon Cate and I took Mabel for a walk and I asked Cate about taking the clip of papers (a.k.a., the bus route). Her response was typical: "S'wasn't me, s'was Caroline." Who knows if she even remembered taking it, but regardless, Cate never accepts the blame for anything. Her first response is always to blame someone else, her second is to deny, deny, deny and every once in a blue moon, if she's really backed into a corner, she might respond with an abrupt: "I said s'was sorry."

"Cate you need to tell the truth," I said calmly, even though I knew it was like convincing a brick wall to soften up a little. "I'm not mad. Just tell me if you took the bus driver's list." Her reply was exactly what I expected: "S'Mom, like I said, s'wasn't me." *Am I ever going to be able to trust you?*

Still, I knew I had to try and trust her, to let her do some things on her own the way other kids her age did. It wasn't fair to hold Cate back just because it made me nervous when I gave her those tastes of freedom. Though I looked for safe independent experiences for Cate, covering what I think are all the bases, she always did something I didn't see coming. In allowing her to sit at the back of the bus, I didn't anticipate she'd open the emergency door. She knew not to do that. And I certainly never thought she'd steal the bus driver's route in accepting her punishment to sit at the front. Then again, this was just Cate for whom every stage has not been exactly what I expected. I had the wrinkles and the laugh lines to prove it.

Noelle and I met in my town's center one afternoon to pick out a wedding gift for a friend and catch up with each other. She had just spent a marathon week on a closing for work and was eager for the company and a change of scenery. We walked along, peering into shop windows and sharing stories of the days since we'd last seen each other.

We turned the corner from Main Street to Farmington Avenue, and up the sidewalk came a blonde-haired woman with Down syndrome. She was completely pulled together with a quick, city walk. Her eyes were aimed straight ahead of her, a hand clenched onto the strap of her pocketbook that was neatly hooked over her right shoulder. We stared in quiet awe as this very capable-looking woman continued past us.

"Did you see that?" Noelle asked when the woman was beyond earshot, turning to me with an expression of joy and surprise. "She's amazing!"

"Absolutely fabulous," I said and we both watched her walk off, peeking into storefronts now and again when something caught her eye.

"She's just out shopping on a beautiful afternoon," Noelle said, the two of us still staring, stunned by this woman.

We continued along after a time, walking side-by-side in silence as if through the hallways of St. Mary's School. The difference today was our silence was self-imposed, each of us mindful of what we'd just witnessed. Although neither of us said a word on the subject while I walked Noelle to her car and we bid each other goodbye, I know in our hearts we both hoped it would be Cate someday.

ℒ—

Cate at 11: Presented an oral powerpoint presentation to the class about seals; can verbalize all her thoughts, but writing sentences is still difficult; can tell time to the five minutes; can add two single digit numbers together; can not yet subtract from ten; still working on tying her shoes; draws people with a head, body, arms and legs (adds the fingers to the whole arm); can ride a two wheeler independently without training wheels.

Later that schoolyear, a letter came home from Cate's teacher explaining that this year's health curriculum would include the topic of sexual reproduction. *What's she going to think of this?* I mentioned the letter to Tim when we were crossing paths that night in the kitchen. Even though he was the father of three girls, this wasn't his favorite topic. "Uh, I'm gonna let you handle that," he said, assuming this was my territory and quietly retreated to the garage. Cate was rummaging through the refrigerator when I took her by the hand. "Come here, Sticky. Sit down."

"S'mom, what?" she asked, swiping the bag of hot chips off the counter while I took a deep breath. *Okay, here goes.* "This year in school you're going to learn about your body, boys' bodies, and what happens to your body when you get older." I explained with her munching away. "Do you have anything you want to ask me about?"

"S'I have a s'juice box?"

Okay, zippo, all done with that.

I had totally forgotten about it until a few weeks later when I picked up the girls from school and as usual, all three were talking at once. Amidst the chatter I heard Cate say, "Mrs. Leathe talked to the girls today."

"Ooooh!" Caroline said in her adolescent way, psyched to know something before I did. "They had the big sex talk."

I hit the brakes. "Oh, Cate, what did she say?" I asked half-hesitating to hear, the way you look at a car wreck, but don't really want to see what happened.

"I dunno," she said poking a straw into her Capri Sun. "Girls in skins. Eggs in bodies." *What?* At first all I could think of was that Hannibal Lector movie where the serial killer was making something out of female skins. After a few minutes of Caroline and me trying to decipher what she meant, we settled on two topics: acne and taking care of your skin and ovaries and getting your period. *Okay, we can handle those.*

After dinner that night, I told Tim about the conversation with Cate in the car and he got the shivers, trying to shake off any thought of his girls growing up or having to cope with what was coming.

"Do we need to talk about this," he asked and started putting dishes in the dishwasher to get off the subject. I sat at the kitchen table and pulled out Cate's homework to find a basic study sheet with a few words about the water cycle and the word reservoir was on there. "Reservoir?" I said, surprised. "Why does she need to know what that is?" And then thought to myself: *What's a reservoir anyway?*

If I hadn't recognized that Cate was growing up before, it hit me now in reviewing the highlights of her school day. *Okay so she had the sex talk and is learning about reservoirs—both of which are beyond her.* I began to breathe more quickly picturing Cate in the middle of all of this. Getting bits and pieces of what her fifth grade classmates were learning. *And here I still tie her shoes. Sometimes I help her get dressed. I cut her pancakes.*

While I wanted Cate to learn as much as she could academically, I recognized the bigger goal was that she have the skills to be able to live her life independently. She needed to be strong in math in order to use money to go shopping, make change, and not be cheated. She needed to read at a fifth grade level to understand a newspaper and use public transportation. She needed to be able to speak well enough to be understood by people who didn't know her. And there were probably a hundred more important skills.

I knew I couldn't baby Cate all the time, even though I did more than I should. That this wasn't going to help her have the kind of life I'd like her to have. A life very different from the one I had envisioned when she was a baby.

I called Ange about the day and our conversation evolved to Cate's future, where my brain still naturally gravitates. "I've always thought we'd put on an addition when Cate grew up so she could have her own space, but still be with us."

"I think Cate might have other plans."

"But I can't imagine her not living with us, Ange. Doesn't she need Tim and me as much as we need her?"

"I've always thought that Cate was born with wings. Just like the rest of us."

"I know, you're right. My daughter with her my-way-or-the-highway, bus-driver-be-damned attitude probably isn't going to settle for some nice, prearranged future."

"And that's a good thing."

"But how will I ever let her go?"

"Vodka," she said and we laughed. "But, seriously, I don't think moms ever really let their kids go. You'll always have that big piece of Cate."

"I guess, but there's so much that goes into a day, so much to worry about: the showering, the laundry, the cooking, the transportation to and from work. Oh my God, work—showing up on time, staying focused, having a good attitude, not taking a two-hour lunch."

"Aw, reminds me of your dad, and he did fine even though he probably never got to work on time, and was more focused on telling jokes than working."

"It's so true—and those long Little Italy escapades he'd take me on when I worked with him, and we only had a half-hour for lunch."

"You'll get her there, Noelle."

"Yeah, I will."

And I did believe it, more and more every day. Cate was a person who was going to do something with her life (what exactly I had no idea), but it would be something she wanted to do. A few years ago, such uncertainty would have thrown me into a full-blown anxiety attack. But now I knew that I needed to hold Cate's future in the same realm as Caroline and Claire's: to keep my expectations high, but entirely undefined. To encourage and teach, yes, to dictate, no. I needed to be confident that Cate would be okay, the way I assumed Caroline and Claire would be.

❧

Noelle called me one evening a few weeks later, desperate for a shopping partner. The three times a year we go shopping, one convinces the other to tag along because it always winds up being a fun adventure. So I said yes, hoping that it wouldn't involve looking for stylish shoes to fit her size 5, triple-E feet because they didn't exist. Believe me, we've looked.

"Actually, I need a pair of black high heels for a meeting I have in New York tomorrow. Please still be my friend."

"You have to know the only possible reason I'm going to endure this torture is because I love you."

At that late hour and with those difficult parameters (small wide feet and no time), it unfortunately meant a trip to the mall, a place where you could easily get distracted by things you didn't need. My goal was to keep us focused. Not two minutes into our mission, we ran into Father Mike, the new parish priest at Noelle's church. He was fumbling with his cell phone and looking a little stressed.

"Father Mike, what are you doing here?" Noelle asked, far more interested in his objective than ours. "Well, I was actually trying to call my mother to ask her opinion about a couch I saw for the rectory. Macy's is having a sale and what we have is in terrible shape."

"Oh my goodness, we'll help you with that," Noelle said, immediately going off-task. "This is my best friend, Angela. She's got a great eye and actually has picked out most of the furniture in my house."

An hour later, after steering him away from the ugly sofa he'd picked, finding one we liked, and encouraging him to buy a side chair as well, we suggested he set a budget and negotiate with the salesperson. As if it were legal advice, Noelle directed, "Here's what you say: I want all of it—the couch, the chair, and delivery—for this price. I'll buy it today or I'm walking." Father Mike was convinced, but the salesperson wasn't. So we walked.

At this point I thought that we would politely go our separate ways, but we wound up in a conversation about the upcoming presidential election. Father Mike said a parishioner recently chastised him for promoting a political party in a sermon, but that he was just sharing Catholic doctrine.

"Jesus, I can't believe that," Noelle said and I didn't know whether to laugh out loud or jab her in the ribs. *He may be wearing jeans, but he's still a priest!* We went off on three other tangents and then somehow landed on the topic of purgatory.

"Do you really believe in that, Father Mike?" Noelle asked. My thoughts jumped to the fact that it was actually his job to believe it.

"Oh, yes," he quickly said. "That's where most of us wind up."

"What is it exactly?" she asked, genuinely interested in his reply.

"I like to think of purgatory as having really bad seats at a concert. You know, you can hear the music, but can't see the stage."

I loved the analogy of this place (where your soul is purified before going to heaven), and actually would have enjoyed talking with him a while longer. But it was 9:30 p.m. and the mall was closing, so I interjected, "Well, it was so nice to meet you."

Noelle shot me a look as we said our goodbyes to Father Mike. We stepped into The Walking Company store just before they locked the gates. "What's up with you?"

"The mall is about to close. Don't you need shoes?"

"Whatever, it really doesn't matter," she said and then asked, "Remember that ring I got you a couple years ago? The one that says, 'Live on the edge.' You've gotta wear that way more often."

"Yeah, yeah, yeah—hey, what are these?" I asked, pulling a chic, patent leather Mary Jane pump off the shelf.

Noelle slipped it on her foot for a perfect fit just like Cinderella. "See, Ange. You've just gotta believe."

ॐ

Like most kids, Caroline and Claire naturally have become more independent as they've gotten older. The simple things I used to do for them or help them with, they began doing on their own one day without me even taking notice. Everyday things like picking out their own clothes, taking a shower, tying their own shoes, making brownies, calling a friend. The difference with Cate was that whenever she did the same things on her own, it usually made me cringe.

She'd walk downstairs ready for school wearing the chocolate lab outfit I detest (brown furry sweater, brown leggings, brown furry socks, brown headband). I'd watch her step out of the shower with a head full of shampoo and proceed to put her pajamas on backwards. I'd get a phone call from Syd's mom telling me that Cate called at 4:30 a.m. to see if Syd could play.

The outcomes weren't much better when I began giving her responsibilities outside of the house, like sending her on errands to my neighbor Paula's house. I might send her for milk or an egg to have her return twenty minutes later eating a lemon and holding a PlayStation game.

"Cate, where's the stuff I asked you to get?"

"S'what stuff?"

What I didn't foresee was that it opened the door for Cate to think she could go next door whenever she wanted to, on a mission for me or not.

Our phone rang at 5:00 a.m. one Saturday morning. It was my neighbor Paula's husband, Bill, calling to let me know that Cate was at their house. I must have still been asleep and answered him, "Cate, oh, okay."

Trying to catch me he said, "Wait, Noelle, don't hang up... she's gonna tell you I was naked, and I swear I had my boxers on."

What the heck is he talking about?

"I let Dutch out and went back to sleep. When I heard him inside, it didn't make sense. So I went downstairs and Cate was in the kitchen. She asked me why I was naked, but I swear I had my boxers on."

Poor Bill was worried I thought he was Chester the Molester when it was my daughter who broke into his house. (She can remember their security code but still has the word "of" in her hard word book—grr.) She walked in the door five minutes later wearing a *High School Musical* nightgown, her hair looking like squirrels were nesting in it. "Why in God's name did you go to the Teed's house?"

"S'Mom, my tooth s'loose."

My neighbor Paula is a dental hygienist, so all my kids have done the same, hoping for an immediate extraction—just not at 5:00 in the morning.

This is where the thought of letting Cate be independent always made me stop. Not only was she unpredictable, her judgment was off. You don't walk into someone's house at 5:00 a.m. to tell them your tooth is loose. Debating in my brain over whether or not there would be a better time for her to practice independence was futile. Bottom line: if I didn't continue to give Cate the opportunities to be independent, she never would be. And that wouldn't be fair to her.

One morning I asked Cate to help me make scrambled eggs. I gave her the discrete steps: getting the eggs out, getting a bowl and fry pan, cracking the eggs, etc. I had her put the bread in the toaster oven. When the buzzer went off signaling the toast was done, she opened the toaster oven and put her hand right on the heating element and burned her fingertips.

"You only touch the bread, Cate, nothing else." *I should have told her that first.*

The next morning I heard lots of banging. When the noise continued I decided to see what was up. I found Cate in the kitchen making eggs, wearing the blue chenille robe my sister gave her last Christmas (if it wasn't in the wash, it was on her body). At least a dozen eggs were cracked and poured into various pots—big saucepots, little saucepots, a casserole dish, the Bundt pan—with egg drippings and shell fragments all over. One egg even made it into the silverware drawer.

"Cate, please, only do this when you ask Mommy."

"Sorry, s'Mom."

I turned on the coffee machine and said, "Let's start over." I taught her again how to make eggs, one simple step at a time, adding to my list of rules that you only use two eggs and you can never turn on the stove. "You need to come get me first." (I will forever have this nagging fear that she'll drag her shirtsleeve through the flame.)

With this second cooking lesson, Cate's confidence in the kitchen grew along with her egg-making prowess. She soon expanded her repertoire to include waffles, cereal, sandwiches, and other seemingly harmless meals, including packing lunches, which was more of a hassle for Tim than a danger to her. Tim was lunch-man unless he worked late, and then the hated job fell to me.

Tim arrived home one night after the kids had gone to bed, and he came into my office to ask if I'd made lunches.

"Actually, I didn't get to it yet," I said, annoyed at the thought that I should be in my office at this god-awful hour and already have made lunches. He ducked out of my office to avoid the derogatory words about to fly from my mouth and a few minutes later yelled from the kitchen, "Come here, Noelle. You've gotta see this!"

When I got to the kitchen, Tim opened Cate's lunch box to show me the contents: exact change for milk, yogurt with a spoon, whole ham sandwich (uncut), and a napkin. She didn't do as well for Caroline who had a jar of relish and Claire who had ten cents for milk and a Mike's Hard Lemonade. The Department of Children and Families might not agree, but I really felt like we were making progress.

～ฺ

Ryan's sixth grade special education teacher understood him and his learning disability in a way no one had. It was a year of teamwork between her and us; with e-mails back and forth every few days to stay in touch on his progress. This was personalized instruction as I'd never seen it, using prior data on standardized test scores like items on a to-do list. "Let's work on these areas," his teacher, Leslie, offered.

How I wished it would continue and yet here we were at another end-of-year PPT meeting. Leslie took Rob and me aside before we left to acknowledge a note I'd written to her boss about her efforts.

"Thank you for your kind words, but it's not me. You must realize you have an incredible son." I attempted to hold up my guard, but failed miserably as the tears surfaced while Leslie continued.

"I think about him on Saturday afternoons when I see my own brother in the garage building something. When I saw Ryan ushering in his tuxedo at the school play, I pictured him at the junior prom. He's a great kid. I don't often have a student like Ryan or this kind of relationship with parents. And your younger son—he's a cutie. Does he come to middle school next year?"

"He'll be here in two years, and I hope he's on your team. He's different from Ryan, who has more of my creative side. John's creative, too, but he's got that Martin math mind."

"That must be the joy of being a parent—seeing the uniqueness in each child."

"Well, I didn't realize that in the beginning. With two boys two years apart, I began mothering them with this same-same mentality. Understanding each child, raising each child to find his own gift, to understand who he is and what makes him happy? That came over time."

I hugged her before leaving the room and in walking to my car, I was overcome with gratitude. I dialed Noelle's home number as if it were reflex and told her about our meeting.

"You know, Ange, she was celebrating Ryan in a way no other teacher has. It was always that he didn't fit into their box."

"She saw the whole person, that there isn't just one path. Sitting in some lecture hall is not who Ryan is. He'll go to college for art, maybe get into graphic design, or animation—there's so much he could do. And, for John, who knows? With his penchant of sticking to a position, he may wind up in your profession."

"As any lawyer will tell you, I hope not," Noelle said with a chuckle and then cautioned, "Just don't get too caught up in exactly what your boys should become. That's their journey."

⚬

By the springtime, I noticed that the moms in the neighborhood weren't standing with the kids in the morning. I was used to walking Cate and Claire out with the dog, but it seemed now was the time to let them wait for the bus without me hovering over them. Things appeared to be going well (which should have tipped me off that they weren't) when I got a call from the school secretary asking how I answered my phone.

"What?"

"Cate brought your home phone to school today, Mrs. Alix."

When I asked Cate about it later she said, "S'wanted to call you, s'Mom."

So in addition to the zillion other things the morning entailed, I now had to frisk Cate in search of contraband before she left for school. I looked in the pockets of her jacket, combed through her backpack, checked out the lunch box. You'd think she might catch on, but every day there was a new find: random pictures, her Game Boy, the portable DVD player, Caroline's wallet. Again, I mistakenly assumed that this was a fail-proof strategy until I got an 8:30 a.m. call with "Town of Simsbury" on the caller ID. *Geez Louise, has school even started yet?*

"Hi, Noelle, it's Mary Ellen," the school nurse said. "I just wanted to make sure you wanted Cate to take a nap today."

"You've got to be kidding, Mary Ellen."

"Cate came in off the bus, went to the bathroom in my office and walked out with her nightgown and robe on. She said that you said she could take a nap and proceeded to find a blanket and lie down on a cot."

"Mary Ellen, c'mon. And not for anything, I can't get that silly robe off her."

"I knew it. Okay, so I'm going to tell her she needs to get dressed and go to class."

"You're a saint Mary Ellen," I said, realizing we were both played as fools in Cate's premeditated plan. I had no idea what she wanted to miss that day, but it involved duping me. For the balance of the day, I was preoccupied with wondering how she got the nightgown and robe by me. *I thought I checked her backpack this morning.*

A few weeks later, the girls left for the bus stop when I realized Claire had forgotten something so I went out after her. I caught Cate in the garage quickly grabbing something and stuffing it into her backpack. *That's how she does it!* "Hand it over, Stick," I said as she let out a sigh, passed me a video, and said, "S'Mom, I s—a—y watching *Home Alone* today."

For all of my expectations for Cate when she was a baby, now only one remained: she'd always be one step ahead of me.

There probably wasn't much to hold Cate back the way I used to think everything would. Though the possibilities for her weren't limitless (the whole world wasn't her oyster), they were far more varied than I pictured even just a few years ago when I projected my own hopes for my kids on them.

In first grade, Caroline wrote a story about what she wanted to be when she grew up. To my horror, it was a dog-walker. Even though this profession pays a decent salary in Manhattan, it wasn't enough for me. I pictured her becoming a doctor, setting what I thought was the highest possible goal for her at age two. At the time, I couldn't help but delicately encourage her to set her sights higher: "How about becoming a veterinarian, Caroline?"

I had the same line of thinking about Cate years ago when the manager at our grocery store approached us. Cate was frantically self-scanning items and stuffing them into bags. "There's our favorite little bagger," he said.

As the kids have gotten older the "What do I want to be when I grow up?" conversation has continued, but my perspective has changed. The other day when it came up at the dinner table, Cate chimed in. She told us she wanted to have five jobs, "S'work at Dunkin' Donuts, s'McDonalds, Shop Shop Shop, bagel store, and s'be a gym teacher."

Caroline sees not the improbability of holding five jobs simultaneously, but the practically of it. "Mom, Cate could never work at all those places. Imagine how fat she'd be."

To which Cate replied, "Caroline, cut it."

Later that week in braving the basement to clean up the craft table (a nice name for this junky old table we repurposed), I found a piece of paper with Claire's handwriting in purple crayon. The title, "Things I want to be when I grow up," was underlined three times and followed by this ten-point list:

1. Photographer
2. Designer with my friend, Gabby
3. Model
4. Actress
5. Singer
6. Singer/actress
7. The next Miley Cyrus or Beyoncé
8. Softball player
9. Do famous people's hair or makeup
10. When 16, work at Best Buy

There was a side column that was boxed out and entitled, "Definitely Not:"

1. An ER doctor
2. A professional bowler
3. Someone without a job

I burst out laughing at this insight into Claire's dreams. *I always wanted to be a hairdresser, too.*

Every now and again I catch myself daydreaming about what the future might hold for my girls. As for Cate, I picture her having a life of her own, an independent life, a life where she'll have a job, an apartment, maybe a husband, who knows? All I can say for certain is that I want Cate to have a great life, a happy life, a life she wants. And now whenever she has a bad day, or a day when she's in over her head I think: *Damn, there's a lot of work I have to do to get her there.* I guess we both still have our mountains to climb.

21

ACCEPTANCE

Jimmy the Chin

I believe
fate smiled and destiny
laughed as she came to my cradle
"know this child will be able"
laughed as my body she lifted
"know this child will be gifted
with love, with patience and with faith
she'll make her way."

Natalie Merchant
Lyrics to *Wonder*

ate's erratic sleeping pattern had been a major issue de jour for me ever since she was little. Come evening, she'd typically fall sound asleep around 8 p.m., sleep pretty well until about midnight, then become restless—sitting up, lying down, getting up, lying down again—until she got up for the day around 5 a.m. Such poor sleep probably impacted her at school, where some days it was as if she put in a full day before even getting there.

Tim and I were accustomed to her nighttime routine, having had no deviation from it in ten years, and assumed this was just how Cate was wired. But at the insistence of the pulmonologist, I made an appointment for her to have a second sleep study. Cate's first one was performed when she was about three years old at a Boston clinic the day before we rushed her to the ER with RSV and double viral pneumonia. So the results were inaccurate.

The unpleasant memory of that first sleep study prevented me from scheduling another one until now. And yet, the latest threat from the pulmonologist that they would remove the prescription from her file (such that we would lose the opportunity to have the test done) lit a fire under me. I found a sleep center in Connecticut that was not only forty-five minutes away, but also had a cancellation so we could get right in.

Cate and I arrived at the facility for our preliminary visit to meet with the sleep doctor. After all the questions and intake, he took us to see the room where the sleep study would be performed. Cate thought it was a hotel room and was excited; you could bring food, watch movies, and go with your mom without having to share a bed or the TV with your sisters. Cate couldn't wait.

The packing began that afternoon even though the sleep study wasn't for another month. She packed her robe, books, bathing suits, pajamas, picture frames, movies, towels, flip-flops—you name it. For the next month, I unpacked that damn suitcase every afternoon, only to find it packed again come evening. As was the case with all of Cate's jobs, I ultimately gave up and let her keep the suitcase packed, pulling things out when she needed them.

When the day for the sleep study arrived, Cate was ready to go before school started. She'd written a permission note that said she was leaving early to go to the hotel with her mom, even though we didn't need to be there until 7 p.m. In leaving for the bus, she alerted me that we still had to go to Stop & Shop for her favorite snacks: "S'Mom, s'need Smarties, s'lemons, and hot chips." While I wasn't looking forward to sleeping in a chair all night, Cate's excitement was contagious.

When we got to the room at the sleep clinic, Cate broke open her suitcase to unpack. She set the pictures on the dresser, lined up her movies on the end table, placed her stuffed animals on the bed, and put four pairs of shoes in the closet. She then shimmied into her Dora the Explorer nightgown, which she insisted on wearing even though it was four sizes too small, and pulled out a lemon.

"Cate, if you wear this silly nightgown, the deal is you have to—I mean have to—wear your underwear."

"S'Mom, s—a—y, I s'wear my underwear."

The sleep tech came in to hook her up to the probes. It was similar to the first time, but because she was older and you could kind of reason with her, the hook-up was a lot easier (the whole process takes almost an hour). There was a camera above her bed and an intercom where the tech talked to us from his remote observation room. It reminded me of Big Brother when his voice came out of nowhere. I jumped about four feet in the air when he saw me struggling with the DVD player and said without warning, "Ah, you insert the DVD into the slot on the side of the TV." I looked up with a smile after catching my breath and waved to the camera. "Okay, thanks."

Cate was loving life—lying in her bed, eating hot chips, and watching *Madagascar*—all the while looking like a pampered robot with the probes and wires attached to her head, face, and body. I was engrossed in my book club book, when I heard the covers of her bed begin to rustle. I immediately looked over to see her submerged under the covers and moving about.

"What are you doing? Seriously, Cate, what are you doing?"

She popped out from under the blankets, stretched her underwear like a slingshot, and fired it off at Big Brother.

I jumped out of my chair, "Cate!" and then apologized to the camera, "I'm so sorry." Laughter came over the intercom and eventually the tech said, "I don't mind. She's a funny one, isn't she?"

Cate's hotel stay ended when she woke up the next morning at 5 a.m. We wouldn't receive the results of the sleep study until six weeks later when the sleep doctor called to tell us that Cate did have sleep apnea. "This isn't uncommon in patients with Down syndrome, Mrs. Alix," the doctor explained. "You'll need to schedule an appointment with my office to have her fitted for a continuous positive airway pressure machine. We call it a c-pap for short." *Another machine?*

Ange said that her brother, Alex, was fitted with a c-pap at a clinic in Boston for his sleep apnea, "Calls it his Big Papi, or when he wants to get technical, his Constantly Pestering All Post-evening machine."

"That's pretty funny, but what do you think that last one means?"

"I think it wakes him up sometimes."

The promise that the c-pap might be the proverbial smoking gun was hope enough to give it a try, though our anticipation was quickly squashed in discovering firsthand what Alex meant. The machine was cumbersome and unsuitable for someone like Cate who sleeps facedown on her belly and breathes through her mouth. The hose popped off almost every half hour and jumped around the room like a hissing snake.

Every time it happened, Caroline would walk around their bedroom, arms stretched out zombie-style in search of the switch to shut it off. Cate was usually wide-awake in the midst of this, offering no help to her sister and scolding, "S'what the heck, Caroline?" Our family gave it a good team effort as I promised her doctors we would, but it just wasn't working. We were getting way more sleep without this frustrating machine. I guess there are some things you just can't fix no matter how hard you try.

~~

Cate at 12: Reads at a second grade level; writing sentences; skip counts by twos and fives up to one hundred; can add three-digit numbers and can subtract two-digit numbers; when asked what an island is, answers "go on vacation"; folds and puts away laundry; has phonetically begun decoding words; can multiply by twos, threes and fives.

I ran into Ange at St. Mary's Church in Wappingers Falls between services on Easter Sunday, our family on the way in, hers on the way out. My mother had us there outrageously early because you know, "If you don't get there at least forty-five minutes ahead of time on Easter, you'll never get a seat." In indulging my mother I got there with plenty of time to talk to Angela, as opposed to my usual Sunday routine when I leave my house the same time mass starts.

"When's the last time I saw you in this neck of the woods?" I asked Ange who became strangely serious all of a sudden. "Noelle…," she said, putting a hand on her heart, unable to say anything else.

…Oh, gosh. For my dad…

"Hey, Frangela," Cate said, thankfully changing the subject.

"Hi Cate, having fun at your Me-Ma's house?"

"Uh huh. How s'Ryan and s'John?"

"Good, but they didn't want to have to put church clothes on today."

"S—a—y s'Mom don't want to s'wear my tights s'today."

"Yep, a good battle this morning," I said, rolling my eyes at Ange. "Church should be interesting."

It came as no surprise that Cate was done with church after Ange and I said goodbye that Easter morning, well before the services even began. I did my best to hang in there with her even though there was plenty working against us. Cate's tights had her insane. The altar servers overdid it with the incense, and she just plain didn't want to be there any more. I gave up before the priest started his homily and took her outside. In passing through the church doors Cate whispered in her magnified voice, "S'Mom, s'wanna see Pop Pop's case."

I don't know why, but his grave doesn't mean much to me even though he meant everything to me. I still think about him at least ten times a day, and talk to him in my thoughts wherever I am, but this wasn't a place that brought me comfort or drew me to him in any way. Still, the girls always like to stop by. Many times when we visited my mom, we'd go to his grave after church and, honestly, it was never sad. When we stood there, I could almost hear his voice saying, "Jesus, don't you people have something better to do?"

Cate and I walked over to my dad's grave, and she got on with her usual routine. She picked some grass and clover that was on the ground at her feet and put it on his headstone and said, "Hi, Pop Pop," and proceeded with this phony kind of cry where she puts her hands over face, and blows in and out of her nose, saying, "I miss Pop Pop." Cate then meandered around looking at all the other headstones, touching all the trinkets people had left behind.

As I was standing there watching Cate, I saw a woman holding a baby on her hip in the row of gravestones behind us. Her eyes were teary when she looked up at me and said, "Kim?"

"No, it's Noelle, Kim's sister."

"Oh, hi, Noelle," she said. "Remember me? It's Marie Cocolicchio." I remembered her well as a friend of Kim's from St. Mary's, and I walked over to ask if she was okay.

"Not really, I'm visiting my mom who died about a year ago."

"Oh, Marie, I'm so sorry," I said and reached out my hand and gently squeezed her forearm. We talked a bit about her mom and her battle with breast cancer and how her dad was doing. She asked me how my parents were and I told her my mom was well, and that we were here to see my dad who was buried in the next row.

"Oh my goodness, I didn't know. I'm so sorry."

"Oh, don't worry. It's been a while, and it really is okay…I mean that."

"Does it get better? I'm still having such a hard time. I have no idea how I'll raise my kids without her. She was the center of our family. I talked to her every day. I loved her so much."

My eyes welled over because I could feel exactly what she was saying, connecting with her on every point. I'd been there, I loved my dad the way she loved her mom. "I have to tell you that it does get better. There will come a time when you'll think of your mom without first having that overwhelming feeling of sadness wash over you."

"I can't imagine getting there."

"I didn't think I'd ever be okay either," I said and took her free hand. "Please, please know that time heals, faith heals, the people you love heal you."

Cate meandered back toward me and I introduced her to Marie. Marie asked her if she liked Troy from *High School Musical* because of her "T" necklace. (He was the teenage heartthrob from the movie.) Marie was as natural with Cate as if she had known her forever. That quality, that natural way that certain people have with Cate, draws me to them immediately.

I could see groups of people walking towards their cars (a sign that mass was over), so I said goodbye to Marie and her children, gave her a big strong hug, and asked her to keep in touch. I took Cate by the hand and as we began to walk away, I heard Marie ask, "Do you think my mom sent you here to make me feel better?"

I stopped and turned to face her. "Yeah, I kind of do."

And I did believe it, but I also knew that Cate brought me to the cemetery that day, to a new place in my life. It was such a good feeling. In making our way to the car, I smiled with the thought of having run into Ange that morning. That I had shared with Marie what my best friend had shared with me.

∽

I jumped into the shower at our Cape Cod rental after the kids went to bed one August night during our annual vacation there. It had become my ritual, since this was a time when there would actually be some hot water.

"It's all about the location," my mother-in-law encouraged me when I first came to the little village of housekeeping cottages on the edge of Cape Cod Bay. (My in-laws had rented here for fifty summers.) I smiled thinking how much I'd come to love this spot and the renewal it offered my soul every year.

I ran soapy hands over my body, stopping at my chest to do a breast self-exam since it had been a while. On finishing up, I felt something that hadn't been there before. "What's this?" I said aloud and hopped out of the shower to tell Rob.

"It feels like a pea," he said, and I shifted up next to him in bed, the words he used lingering in the air like ocean mist.

"My mom said her breast cancer felt like a pea," I said and then fell silent for a long time, hanging on the stillness of my last breath. I was mindful of the words Noelle had told me once. *Life can change in an instant.*

"I don't know what this is," I said, running my index finger over the pea.

"Don't think the worst," he said, trying to divert my thoughts that were already going down that unknowing road. My mother had breast cancer when she was forty-four, and I was well aware this placed me in a high-risk category for developing the disease. "Definitely get it checked," Rob said calmly, "but I bet it's nothing." Still, I couldn't help but think about my mom and that maybe it was my turn.

For all I knew about the fragility of life, I'd never had to contemplate the fragility of my own life in such a real and personal way. And while it was frightening as a mom to consider that I might be sick, I also had the sense that I could handle this, whatever it was. I'd implicitly come to understand that life was all about uncertainty. So although I was concerned, I was not afraid.

The nurse I spoke to in the morning told me not to rush home, that I'd be okay waiting a week, no matter what this was. "Enjoy your vacation," she said, and I tried to. I spent time with my family on the beach, playing games, planning daytrips, eating dinner out, taking in every second I possibly could. However the lump didn't stray far from my mind.

I called Noelle as soon as I got home. "How I've missed my friend," she said on hearing my hello. "How are you? How was the Cape?" asking one question after the next.

"We had a great time, beautiful weather, but..." Part of me hesitated, wanting to tell her, but not wanting to make a big deal of this. "I found a tiny lump in my breast a few days after we got to the Cape. And you know me, I'm going to have some tests just to make sure everything's okay."

"I'll go with you."

"That's okay. You must be busy with work."

"Don't worry about that," she said. "When do you need to leave?"

"Friday morning at 9:30."

"I'll be there."

❧

While it was a surprise to see Noelle's red minivan pull up to the curb of my house at 9:30 a.m. sharp on Friday morning, it also made me smile. She had made a promise and for as long as I can remember, her promises were for keeps—even if it meant she had to be on time. "I'll stay as long as I can," Noelle said, not telling me about the conference call she was currently missing.

We left in separate cars and I met her in the lobby of the medical building, across from the children's hospital in Hartford where we parked during the year of pneumonia. "Why do you still not turn left in the garage to sneak a low parking spot?" she asked. "You're just getting here, and I've already got my coffee." She handed me a chamomile tea and went on her caffeine rant. "I'll never understand how you don't need caffeine in the morning. Shit, if I could get it intravenously I would."

My name was called at the radiology lab, and we followed a woman to the changing rooms. "Are two of you having tests?" the technician asked somewhat confused. "No, I'm just coming along," Noelle said and took a seat in an open dressing room. Meantime I slipped into the one-size-fits-all gown and walked to the mammography room and then into a separate room for an ultrasound.

"You'll know what this is by the time you leave today," the ultrasound technician said, and asked me to lie down on the hospital bed in the room. She rolled the sensor back and forth over the lump, staring at the image on the screen, clicking every now and then to take a picture. "Let's hear what the radiologist has to say," she said. "Can I turn the music up for you?"

"No, thank you. I'm fine," I said. And, I was fine, while I lay there alone, strangely peaceful as if still floating on my back in the warmth of Cape Cod Bay. My mind was clear, without the need to think about anything the way it usually did. After only a few minutes, the technician burst into the room, "It's a cluster of cysts," she said the way you blurt out a secret you can't possibly keep. "You're fine."

Noelle shot up when I opened the door to the changing rooms. "I'm okay, just some cysts," I said, and she grabbed hold of me as if I'd been lost. "I knew it," she said, and we tightened our grip on each other.

"Even if this was different news, you would have been okay. We would have done it together," she said before loosening her embrace.

I brushed tears from my face, took a deep breath and closed my eyes. *Thank you, God, for giving me such a good friend.*

"What a great day," Noelle said and continued on. "You're okay, and isn't that Josh Groban singing? I love him." She turned her head to listen, and I continued to wipe my face. "You are loved," he sang.

In closing the curtain to dress, I pictured how different this could have been. There were plenty of women in my shoes— women I knew very well—who were now being sent for biopsies, having chemotherapy, or preparing for surgery. I committed myself then and there to live my life with a sense of urgency. Special moments, plans, and dreams could only happen if I put myself out there. *We only have the time we are given.*

I stepped out of the dressing room while Noelle was scrolling through her phone.

"Aren't you cute with your matching polka-dot flip-flops," the ultrasound technician said in passing by the two of us. Noelle and I looked down to see we'd unknowingly bought similar sandals that summer.

"You must be friends," the technician happily concluded.

Noelle and I glimpsed at each other and replied, "Yes, we are." And I knew as we walked out of the building side by side that we always would be.

———

Cate was in sixth grade and had been obsessed with *High School Musical* for the past year. She had CDs, DVDs, socks, pajamas, T-shirts, a backpack, and the life-size cardboard cutout of Troy. This was definitely an instance of the apple not falling far from the tree. I'd been infatuated with Shaun Cassidy in my day, owning some of the same type of memorabilia. Cate knew the exact day the sequel was to premier along with the release date of the video. She was a marketer's dream.

Tim and I never got around to having her birthday party that year, and Cate never let us forget it, often asking us, "S'when s'my birthday party again?" One fall weekend, the third *High School Musical* movie was coming out in the movie theatres, a fact I was well aware of because Cate told me every day that week, "S'Mom, *High School Musical 3* s'in the movies on Friday." I told her that maybe I would take her and Claire on Sunday, after Caroline's soccer game. She was ready to go early Sunday morning, standing at the edge of my bed to ask, "S'Mom, s'when we leaving? Ask Syd to go? S'need to bring snacks."

"Cate, all right, all right, but we're not going until later," I said trying to appease her. "Please, let's just go back to bed."

"Okay, s'Mom" she said and headed downstairs.

We went about our day, going to church, CCD class, and Caroline's soccer game. I was talking to my friend, Jeanne, on the sidelines at the game when she mentioned, "So you're having Cate's birthday party today?"

"What?"

"Oh, my neighbor mentioned her daughter was going to Cate's birthday party today," she said kind of embarrassed. "Maybe I got it wrong."

"Yeah, I don't know. I planned on taking the girls to the movies later, but that's about it."

Tim, the girls, and I came home from the game and my answering machine was flashing with a bunch of new messages on it. The first was from a mother I didn't know: "Oh, hi, I'm Bridget's mother. Bridget wasn't sure whether she was supposed to get dropped off at your house or at the movies for the party. Can you give me a call?"

Holy shit.

I was now clued in, and by the fourth such message, a light went off in my brain about the logistics of how Cate could throw a birthday party for herself. About a week before, she came home from school with a telephone address book into which her friends wrote their names and phone numbers. Cate wouldn't have been able to pull this information from the school directory on her own.

I went downstairs to the basement to find Cate playing her PlayStation games and asked whom she called.

"S'my friends."

"What did you ask them?"

"Duh, s'go to my birthday party."

"CATE, THIS IS NOT A BIRTHDAY PARTY. YOU WERE BRINGING ONE FRIEND TO SEE A MOVIE. HOW MANY PEOPLE DID YOU CALL?"

There was no response, so I quickly phoned Syd to find out what she knew and she said, "Oh yeah, Cate called me this morning about the party." I had her contact all the girls she thought Cate might have called (thank God for Syd!) and I called the parents back who had left messages. About an hour later, three girls showed up at my house and then five more at the movie theatre, each carrying a present for Cate. I was mortified with the thought of all of these mothers racing around town in the ninth hour to buy birthday gifts for my daughter when it wasn't even her birthday.

Tim and I had each of the girls call their parents after the movie to see if we could take them out to pizza in an attempt to make it the real birthday party they thought they were attending. Each girl took a turn with my cell phone, and I could only imagine what the parents must have been thinking: "What's wrong with these people, throwing a birthday party on the fly? No invitations, six hours notice, and oh, now they're going out for dinner."

We went to a pizza place near home and the girls sat at one big table. They were all friends with Cate, but not really friends with each other. When the pitcher of Sprite came and the waitress poured them each a glass, Cate broke the ice by standing up to give herself a toast. Brushing the hair out of her face, she lifted a glass and said, "My peeps—I s'love you guys."

Wow, she watches way too much TV.

We took the girls home one by one. After I apologized to each parent, I had Cate do the same and return the gifts. Door after door we met with the same response: lots of laughter and

"No, no, no. Cate, you keep the gift." Cate's personal telephone book has since been confiscated and hidden in an undisclosed location, and you can trust that I'll think twice before I ever blow off a birthday party for her again.

☙

It was the first Saturday of June and Cate was awake early as usual. She came upstairs with half a watermelon wanting a snack and I don't really recall what Tim or I said, but she left our room and headed back downstairs. I was immobile as I felt Tim get out of bed. The next thing I heard was Tim shouting, "Cate, you could cut off your fingers." He found her with a cleaver lodged in the watermelon.

He returned to our room after handling that fiasco and said he thought he needed to start exercising. "You haven't exercised in fifteen years. What am I missing?" I asked, still not able to open my eyes. "You know, Tim, I wonder if I have cancer or something because I'm so tired at night and I can't get out of bed in the morning."

"You think you're sick? I think you're finally well," he said with more energy than I could possibly muster at the moment. "Want to go for a walk?" he asked and added, "We can take Mabel."

"What about Cate?"

"Right, she can come, too." *What the heck is wrong with him? Was he going to leave her here? Caroline won't be up for seven more hours and Claire's still sound asleep.*

The thing was, he'd actually backed himself into a good idea. I'd recently taken Cate for her annual physical where her pediatrician grilled me for most of the appointment about Cate's weight. I was crushed by the talk and the importance of this one particular matter for there were so many other things to keep track of. Yet there was no denying the truth of it, when I looked at Cate who was basically naked in the exam room—the cereal snacking, the juice box insanity. Cate hadn't grown any taller in the past couple of years, just wider.

"I have two words for you: Operation Slimdown," I said, staring her down.

She started rubbing her belly with both hands the way people do a Buddha for good luck and said to me, "Have three words for you: S'no Operation Slimdown." I wasn't sure if I was more shocked by the comment or her math skills when she turned to her doctor and said, "I s'love my fat belly."

Ah, yes, this was Cate in a nutshell.

After this mental digression, I was wide-awake and eager for a walk. I threw on a pair of shorts and a T-shirt and was sitting at the bottom of the stairs tying my sneakers when Cate walked over holding Mabel's leash. She was ready to go, dressed in flip-flops and her robe, the pockets of which were stuffed with two lemon halves and a juice box, you know, for the road.

"S'Mom, when s'my graduation party again?"

"Cate, remember it's not a party for you. It's a party to say thank you to all of your teachers for helping you in elementary school."

"S'not just teachers, s'Mom. Asked lunch ladies, s'Miss Jarvis, s'Miss Kolowski."

"You didn't ask for presents, did you?"

"Uh…"

"Caaate!" I said as I rolled my eyes and looked up at Tim who was standing there laughing. *I'll have to deal with that Monday morning.*

We were about to leave, when Tim nudged me with his elbow and said, "I guess Jimmy the Chin is coming."

"Oh, yeah, she kinda does look like that mobster that wore the bathrobe," I said and laughed. "But isn't that guy's name, 'Vinny the Chin?'"

"Noelle, you're so literal," he said to which I offered no rebuttal. When you're right, you're right. So out we went into the dawn for a little Operation Slimdown. Tim setting a pace, swinging his arms to work up a sweat, Mabel and Jimmy the Chin sauntering along going nowhere in particular, and me smack in the middle. I looked back at one point to see Cate taking off her robe and I lost my breath. Underneath was the T-shirt she slept in, and, well, nothing else.

"Cate, oh my God, put your robe back on."

"But, s'Mom, I'm hot."

"Well then you should have worn underwear," I said and heard Tim say from up ahead, "Yeah, and pants."

We continued along and I recalled the dysfunctional family walks we took around the neighborhood when we first moved to Simsbury. They weren't all that different from this one. And here I was, not fazed by much anymore, not needing to explain my life to anyone, just enjoying it. So much laughter, so much learned, so content.

With Gratitude

We believe *Just Cate* isn't just ours. It belongs to every person who has helped us on our writing journey. Deepest thanks to our mentor and friend, Jenny Minton, who, nearly a decade ago, saw the glimmer of a story in a few early chapters and has guided us along ever since. Best to our new friend and graphic designer, Liz Panke, for not only giving *Just Cate* a visual image in print and online, but for being so passionate about our work, and so patient with us along the way.

Thank you, Michele DeFilippo and Ronda Rawlins with 1106 Design, along with the folks at Lightning Source, for all the handholding to bring this book to life. You helped two novices meticulously create a beautiful book—the book we knew in our hearts *Just Cate* would be.

To Matt Boline and Melissa Carden, for their incredible generosity and creative talent, producing our book trailer because they believed in our story as much as we do—words cannot express our most heartfelt thanks to you. And with all that we are, thank you, Renee Hartshorn, for designing our first website while you were in Dubai, working nights to keep up with our days.

Cheers to Linda Cashdan for word doctoring our first draft, encouraging us to weave our voices more closely together to tell our story. Our deepest gratitude to close friend and spiritual guide, Nina Whitnah, for proofing our final manuscript with grace and intimate knowledge of both *The Chicago Manual of Style* and *The Holy Bible*.

To the many people in publishing and media who helped us out of kindness because they wanted to, our enduring thanks: Terry Walters, Mary Jones, Liz Welch, Stacey Battat, James Tully, Ellyn Spragins, Megan Meany, and Lisa Swayne.

To Tara Gilvar, Becky Hull, and Marie McNamara with B.I.G. (Believe, Inspire, Grow), kudos for helping us chase our dreams and for connecting us to so many talented B.I.G. members, most especially photographer Jane Shauck. We cannot thank you enough, Jane, for your beautiful photos that have brought *Just Cate* to life. And thanks also to branding expert, Stacy Silk Rome, for giving us a marketing road map.

To our friends and family who read our work at various stages of completion, and/or who offered help out of the goodness of their hearts—Nancy Murray, Linda Scacco, Andrea Ellen, Paula Teed, LFM, Chris Manning, Kristen Herzog, Cathy Clifford, Maureen O'Brien, Susan Autuori, Kathleen Fogarty, Scott Watrous, and Jane Scott Ashley, and so many more we wish we had space to include—we so appreciate your insights, honesty, and help to see our dream through.

Bear hugs and thanks to our book clubs for your enduring support and friendship. Noelle's group: Leslie Congdon, Ginger Gillespie, Ann Grote, Ann Hoffman, Kristin Horrigan, Marie McNamara, and Michelle Sullivan. And, Angela's group, including "The Road Crew:" Carol Dupuis, Karen Connal, Amy Fisher, Karen Brown, Joan Green, Karen Humphreys, Renee Hartshorn, Nancy Murray, Claudia Oakes, and Suzanne Schumann. We love each and every one of you.

And to our husbands, Tim Alix and Rob Martin, thank you for believing in us, especially on hard days when we wondered how it would ever happen. We love you more than we can possibly say.

In closing, special thanks from Noelle to the people who have been essential in her life with Cate: I give all my thanks to my family—my mom, my sister, my brother, all my aunts, uncles, and cousins—and you, Dad. I love you. To the incredible people who've worked with Cate (and me!) all these years, in particular: Deb Cervas, Beth Somen, Ellen Yazmer, Helen Donaher, Rita Daves, Val Soja, Tracy McConnell, Kim Erickson, Donna Trainor, Jane Panarella, Karen Wilbur, Sue Lemke, Patricia Peters, Michelle Hester, Mary Ellen Leathe, as well as all of the teachers, paraprofessionals, school staff, neighbors, and coaches who have taught Cate, cared for her, and encouraged her to walk the straight and narrow—thank you for helping me help Cate live the life she is meant to live.

Permissions

About the Authors

Noelle Alix is a storyteller having learned the craft well from her late father, a compassionate, irreverent Irishman. By day, she is a finance attorney with Vinson & Elkins LLP, and by night she coauthors with Angela Martin the blog, *Simply What Matters Most* at *www.justcate.com*. She lives outside Hartford, Connecticut with her husband, three daughters, and basset hound, Mabel.

Angela Martin is a writer, blogger, binge poet, and friend. She has been quietly writing since childhood and currently is a guest speaker for a creative writing class at the University of Hartford. An advocate for educating every child, Angela has volunteered extensively in her church, her kids' schools, and her community. She lives ten minutes away from Noelle—the same as when they were growing up—with her husband, two sons, and golden retriever, Dixie.

For speaking engagements, contact the authors at their website, *www.justcate.com*.

CPSIA information can be obtained at www.ICGtesting.com
Printed in the USA
LVOW041028290512

283720LV00002B/6/P